TECHNOLOGY AND MEDICAL PRACTICE

Theory, Technology and Society

Series Editor: Ross Abbinnett, University of Birmingham, UK

Theory, Technology and Society presents the latest work in social, cultural and political theory, which considers the impact of new technologies on social, economic and political relationships. Central to the series are the elucidation of new theories of the humanity-technology relationship, the ethical implications of techno-scientific innovation, and the identification of unforeseen effects which are emerging from the techno-scientific organization of society.

With particular interest in questions of gender relations, the body, virtuality, penality, work, aesthetics, urban space, surveillance, governance and the environment, the series encourages work that seeks to determine the nature of the social consequences that have followed the deployment of new technologies, investigate the increasingly complex relationship between 'the human' and 'the technological', or addresses the ethical and political questions arising from the constant transformation and manipulation of humanity.

Other titles in this series

Contested Categories
Life Sciences in Society
Edited by Susanne Bauer and Ayo Wahlberg
ISBN 978 0 7546 7618 8

The Genome Incorporated
Constructing Biodigital Identity
Kate O'Riordan
ISBN 978 0 7546 7851 9

Technology and Medical Practice
Blood, Guts and Machines

Edited by

ERICKA JOHNSON
Division for Science and Technology Studies,
University of Gothenburg, Sweden

BOEL BERNER
Department of Thematic Studies – Technology and Social Change
Linköping University Sweden

ASHGATE

Published by
Ashgate Publishing Limited
Wey Court East
Union Road
Farnham
Surrey, GU9 7PT
England

Ashgate Publishing Company
Suite 420
101 Cherry Street
Burlington
VT 05401-4405
USA

www.ashgate.com

British Library Cataloguing in Publication Data
Technology and medical practice : blood, guts and machines.
 -- (Theory, technology and society)
 1. Medical innovations--Social aspects. 2. Social
 medicine.
 I. Series II. Johnson, Ericka, 1973- III. Berner, Boel.
 362.1'042-dc22

Library of Congress Cataloging-in-Publication Data
Technology and medical practice : blood, guts and machines / [edited] by Ericka Johnson and Boel Berner.
    p. cm. -- (Theory, technology and society)
 Includes bibliographical references and index.
 ISBN 978-0-7546-7836-6 (hbk) -- ISBN 978-0-7546-9652-0 (e-book)
 1. Medical technology--Social aspects. 2. Medical personnel and patient. 3. Social medi-cine. 4. Feminist theory. I. Johnson, Ericka, 1973- II. Berner, Boel.
 R855.3.T565 2009
 610.28--dc22

                                                                                  2009033015

ISBN: 978-0-7546-7836-6 (hbk)
ISBN: 978-0-7546-9652-0 (ebk)

Mixed Sources
Product group from well-managed
forests and other controlled sources
www.fsc.org Cert no. SA-COC-1565
© 1996 Forest Stewardship Council

Printed and bound in Great Britain by
MPG Books Group, UK

Contents

PART 3 LINKING BODIES AND MACHINES

List of Figures

Notes on Contributors

Boel Berner is a professor at the Department of Thematic Studies — Technology and Social Change, Linköping University, Sweden. Her research has involved studies of technical knowledge and expertise in diverse areas, such as engineering work, household technology, technical education and risk. She has also published extensively on issues of gender and technology. Current work concerns blood transfusion practices, risk and citizenship. Her publications in English include the edited volumes *Gendered Practices* (1997), Almqvist and Wiksell International, *Manoeuvring in an Environment of Uncertainty* (with Per Trulsson, 2000), Ashgate, and *Constructing Risk and Safety in Technological Practice* (with Jane Summerton, 2003), Routledge.

Dawn Goodwin is a lecturer in the School of Health and Medicine at Lancaster University, UK. Her research interests include collaborative work practices and human-machine/material interactions in healthcare, and the imaging, visualization and simulation technologies used in medical education. Her recent work draws on STS, ethnomethodology and medical sociology to study the practices of diagnostic work. This has culminated in the publication of an edited collection, Buscher, M., Goodwin, D. and Mesman, J. *Ethnographies of Diagnostic Work: Dimensions of transformative practice* (in press), Palgrave Macmillan.

Ericka Johnson is a researcher at the Division for Science and Technology Studies, University of Gothenburg, Sweden. Her research has explored how the gendered body is constructed in and by medical technologies. She is the author of *Situating Simulators. The integration of simulations in medical practice* (2004), Arkiv förlag, and *Dreaming of a Mail-Order Husband* (2007), Duke University Press.

Petra Jonvallen is assistant professor at the Department Human Work Sciences at Luleå University of Technology, Sweden. Her previous research has analysed tensions between the pharmaceutical industry and health care services in the realm of clinical trials, where she highlighted the relationships between the biomedicalization of body weight and the production of obesity drugs. She has published *Testing Pills, Enacting Obesity. The work of localizing tools in a clinical trial* (2005), Linköping University Press, and Compliance revisited: pharmaceutical drug trials in the era of the contract research organization, (2009), *Nursing Inquiry*, 16(3).

Corinna Kruse is a researcher at the Department of Thematic Studies – Technology and Social Change, Linköping University, Sweden. Her work examines science and technology as cultural processes. She is the author of *The Making of Valid Data. People and machines in genetic research practice* (2006), Linköping University Press.

Maggie Mort is reader in the Sociology of Science, Technology and Medicine at the Department of Sociology and Division of Medicine, Lancaster University, UK. Her research interests include human machine relations in clinical practice; telecare and telemedicine, and participatory ethnography. Her publications include *Building the Trident Network: A study of the enrolment of people, knowledge and machines* (2002), MIT Press, Making and Unmaking Telepatients: identity and governance in new care technologies (2009), *Science, Technology & Human Values*, 34(1), 9–33 and Beyond Information: intimate relations in sociotechnical practice (2009), *Sociology*, 43 (2), 215–231.

Rachel Prentice is an assistant professor in the Department of Science and Technology Studies, Cornell University, USA. She is the author of *Bodies of Information: An ethnography of anatomy and surgery training and practice* (forthcoming), Duke University Press.

Celia Roberts is a senior lecturer at the Department of Sociology, Lancaster University, UK. She is the author of *Messengers of Sex: Hormones, biomedicine and feminism* (2007), Cambridge University Press and *Born and Made: An ethnography of preimplantation genetic diagnosis* (with Sarah Franklin, 2006), Princeton University Press.

Kerstin Sandell is an associate professor at the Center for Gender Studies at Lund University, Sweden, in the field of feminist technoscience studies. Her work includes the ethnography *(Re)creating the normal. Breast operations and burn reconstruction in plastic surgery practices* (2000), Arkiv förlag, as well as writings on feminist theory and intersectionality, most recently: A feminist re-reading of theories of late modernity (with Diana Mulinari, forthcoming), *Critical Sociology*.

Lucy Suchman is professor of the Anthropology of Science and Technology and co-director of the Centre for Science Studies at Lancaster University, UK. Her research has involved ethnographic studies of sites of technology production and use, including theoretical and practical problems at the interface of humans and machines. She is the author of many works, most recently *Human-Machine Reconfigurations: Plans and situated actions*, 2nd expanded edition (2007), Cambridge University Press.

Jenny Sundén is associate professor and researcher at the Department of Media Technology and Graphic Arts, Royal Institute of Technology (KTH), Sweden. She is the author of *Material Virtualities: Approaching Online Textual Embodiment* (2003), Peter Lang, and a co-author of *Cyberfeminism in Northern Lights: Digital media and gender in a Nordic context* (with Malin Sveningsson Elm, 2007), Cambridge Scholars Publishing.

Acknowledgements

We would like to thank Vinnova (The Swedish Governmental Agency for Innovation Systems), the Division for Science and Technology Studies, University of Gothenburg, the Department of Thematic Studies — Technology and Social Change, Linköping University, and the Department of Science and Technology Studies, Cornell University, for funding to support this anthology. Thanks are also extended to the Campus Varberg library for summer work space and to Corinna Kruse for a careful final editing job.

Introduction

Technology and Medical Practice: Blood, Guts and Machines

Ericka Johnson and Boel Berner

This book is an examination of medical technologies through the lens of medical practices. It is also the reverse: a study of medical practices refracted through an examination of medical technologies. It presents examples of how practice shapes and is shaped by different medical technologies, and the way these technologies and practices create specific, local understandings of the normal and pathological, bodies and machines. Employing what Mol terms praxologies (Mol 2002), it attends to practice to problematize the idea of medical technologies as universally applicable and bodies and practitioners as neutral users. The authors collected here approach medical technologies by paying close attention to the specificities of technology use and the understandings and knowledges that are created in the intra-actions (Barad 2007) between technologies, bodies, and medical professionals.

We do this by looking at different technologies, using different methodological approaches and conducting our research in different sites. Empirically, one encounters pharmaceuticals, ultrasound scans and anaesthesiology readouts in the book. Simulators appear and take many forms (all claiming to represent the same body). Foetal monitors are covered in blood, blood transfusion devices developed, and laboratory equipment defined. To capture these technologies and the practices in which they are embedded (and which they also create), some have been approached ethnomethodologically, others with periods of ethnographic observation. Interviews were held with users, designers and practitioners, and discourse analysis conducted on medical literature and marketing material. 'The field site' has proven to be varied, from medical journals to operating theatres, from maternity clinics to research laboratories. Medical practices can and do happen outside the clinical setting so following the technologies in use has meant that also we as researchers have had to be flexible in defining our sites. Some of us have worked directly in hospitals, others in laboratories, and others in educational settings or with archival material. And most of us have had to conduct research in several different places as we followed our technologies.

Yet, for all the variety found in our field sites and research objects, there are also similarities between our approaches. First and foremost is that the authors all take technology seriously. The technology is an integral part of, and often even an actor in, the constellations of practice that we analyse. And so, too, is the practitioner. This book is about technology and medical practitioners much more than it is about patients or even bodies. While patients and bodies (and policies and pathologies) appear in the texts, in many ways they are supporting characters to the main actors: practitioners and technologies.

Another similarity is our disciplinary position. If, methodologically, we are inspired by more traditional approaches taken from established fields like sociology, anthropology and history, theoretically our work is located at the intersection of two interdisciplinary conversations, feminist science studies and science and technology studies (STS). In the chapters that follow we draw inspiration, use theoretical tools and participate in conversations from both.

Theoretical Inroads

Much of the work here could be categorized as a feminist science studies approach to medical technologies and practices. The research it draws inspiration and presents empirical material from areas traditionally associated with feminist science studies: reproductive health and the female body (see for example Barad 2007, Haraway 1991, Martin 1992, Oudshoorn 1994, Rapp 1999, Waldby 2000). In the pages that follow one finds hormones and blood, virtual uteri and palpated ovaries, pregnant bodies and birthing women. Likewise, the reader will find analyses that have grown out of longstanding feminist concerns with the implications of science and technology for women. The chapters in part one, for example, deal with how technology is implicated in the construction of the normal and the abnormal, and how it is used to coordinate certainty and medical truth, a common subject of feminist science studies work and critique. The authors writing in part two examine the way bodies shape simulators and simulators shape bodies. Largely inspired by feminist science studies work on the body, these chapters show how simulator technology constructs very specific knowledges about and representations of the (female) body. And the chapters in part three touch on lived experiences of and emotional reactions to bodies and medicine, topics also familiar to those working within feminist science studies. Some of the chapters have also integrated more recent work within feminist science studies, for example the ideas of Karen Barad, to understand how knowledges and artefacts become in, through and by practice.

We also position our work in the field of STS and Medicine, and claim that perhaps the book's main contribution is a focus on the practices surrounding medical technologies (cf. Berg and Mol 1998, Berg and Timmermans 2003, Heath, Luff and Sanchez Svensson 2003, Olin Lauritzen and Hydén 2007) while expanding this through our integration of theories, ideas and politics from feminist science studies. This positioning can be read as an attempt to direct attention towards the specific, often mundane practices and policies that are used to integrate technical developments into medical contexts.

Medicine is plural and heterogeneous. In *Differences in Medicine* (1998), the disunity of medicine is explored by investigating medicine's practices and performances. The point of departure there was that medicine is not a coherent whole but rather 'an amalgam of thoughts, a mixture of habits, an assemblage of techniques' (Berg and Mol 1998: 3). Medicine is multiple. It is diverse and filled with differences, differences which lead to tensions and also coordination work (Berg and Mol 1998: 8). This understanding has also permeated much of the work that is presented in the following chapters. From STS we take an understanding of technologies as flexible, as well as the practices they influence. These are staples of STS thought, and in our work they are applied to the development of technologies in medicine.

In line with an STS informed approach, many of the contributors to this book employ ethnographic methods, which carry with them a respect for everyday encounters, an awareness of the ambiguity of technologies, and an exploration of how technology embodies and changes practice. Many of the authors draw attention to the details of clinical work and research, analysing the adoption, integration and learning of technologies in medicine. And, as mentioned above, many of the contributors are also influenced by work in feminist science studies, which facilitates theoretical discussions about the body, the (ab)normal, the abject and performativity to be integrated into more mainstream STS and Medicine approaches. Finally, our work not only delves into the integration of new, often high-tech machines as they are introduced into medicine, it also reflects over the development and spread of new medical practices, and how these are influenced by and introduced into new technologies (cf. Brown and Webster 2004).

Contents

The book is divided into three parts. Part 1 deals with how medical practices and technologies are used to know and to create knowledge about patient bodies and how technology and practices together are used to create certainty (and uncertainty) in medical practice. The research here addresses questions like: Who is the patient? What is normal? What is abnormal? How can technologies change these definitions? How are certainty and accountability achieved in technical practices? In the first chapter, Celia Roberts' work moves us into the contested terrain of puberty. She explores how the pubescent body is presented, defined, and ultimately manipulated in contemporary biomedical discourses. Among other things, she discusses why the machine metaphor is sometimes employed to represent the pubescent body, but also how the technologies of biomedicine are used to change these bodies. Her work illuminates the blurred boundary between the 'social environment' and the biological body in these discussions. It touches upon the flexible constructions of 'statistically normal' puberty that vary between countries, races and social classes, and the political implications that acceptance of these normal/pathological distinctions carries with it. She ends her chapter with the challenge to leave aside the idea that pathology is open to intervention and instead suggests that we work towards facilitating health and happiness for individuals.

In the second chapter, Kerstin Sandell examines how Swedish midwives learn how to conduct routine ultrasounds in the 17th week of pregnancy. Sandell's work combines extensive ethnographic observations of ultrasound practices with the concept of professional vision. Never far from discussions about what is a 'normal' foetus and what abnormalities appear on the screen, Sandell shows how midwives use ultrasound technology to simultaneously construct knowledge about the body, the objects of knowledge, and the professional identities of the knowers.

In Chapter 3, Dawn Goodwin and Maggie Mort use ethnomethodological data of anaesthetic practice to discuss how coherent bodies are made, options are reduced and a single path of practice emerges out of what are really multiplicities, disunities and incoherences of bodies, objects and knowledges in anaesthetic care. They argue that health care practitioners work in a culture in which certainty – of knowledge, diagnosis and actions – is highly valued, yet also an unattainable ideal. They show how this conflict is resolved in practice, relating these concerted efforts at alignment with the demand for accountability placed on health care workers.

The authors in Part 2 explore how patient bodies are represented by medical technologies. All three of these chapters deal with simulators that recreate the female reproductive organs. These chapters look at how medical practices are captured 'by' technology (and problematize this concept in doing so) and how these practices are then reinterpreted in other contexts. Rachel Prentice's work, in Chapter 4, explores the development of a virtual reality simulator designed to teach the physical aspects of minimally invasive surgery. Closely examining the interplay of engineers, computer programmers and surgeons, she shows how a surgeon's physical experience can become mathematized when programmers reconstruct it for computers. Her chapter displays the practices employed when researchers construct 'body objects', representations of bodies and body parts that are engineered to inhabit computer programs. She argues that surgical learning occurs at the interface of bodies and instruments, through simultaneous sculpting of the surgical site and training of the surgeon's body.

Jenny Sundén approaches this subject by analysing a birthing simulator. Her posthuman, feminist understanding of technobodies critically explores how both life and death are simulated in a birthing machine. Sundén reads the simulator inspired by discussions about intersectionality to point out that this particular reproductive machinery and the birth-giving body it simulates is entwined with issues of sexual difference and sexuality as well as race and national belonging.

In similar lines, but with a different theoretical approach, Ericka Johnson discusses how phenomena of knowing bodies are recreated in simulators. Analysing the body of a gynaecological simulator, she shows that simulators reproduce the *experience* of medical practice, even though debates about their validity tend to focus on anatomical structures. At the heart of this conflated discourse lurks the distinction between ontology and epistemology, of what is known and how it is known. She ends her chapter by suggesting that if one understands medical simulations as reconstituted practice rather than representations of ontologically independent human anatomies, one must also ask *whose* experience is being represented by the simulator. As Prentice's chapter discusses, simulators are often designed through collaborations between computer scientists, engineers and medical doctors. In these work constellations, the patient's experience of a medical practice is not merely silenced, it is never even considered. But, taking another lesson from STS, Johnson reminds us that it could be otherwise. One could imagine a simulator which integrates patient-specific phenomena of knowing medical practices.

In the final part of the book, the authors examine how bodies and machines are linked together and the relationships they form. Petra Jonvallen approaches the question of emotions and the abject in her analysis of emotions in the birthing room, presenting research she has done on the integration of a new, electronic foetal monitor into the Swedish health care. In this chapter, she studies how an evidence-based technique was being introduced into birthing practices and why it was difficult to introduce the method despite there being scientific evidence of its merits. Jonvallen describes how the practices of managing emotions and responses to the life and death of the birthing room combine with the introduction of new technologies, and how technologies and emotions can, following Mol (2002), co-produce multiple bodies.

Corinna Kruse's chapter on certainty in the biomedical laboratory uses results from an ethnographic study of a biomedical laboratory to discuss the 'cuts' (Barad 2007) needed to construct machines and humanness. Her work demonstrates that these boundaries are fluid and the cuts both seemingly arbitrary and time and context dependent.

Boundaries and 'cuts', though of a very different kind, also play large roles in Boel Berner's chapter on the technological infrastructures of blood donation. Detailing the cultural and historical context within which specific actors work, she shows that different actors and technologies, based in varied organizational contexts, have changed the character of blood donation. Similar to the hybrid historical approaches found in Timmermann and Anderson (2006), Berner explores the development of blood transfusion systems in Sweden through historical documents but in an analysis coloured by theoretical ideas about sociotechnical assemblages, actors and artefacts found in STS.

Finally, Lucy Suchman's commentary on the various chapters emphasizes the moving interface between bio and techno, bodies and machines in modern biomedicine. She reflects upon how medical practices are restaged and/or transformed in meetings between medical professionals, patients and their kin as bodily encounters that are crucially mediated and made sense of through machines. The body/machine boundary is thus reconfigured as something performed in time, as the interface through which subjects and objects are both differentiated and aligned.

Contributions

Read as a whole, these chapters show how a study about technology and medical practice is also a study of medical knowledges. The normal and the pathological are shaped in knowledge practices in which technology is an actor. Simulator technology becomes a prism to see how knowledge is constructed about the body, and how local knowledges can be presented as neutral and universal through techno-practices. Bodies and machines are linked through local knowledge practices which integrate machines and bodies, and which make machines and bodies work. Emotions are felt and explored, the definition of what is a machine and what is a human is developed, and bodies are literally linked together. Throughout, our work examines and demonstrates alternative forms of knowledge production, a standard of feminist science studies and STS, showing that ways of knowing are not universal. We are helped in this task by one very important practicality: the book contains contributions from researchers active in Sweden, the UK and the US, countries that have very different health care provision systems and ideologies. How these systems and ideologies interact with technological development differently, and the different expectations and demands they place on those working in and receiving care by the systems becomes apparent when these chapters are collected together. By showing that the medical truths implied by, through and in new technologies change as they move across various groups and into heterogeneous practices, this book questions the very idea that medicine can collect a database of 'best practices' that will be 'best' for everyone, everywhere. It debunks the idea that 'evidence' from one setting will necessarily be applicable in another and shows the importance of respecting local practices in policy decisions. Or, as Lucy Suchman concludes in the Epilogue to this book:

> Like bodies (and machines), the singularity and coherence of 'medicine' is articulated not as a prior condition but as an effect of professional and bureaucratic discourses that are enabling of institutional arrangements, but also obscure the messy contingencies, internal contradictions, affective complexities and practical achievements of medicine-in-practice (Suchman, this volume p. 206).

As she also argues, 'To do justice to these realities requires multiple forms of engagement, from specific locations in the midst of temporally unfolding encounters and events, to close readings of historical and organizational records, to theoretically informed reflections on conceptual, practical and political implications' (Suchman, this volume p. 206). Such has been the ambition of the various studies assembled here, and of the volume as a whole. Speaking, as we do, from the intersection of feminist science studies and STS, we hope our perspectives can awaken new ideas and thoughts between and within these fields, as well as among patients, professionals and others who work with medical technologies.

References

Barad, K. 2007. *Meeting the Universe Half-Way*. Durham and London: Duke University Press.

Berg, M. and Mol, A. (eds). 1998. *Differences in Medicine: Unraveling practices, techniques, and bodies*. Durham: Duke University Press.

Berg, M. and Timmermans, S. 2003. The practice of medical technology. *Sociology of Health and Illness*, 25 (Silver Anniversary Issue), 97–114.

Brown, N. and Webster, A. 2004. *New Medical Technologies and Society: Reordering life*. Cambridge and Malden MA: Polity Press.

Haraway, D. 1991. *Simians, Cyborgs, and Women: The reinvention of nature*. New York: Routledge.

Heath, C., Luff, P. and Sanchez Svensson, M. 2003. Technology and medical practice. *Sociology of Health and Illness*, 25 (Silver Anniversary Issue), 75–96.

Martin, E. 1992. *The Woman in the Body: A cultural analysis of reproduction*. Boston: Beacon Press.

Mol, A. 2002. *The Body Multiple: Ontology in medical practice*. Durham: Duke University Press.

Olin Lauritzen, S. and Hydén, L.-C. 2007. *Medical Technologies and the Life World. The social construction of normality*. London and New York: Routledge.

Oudshoorn, N. 1994. *Beyond the Natural Body: An archaeology of sex hormones*. New York and London: Routledge.

Rapp, R. 1999. *Testing women, testing the fetus. The social impact of amniocentesis in America*. New York: Routledge.

Timmermann, C. and Anderson, J. 2006. *Devices and Designs. Medical Technologies in Historical Perspective*. New York: Palgrave Macmillan.

Waldby, C. 2000. *The Visible Human Project: Informatic bodies and posthuman medicine*. London: Routledge.

PART 1
Judging Bodies

The discourse of medicine relies on certainty, but the messiness of practice presents ambiguity. This paradox becomes particularly apparent when discussing the normal and the pathological. How do we know what is normal? How can we determine what is abnormal? These are questions inherent in medicine (see Canguilhem 1991, Fausto-Sterling 2000, Oudshoorn 1994, Waldby 2000). However, as the following chapters show, technology can sometimes bring these concepts into focus in interesting ways, highlighting how the (ab)normal is defined in context and through concerted, cooperative work. Technologies can be used to redefine the normal and the pathological for practitioners and patients alike, the starting point for the first three chapters in this book.

In Chapter 1, Celia Roberts presents an analysis of how pubescent bodies are defined in contemporary biomedical discourses. Her critical reading of medical papers, textbooks and media reports examines the changing definition of 'pathological' puberty (early, late and undesired puberty), and the increasing numbers of bodies which are being included in that category. Drawing on science and technology studies, social studies of health and medicine and feminist theory, she uses examples to discuss norms and interventions in biomedicine. Roberts' work is fascinating in that it shows how the definition of pathological is both flexible over time and across cultures, for example, how breast development at age eight is redefined as normal in the US to avoid the costs of mass screening but that breast development at eight is still considered pathological in the UK. Her work also points to disturbing examples of biomedical practices, as when she discusses the hormonal treatments advocated for Gender Identity Disorder, a medical procedure used to delay puberty in children who may possibly wish to change their sex as adults. Roberts demonstrates that Gender Identity Disorder is presented within a discourse of 'acceptable' behaviour for girls and boys which pathologizes non-normative gender identities and requires adherence to a narrowly defined script of acceptable behaviours.

Roberts is discussing the construction of pathology, but she shows that medical practitioners are not blind to the changing definition of normal occurring in their practices. Her material indicates that practitioners are aware that norms are not the same as normal, optimal health. Roberts calls for research which also engages parents, teachers and children in examining how everyday puberty is lived and ordered, encouraging us to view puberty as a transition to adulthood rather than leaving it as a question of normal and pathological bodies.

Kerstin Sandell's study discusses how practitioners grapple with the normal and the pathological in their everyday work practices. Through ethnographic study of routine ultrasound screening, her chapter shows that a distinction between the normal and the pathological is taught and made by midwives in the examination room. Her research presents the details of work that maintain an aura of objectivity around the exam, an exam which serves to decide what abnormalities lay within the jurisdiction of medicine and are thereby treatable.

Sandell's close ethnographic study of learning practices describe how the work practices of midwives are seen by them as necessary for observing and determining the (ab)normal and teaching this ability to newcomers. Of primary importance is the assumption that an individual midwife's ability to recognize the normal and the pathological is dependent on his/her exposure to many real foetuses, a cumulative knowledge that grows out of many visual impressions. This plays in stark contrast to the idea of learning the normal through books, anatomies and other text-based material. But learning to see the normal through practice is also dependent on the technological capabilities of the ultrasound machine. Newer, more advanced ultrasounds will potentially enable different views and the discovery of more deviant, 'abnormal' scans. How this should be integrated into the existing work practices is a point of negotiation between midwives and obstetricians, but it also involves careful handling of the feedback given to parents during the exam.

Sandell's chapter presents an interesting material element to establishing the normal/pathological. Within the Swedish practice of state funded, routine, ultrasound scanning in week seventeen, 'results' of a normal scan are not saved. Except for the 'snapshot' image sent home with the expectant parents, there is no storage of raw ultrasound data, still images or video, that can be referred to later should an abnormality appear. Thus midwives are taught to interpret the scans for the parents using conditional statements like 'as far as we can see', or 'ok for now'. This is in strong contrast to the simulator technologies discussed in Part 2. In Sandell's research, the normal comprises a tentative position and an absence of materialized representations, which reflects Roberts' concern in Chapter 1 that there is an overemphasis on the pathological and not enough discussion of the normal within medical practice.

How to interpret technological ways of knowing the body are also examined in the third chapter. Drawing on ethnomethodological analysis of anaesthesiology practice, Dawn Goodwin and Maggie Mort present accountability being achieved in practice through interactions between people and artefacts. In their examples, public consensus is produced and an intervention is legitimated in the interactions between the technologies of anaesthesiology, the clinical team and the patient's body. Their examination clearly shows the distinction between the ethnomethodological sense of accountability and the professional one.

In the material they have gathered, Goodwin and Mort first demonstrate how routines and norms signify accountable practice, but then they show that in the messiness of clinical practice, where coherent narratives and routines are sometimes lacking, much work is done by clinicians to make an intervention accountable. They suggest that there are different accountability communities and that policy-makers, practitioners, ethnomethodologists and science studies researchers understand the concept differently. Is accountability a decontextualized 'account' open to the judgement of others or something that is interactionally achieved between co-participants? Their work adds accountability into the analytical framework espoused by science and technology studies that views incoherences and disunity in medical practices, knowledge, objects, technologies and bodies. Through ethnomethodological detail, Goodwin and Mort demonstrate how practitioners maintain accountability within a paradigm that expects certainty even when certainty is missing in practice, and how routines and accountability are practised even in the face of ambiguity.

Thus, all three chapters deal with how medical practices incorporate technologies to deal with certainty and ambiguity when creating knowledge about and treatments for the (ab)normal body. In them, technology is sometimes used to judge what is normal and create knowledge about the body, but it does not work alone; it interacts with policy guidelines, practitioners, bodies, patients – even patients' families – in creating and defining the normal, healthy patient. Incorporating technology into the analysis of these practices forces us to pay analytical attention to the collective, often cooperative and often very repetitive elements of knowing practices upon which an understanding of the (ab)normal relies.

References

Canguilhem, G. [1978] 1991. *The Normal and the Pathological*. Translated by Carolyn R. Fawcett in collaboration with Robert S. Cohen. New York: Zone Books.

Fausto-Sterling, A. 2000. *Sexing the Body: Gender politics and the construction of sexuality*. New York: Basic Books.

Oudshoorn, N. 1994. *Beyond the Natural Body: An archaeology of sex hormones*. New York and London: Routledge.

Waldby, C. 2000. *The Visible Human Project: Informatic bodies and posthuman medicine*. London and New York: Routledge.

Chapter 1

Defining the Pubescent Body: Three Cases of Biomedicine's Approach to 'Pathology'

Celia Roberts

The pubescent body is usually represented as a body in tumult. For both boys and girls, although with quite different inflections according to sex, puberty is understood as a time of profound and irreversible change. For increasing numbers of children in wealthy countries, puberty is also associated with pathology and biomedical intervention. For these children, puberty comes too late, too early or is fundamentally undesired. In such cases, biomedicine offers pharmacological interventions to bring puberty on or to hold it off till later. Puberty thus becomes a medico-technical experience: a coming together of blood, guts and machines in challenging and highly consequential ways.

In this chapter, I tell stories about puberty in order to critically question how pubescent bodies are defined in contemporary biomedical discourses. The chapter is based on critical readings of diverse textual sources, including medical papers and textbooks, media articles and internet resources. My argument suggests that some pubescent bodies – understood as 'pathological' – are today becoming sites for seriously consequential biomedical interventions; others – understood to be 'normal' – are left to develop without such intervention. Significantly, in the current era increasing numbers of pubescent bodies are meeting established biomedical criteria for 'pathology' (and hence intervention). This paper investigates the effects of this change, and how it is being managed. Engaging with Georges Canguilhem's ([1978] 1991) argument about modern biology's focus on the abnormal in establishing norms, I suggest that there is much to be learnt from the example of puberty about the status of bodies, norms and interventions in biomedicine today.

Technoscientific Understandings of Puberty

In biomedical textbooks, puberty is defined as the process that produces a body able to sexually reproduce. In the 6th edition of *Human Physiology: From cells to systems*, for example, Lauralee Sherwood (2007: 739) writes, 'Puberty is the period of arousal and maturation of the previously non-functional reproductive system, culminating in sexual maturity and the ability to reproduce.' In an era of ever-increasing rates of infertility, this is a rather uncomfortable definition (did people who cannot reproduce as adults not go through puberty?), but it is one that nevertheless holds. A recent scientific review published in *Reproduction*, for example, baldly states that 'Puberty is the attainment of fertility' (Ebling 2005: 682).

In material terms, puberty is described as the process of developing what physiologists call 'secondary sexual characteristics' (breasts, pubic hair, adult genitalia) and of moving into an adult cycle of production of sex cells (eggs and sperm). The biological processes associated with such developments are complex. According to undergraduate physiology textbooks, in late childhood maturational changes and decreased inhibitory mechanisms in the brain increase secretion of gonadotropin releasing hormone (GnRH) from the hypothalamus in pulses during sleep. Over time these pulses become longer until an adult pattern is established. The pulses of GnRH lead to increased secretion of luteinizing hormone (LH) and follicle-stimulating hormone (FSH) from the anterior pituitary, which in turn increases secretion of either testosterone from the testes or estrogen from the ovaries. It is these well-known sex hormones that 'arouse' the dormant reproductive systems, stimulating the development of the secondary sexual characteristics.

Like many hormone stories, this story of sexual development maintains an understanding of sexual difference as binary (see Roberts 2007). Stories of puberty in girls focus on the estrogen-producing ovaries, and stories about boys focus on testosterone-producing testes. In relation to boys, for example, Sherwood (1997: 739) writes that 'Testosterone is responsible for growth and maturation of the entire male reproductive system.' In a section on girls, she states 'GnRH begins stimulating release of anterior pituitary gonadotropic hormones, which in turn stimulate ovarian activity. The resulting secretion of estrogen by the activated ovaries induces growth and maturation of the female reproductive tract as well as development of the female secondary sexual characteristics' (Sherwood 2007: 762). It is important to note, however, that girls also experience changes in androgen secretions at puberty. In pubescent girls, these 'male' hormones are linked, Sherwood (1997: 762) explains, to the growth of pubic and underarm hair, overall growth and 'the development of libido'. Similarly (although much more 'surprisingly' for biomedicine), estrogen also affects male sexual development. 'Recent findings suggest', Sherwood notes (1997: 742) 'that estrogen plays an essential role in male reproductive health; for example, it is important in spermatogenesis and surprisingly contributes to male heterosexuality. Also, it likely contributes to bone homeostasis.' Such 'surprises', as I argue elsewhere, stem from a long history of understanding sexual difference as binary and even oppositional, and have no basis in physiological reasoning or material evidence (Roberts 2007, see also Oudshoorn 1994, Fausto-Sterling 2000).

The hormones released in puberty do stimulate significant biological differences between women and men's bodies, namely, ovulatory and menstrual cycles in women and continuous sperm production in men. The differences between these sets of processes are much discussed: Sherwood (1997: 752), for example, concludes that 'Female reproductive physiology is much more complex than male reproductive physiology. Unlike the continuous sperm production and essentially constant testosterone secretion characteristic of the male, release of ova is intermittent, and secretion of female sex hormones displays wide cyclic swings'. Her use of the non-technical term 'swings' – a word often associated with emotional lability – references a wide-spread cultural interpretation of this difference: women are often understood as moody and fluctuating because of their sexual physiologies, whilst men are seen as constantly desiring and stable. Such differences are, as Sherwood's writing shows, built into discourses of puberty and thus into children's lives at very young ages.

Blood, Guts and Mysterious Machines

Despite this physiological knowledge of the 'blood and guts' constituting it, puberty remains, as physiologists Palmert and Boepple (2001: 2367) write, 'a long-standing mystery' for biomedicine. The two key elements constituting this mystery are described in a review article written by a group of pediatricians and published in *Endocrine Reviews* (Parent et al. 2003). Firstly, in humans there is extraordinary variety in the timing of puberty in the current era ('a 4–5 year physiological variation in age at onset') (Parent et al. 2003: 668) and a similar variation in the timing of puberty across historical periods. In Europe, for example, age at puberty for girls dropped from 17 in 1830 to under 14 in 1960 (Parent et al. 2003: 673, see also Ellis 2004: 926). Secondly, what actually *causes* puberty to start remains uncertain. In their introduction, Parent et al. (2003: 668) write that 'puberty results from the awakening of a complex neuroendocrine machinery in which the primary mechanism is still unclear'. According to these clinicians, then, puberty constitutes a profound paradox: a machine with incomprehensible mechanics (which could, logically, only be a kind of alien entity).

Aliens aside, the use of a machine metaphor to describe the pubescent body is unsurprising. As several authors have argued, from the 18th century on, such metaphors have been ubiquitous in biological discourses (see for example, Canguilhem [1978] 1991, Stacey 2000, Waldby 2000). In relation more specifically to reproduction, anthropologist Emily Martin ([1987] 1992) describes biomedical texts' reliance on cultural discourses of factory-based production in describing menstruation. Menstruation is figured as a kind of failure of purpose (to conceive) and as producing disgusting waste. 'Menstruation', she argues, 'not only carries with it the connotation of a productive system that has failed to produce, it also carries the idea of production gone awry, making products of no use, not to specification, unsaleable, wasted, scrap' (Martin [1987] 1992: 46). Such descriptions, Martin suggests, are linked to understandings of gender and work. The reference to menstruation as failed activity resonates with the 19th and early to mid 20th century idea that women are supposed to be at home reproducing the species, 'providing a safe, warm womb to nurture a man's sperm' (Martin [1987] 1992: 47).

In contemporary biomedical discourses of puberty, mechanical discourses are particularly strong when genes are invoked as stimulating hormonal cascades. Palmert and Boepple (2001: 2364), for example, argue that 'The mechanism(s) underlying the relative suppression and the subsequent pubertal activation of hypothalamic GnRH secretion is unknown but of critical importance. Further understanding of the maturation of GnRH secretion and pituitary responsiveness is vital to understanding the mechanism(s) behind the broad variation in the timing of puberty.' Their suggestion for promoting such understanding is to search for the specific genes that constitute what they describe as a form of 'genetic control' underlying environmental and metabolic factors influencing the timing of puberty, which they suggest are 'critical regulators' of the timing of puberty, 'but their influence is superimposed on significant genetic control' (Palmert and Boepple 2001: 2366). Such understandings of genes as providing a kind of overarching control of complex biological mechanisms have been much criticized as overly simplistic and locked into limiting cultural views both of machines and of individuals' relations with their environments (see, for example, Fox Keller 2001, Oyama 1985).[1]

Puberty's mysterious nature tends to challenge the use of machine metaphors, however, as machines are usually entities that experts at least can understand. Puberty, on the other hand, is riddled with complexities, mostly centring on the relations between individual biological factors (genes and hormonal systems) and 'other' or 'environmental' factors. Unlike many technoscientific descriptions of hormonal or other biological processes that figure the body as an enclosed, homeostatic biological system (see for example, Roberts 2007, Spanier 1995), contemporary biomedical texts describe the causes of puberty in ways that (could) disrupt typical technoscientific distinctions between the biological and the social. Ebling (2005: 683), for example, writes that '[T]he neurotransmitter and neuromodulatory systems that impact upon the GnRH secretory network convey information about metabolic fuels, energy stores and somatic development and, for many species, information about season and social environment.' This mention of 'social environment' is unusual in biological texts about internal bodily processes.

Despite these unusual references to the interplay of biological, environmental and even social factors, biomedical discourses struggle to understand and to represent the importance of non-biological actors in puberty. Parent et al. (2003), for example, discuss an extraordinary range of possible contributors to the timing of puberty, including genes, inter-uterine conditions, insulin sensitivity, diet, exposure to sunlight, environmental toxins and emotional and physical stress, but want to insist that the most important factor is straightforwardly biological (genetic).

---

1   For a more detailed analysis of genetic arguments about early puberty see Throsby and Roberts, forthcoming.

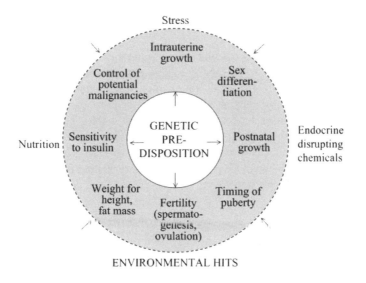

Figure 1.1   Environmental hits

Source: Parent, A.S.,Teilman, G., Juul, A., Skakkebæk, N.E., Toppari, J. and Bourguignon, J.P. 2003. The timing of normal puberty and the age limits of sexual precocity: Variations around the world, secular trends, and changes after migration. *Endocrine Reviews*, 24(5), 686. © 2003, *The Endocrine Society*, reproduced with permission.

Observations and findings from twin studies, they argue, 'indicate that 70–80% of the variance in pubertal timing can be explained by heritable factors' (Parent et al. 2003: 679). Such heritable factors are not simple: indeed, Parent et al. (2003: 680) suggest that 'It is likely that a cascade of genes may determine variations in timing of pubertal onset', but they remain firmly within the body's own systems. In trying to set these genetic factors in relation to the other, less straightforwardly biological factors, Parent et al. provide a diagram constituted by concentric circles, in which 'genetic predisposition' takes the central position. This genetic core affects the other circles in an outward-pointing fashion; genes affect bodies, not the other way around (Parent et al. 2003: 686. See Figure 1.1). Surrounding this individual biological 'core' come other more obviously biological factors (post-natal growth, weight, insulin sensitivity, possible malignancies). Encircling these is a series of 'environmental hits' that pound at the edge of the circle as inward-pointing arrows (stress, endocrine disrupting chemicals and nutrition).

Such diagrams, as Jackie Stacey (2000) has argued in the case of alternative health discourses on cancer, position the individual and his or her susceptibilities within an environmental context of 'risk' (here, 'hits') that are more or less avoidable. The individual body in such representations is positioned as potentially pure: something that is overwhelmed or attacked by 'unnatural' forces. Although the mysterious timing of puberty, in Parent et al.'s model, is 'integrat[ed] … within a spectrum of processes that are influenced by both genetic and environmental factors' (Parent et al. 2003: 686), these factors remain figuratively distinct and hierarchically sited: genes are at the core and the environment attacks the body from the outside. Such representations, I will argue in the remainder of this chapter, fail to come to terms with the disruptive potential of puberty as a site in which distinctions between biology and the social are impossible to maintain. The model of concentric circles maintains a kind of pure, biological norm and figures 'other' (environmental or social) factors as abnormal, something 'outside' that should be resisted. 'Normal' puberty, in this model, is something that is not notably influenced by external factors (these remain merely 'permissive') (Parent et al. 2003: 686), but is largely determined by genes.

Pathology, Normality and Clinical Machines

In his influential work *The Normal and the Pathological*, historian of biology Georges Canguilhem ([1978] 1991) argued that modern scientific knowledge of normal biological processes is established through production of knowledge about, and exclusion of, the abnormal (what he calls normalization). '[T]he norm', (the standard against which bodies are measured), he argues, 'is what determines the normal starting from a normative decision' (Canguilhem [1978] 1991: 245). '[T]he abnormal,' in other words, 'while logically second, is existentially first' (Canguilhem [1978] 1991: 243). This argument has strong resonance in the case of biomedical accounts of puberty. In the biomedical literature great emphasis is placed on children who do not undergo puberty in a 'normal' way – those for whom puberty is early ('precocious'), late ('delayed') or even undesirable (the case of children diagnosed with 'gender identity disorder'). Exploration of these issues underpins biomedical understandings of normal processes of development, and marks out (pathological) bodies in which, in the cases of precocious and undesired sexual development, puberty is *unusually* socially or environmentally affected. For delayed puberty, the opposite seems to be true: children with delayed puberty suffer from genetic conditions which render their bodies unable to respond *enough* to their environments. These bodies, arguably, are not social enough to become pubescent. In all these cases of 'abnormality', the 'blood and guts' of puberty become articulated with the machines of clinical biomedicine: through clinical encounters, assessments and pharmaceutical technologies. In such articulations, these kinds of pubescent bodies become new entities, their instantiations and experiences profoundly enmeshed with socio-technical actors. In all of these cases, biomedicine attempts to bio-chemically produce particular kinds of puberty – to return bodies to a desired normality or, in the case of children diagnosed with 'Gender Identity Disorder', to suspend puberty for some years. These attempts to form certain kinds of pubescent bodies, I argue below, come with particular consequences and costs, both for the children and families involved and for our understandings and experiences of bodies more generally today.

Delayed Puberty

Although there is much more concern about early or precocious puberty, there are some children for whom puberty comes so late it is deemed problematic (that is, beginning after the age of 13 according to internationally agreed standards) (see, for example, Traggiai and Stanhope 2003). These children are usually living with a genetic condition that affects their body's ability to produce or respond to particular hormones, such as Turner's syndrome or Prader-Willi syndrome. For such children, pharmaceutical treatments are widely available. Alonso and Rosenfeld (2002: 26), for example, in writing of 'abnormal puberty', note that 'Girls with insufficient oestrogen can now be treated with physiological oestrogen replacement regimens without compromising final adult height. Aromatase inhibitors or anti-oestrogens are potential treatment modalities for delayed puberty in boys and incomplete precocious puberty in both sexes.' Puberty, in this framework is something that can go seriously wrong but which 'can now be treated'. Such treatments are not without risks. Tests required to assess children's growth include X-rays (to assess 'bone age') and blood tests, as well as karyotyping in some cases. The long-term risks of treatment are also noteworthy. In the case of delayed puberty in girls, for example, Alonso and Rosenfeld (2002: 27) note that more research is needed into 'the development of very low dose oestradiol delivery systems suitable for induction of puberty in short, hypogonadal girls' as anything other than very low doses may reduce the girl's adult height, by affecting bone formation (inhibiting it rather than stimulating it, as 'biological' levels of oestrogens do). Developing the appropriate 'delivery systems' means developing injections, pills, implants or patches that introduce manufactured chemicals in doses and timings as close as possible to 'normal' biological amounts and processes. In these cases, then, children with genetic conditions are provided with pharmacological treatments to simulate or stimulate 'normal' processes of development. Such treatments, arguably, open these children's bodies to 'the social' in very specific ways, rendering their experience of puberty a complex negotiation of doctors, drugs and disciplinary regimes.

Precocious Puberty

On the other end of the clinical spectrum are children who experience puberty 'too early' and whose puberty is seen to be perhaps overly responsive to social or environmental conditions. This condition is described by clinicians and parents in emotive language; in a response to an article in which the British parents of a girl who started puberty at six and a half describe their difficult experiences getting medical help, for example, the commissioning editor sympathetically names precocious puberty a 'frightening condition' and admits that 'Treatment for this rare but devastating condition for parents and children is still somewhat unpredictable' (O'Sullivan, O'Sullivan and Mann 2002: 321).

Although the definitions of this condition are shifting as more and more children experience it, in the United States in 2003, puberty was defined as clinically precocious for white girls if it occurred before seven or eight and for white boys before nine. For black girls, the cut-off age was lower: six or seven years (Parent et al. 2003: 675).[2] As this 'racial' difference begins to indicate, the causes of precocious puberty are complex and unclear. 'Racial differences in the age of puberty constitute a long term mystery: is this difference due to diet, social experiences or something more 'biological'? In the conclusion to their long review, Parent et al. present precocious puberty as a bodily (genetic) response to non-genetic (environmental, social, nutritional) factors; something that occurs only in 'specific situations'. Individual variability in the onset of normal puberty, they write, 'is likely to depend on the genetic control of the expression of signals or signal receptors in the hypothalamus. This process is only slightly influenced by peripheral and environmental signals, which play an essentially permissive role in those conditions. In specific situations, however,' they argue, 'these peripheral and environmental signals may play a crucial role in the occurrence of either abnormal precocious (or delayed) puberty in a subset of the population or increased incidence of precocity (or delay) because of a shift in timing of a whole population' (Parent et al. 2003: 686). Precocious puberty (and some forms of delayed puberty) is the result of unusually strong effects of external factors. This can happen both to individuals and to 'whole populations'.

One of the most fascinating indicators for precocious puberty is migration. As Parent et al. describe, over the last ten years many parents of girls adopted from poor countries (India, Romania or China, for example) have reported that these children (usually girls) go through puberty notably earlier than their peers in their adopted countries (Sweden or Belgium, for example) and their peers in their home countries (see also Virdis et al. 1998). This may have to do with a change in nutrition – often these children are underweight when they arrive in the adopting country (Parent et al. 2003: 682) – but might also be do with the stress of adoption itself (Parent et al. 2003: 683). Interestingly, other studies have shown that children migrating with their biological families also go through puberty earlier than their peers (Parent et al. 2003: 683). These children may not be experiencing significant changes in diet and are not acquiring new parents or experiencing the 'affective deprivation' that usually precedes such a change (Parent et al. 2003: 683), but they are experiencing multiple bio-social changes: new climates, new exposures to daylight, new foods, new social relations. Such children are also experiencing

---

2   I have been unable to find a figure for black boys. Most of the literature focuses on girls: as Parent et al. (2003: 675) state, most precocious puberty occurs in girls (a three to one or four to one ratio), a proportion that appears to be increasing in many studies. British treatment guidelines produced on behalf of the British Society for Paediatric Endocrinology and Diabetes (Kirk 2004) report that 90 per cent of cases of central precocious puberty (that is, precocious puberty not caused by any specific pathology such as a brain tumour) are girls.

a change in exposure to environmental toxins (such as organochlorine pesticides in foods): even though they may be moving from a place of higher exposure, the change might in itself, Parent et al. suggest, provoke a pathological response: '[M]igration may interrupt exposure of foreign children to some EDCs [endocrine disrupting chemicals]. In such conditions, it is unknown whether central precocious puberty could result indirectly from withdrawal of the negative feedback effects of the sex steroids or their environmental analogs and/or directly from accelerated hypothalamic maturation caused by sex steroids' (Parent et al. 2003: 685).

As for delayed puberty, many children experiencing precocious puberty are offered biomedical assessments and pharmaceutical treatments. Such treatments block GnRH receptors in the pituitary gland, holding off the hormonal cascades leading to the development of secondary sexual characteristics. As with the treatments for delayed puberty, there are risks here both in terms of assessments (again, X-rays are commonly used to assess bone growth and MRIs may be used to check for tumours or other pathologies) and in terms of long-term outcomes, particularly in relation to adult height (see, for example, Hirsch et al. 2005, O'Sullivan, O'Sullivan and Mann 2002).

Deciding who to offer clinical assessments to is also an issue of growing concern and debate. A commentary published in *Pediatrics* in 1999 suggested that in the United States, increasing numbers of children experiencing early puberty meant that physicians would soon not be able to provide clinical assessments to those who under earlier clinical regimes would have been offered them. Working with figures from key studies and referring to one of the most common measurements of the onset of puberty (the Tanner Scale) the authors write,

> This totals 195 400 girls <8 years old with at least Tanner 2 pubic hair. There are ~650 pediatric endocrinologists in the United States. If all these girls truly need an evaluation, then each endocrinologist would have to see, on average, 300 of these girls. If we estimate the cost for a basic evaluation as proposed by the authors of an examination and bone age films (including radiologist interpretation) at $250, the cost to evaluate these girls would be $48,850,000. (Herman-Giddens, Kaplowitz and Wasserman 1999: 915)

Their conclusion is that 'Primary care physicians should not blindly use the age of a child as a guide for referral' (Herman-Giddens, Kaplowitz and Wasserman 1999: 915): such 'blindness' would clearly, in their view, overload clinical and medical insurance systems.

This discussion of the costs and practical issues relating to offering assessments to children experiencing early puberty indicates the difficulties associated with the significant changes in puberty in the developed world today. It is, of course, simpler (as has been done in the United States) to alter the threshold of 'normal' puberty, to say, for example, that it is no longer pathological to undergo breast development at eight, than to pour resources into offering screening to so many children. In the UK, interestingly, this alteration has not been made (Kirk 2004) (which is not to say that there are no concerns about cost of screening and treatment) (see, for example, O'Sullivan, O'Sullivan and Mann 2002).

Changing the cut-off ages for 'normal' puberty, Herman-Giddens, Kaplowitz and Wasserman argue, risks papering over the potentially serious nature of increasing rates of early puberty and silencing the '"canary in the mine" for environmental problems' that such rates may constitute (Herman-Giddens, Kaplowitz and Wasserman 1999: 925). As they bluntly state in a pair of final summary statements:

1. Data show that girls are maturing earlier than they did several decades ago and that there are substantial racial differences between white and black girls.
2. These 'norms' are not the same as the condition of being 'normal' in the sense of indicating optimal health (Herman-Giddens, Kaplowitz and Wasserman 1999: 925–926).

This distinction between what is statistically normal and what is healthy returns us to Canguilhem's argument. The paradox of such a distinction has the potential to undermine fundamental biomedical approaches to thinking about bodies that understand norms as constituting health. Although the potentially serious impact on the economics of healthcare is worrying, refusing to assess children because their early puberty is statistically normative may be unwise because such precocity may indeed be unhealthy and, additionally, may provide important information about the environmental conditions in which we all now live. Maintaining categories of 'pathological' puberty (and keeping these categories moving so that they do not contain too many children) means maintaining an idea of 'normal' puberty at high cost: both to the children exposed to potentially risky assessment technologies and pharmacological treatments and to the children who remain in the (newly constructed) norm. Maintaining normal/pathological distinctions, in other words, means diverting attention away from more difficult questions about environmental toxins, the emotional distress of migration and adoption or the effects of high-fat diets on young people, and remaining focused on internal biological systems and hormonal interventions.

Clinically Preventing Puberty

Discourses on delayed and precocious puberty (including those I have produced above) employ a language of simple sex distinctions: speaking of 'boys' and 'girls' as if these are self-evident categories. In other, less prevalent clinical discourses, however, such distinctions themselves become the subject of discussion. For children diagnosed with 'Gender Identity Disorder' (the term now used in psychiatry to describe what used to be called transsexuality), puberty is approached with dread. Whilst young children who do not feel they fit into the standard category of 'male' or 'female' that socially 'fits' their body type can often successfully dress and behave in a way they feel happy with (and, importantly, that does not evoke suspicions in others), at puberty the body can begin to undo such lives. Living as a young boy with girl's genitals is one thing – genitals can be hidden in primary school – but living as a boy with a teenage woman's breasts, figure and menstrual cycles is quite another. Popular media, activist and research literatures all describe the agonies of such experiences (see, for example, Smiley 2007, Gender Identity Research and Education Society undated, Van de Waal and Cohen-Kettenis 2006). Puberty, as noted earlier, is often figured as tumultuous change; for those for whom this is change in the wrong direction, consolidating and building an undesired adult embodiment, it is unbearable somatic treachery.

In the framework of my argument here, the example of children diagnosed with Gender Identity Disorder provides a case of 'extreme' sociality in terms of puberty. Although some might argue that there are genetic causes of transgender identity (or Gender Identity Disorder), there is no biological (genetic, hormonal or other) 'problem' with the processes of pubertal development for children in this group. Their reasons for seeking pharmacological treatments in relation to puberty are 'purely' social: they are about personal and social identity and the profound desire to live differently from what would usually be expected. Even more strongly than in the case of precocity, then, puberty in this third case is understood as something that can be controlled and managed through biomedicine. For this small, yet growing, group of children, their pubescent bodies become experimental sites for intervening in 'normal' biological processes in order to meet intense social desires.

In recent years, some clinics, notably in The Netherlands, Australia and the United States, have begun to offer children diagnosed with Gender Identity Disorder biomedical treatments that delay puberty for several years, so that they have more time in which to make a decision about transitioning between genders.[3] Using pharmacological interventions to interrupt the gonadal effects of GnRH secretion at the point at which puberty has just started (around 12 years of age) means that the child remains small and undeveloped compared to peers (placing the child in a similar position to those diagnosed with delayed puberty) (Van de Waal and Cohen-Kettenis 2006) and subjects the child to other potential long-term risks (in relation to bone density and fertility, for example) (Gender Identity Research and Education Society undated: 3). For these children and their parents, however, such delays are worth risking, firstly because they avoid the suffering of unwanted physical development, and secondly because the treatments produce a body

---

3   In the UK, controversially, such treatments are not allowed (Gender Identity Research and Education Society undated: 3). Indeed, guidelines produced by the British Society for Pediatric Endocrinology and Diabetes (BSPED) (2005) argued that it was necessary for children to experience their post-pubertal bodies as their birth sex before deciding to transition (Giordano 2008). These guidelines are no longer available online, and at the time of writing (July 2009) the website of the BSPED notes that new guidelines are forthcoming (www.bsped.org.uk/professional/guidelines/index.htm).

that can, as an older teenager or adult, undergo directed hormonal interventions to become the sex of choice. The young person's body is thus biochemically constituted as a relatively 'blank canvas' for later, desired sexual development and the hormonal medications and surgery subsequently needed to change the body can be less invasive because the body will be less developed sexually (although there may also be negative consequences: a lack of genital development may mean there is less tissue for surgical genital construction in later life [Gender Identity Research and Education Society undated: 3]). Delaying puberty with medication allows the child more time to make highly consequential decisions about hormonal treatments designed to develop secondary sexual characteristics and surgery to remove unwanted body parts and make others: 'Suspending puberty provides the adolescent, and the clinicians, with an extended period of time in which to examine thoroughly his or her own sense of gender identity whilst being spared the stress of full puberty' (Gender Identity Research and Education Society undated: 3). The slogan for the drug used in this process (*Luberon*) – 'Pause the child within' (Smiley 2007: 2) – is somewhat misleading in this respect. The point is not to 'pause the child', but to allow the young adult time to develop psychologically without being pushed into an undesired biological sex.[4]

For feminist sociologist Myra Hird, this is a troubling process. In an argument that resonates with my concerns about precocious puberty, Hird (2003) asks whether attending to the individual biomedical needs of individual children risks obscuring social issues around gender norms and expectations of children's behaviour. In an ethnographic report of a biomedical conference on recent developments in the field of transgender interventions, she describes the inability of clinicians such as leading Dutch physician Peggy Cohen-Kettenis (cited above) to understand feminist questions about the relation between sex and gender or sociological analyses of sexuality as socially constructed. Hird suggests that the turn to pharmacological control of puberty is linked both with a limiting understanding of sex/gender as binary and, perhaps more disturbingly, a continuing understanding of homosexuality as pathology. Children diagnosed with Gender Identity Disorder, she reports, were described as suffering from individual pathologies that needed to be fixed to ensure happiness. Ambiguous gender identity, as evidenced by atypical behavioural preferences (liking both to play roughly with boys and to wear skirts, for example) was associated with instability and immaturity. The aim of hormonal

---

4   It is interesting to compare these discourses about transsexual children to those about intersex children (children born with physical attributes that do not align with standard biomedical understandings of 'male' or 'female'). In both cases, the ultimate goal is to give children time to grow up and make a decision about their own sexual and gender identity. In the case of intersex children, as has been widely discussed in the sociological and activist literature, creating this time for children means withholding biomedical intervention (surgical or hormonal) (see, for example Fausto-Sterling 2000, Chase 1998, Holmes 2000). Here, the demand is for hormonal treatments, and the prospect of future surgical treatment is framed in positive terms.

treatments of Gender Identity Disorder, Hird argues, appeared at this conference to be to produce children who would behave normatively for whichever sex they 'chose'.

Discussion: Beyond Blood, Guts and Machines?

In these three cases, hormones are used to speed up or to delay puberty. The 'pathological' pubescent body thus becomes something alterable by pharmaceutical hormonal technologies: complex articulations of blood, guts and machines. Such interventions constitute a form of 'reordering life' (Brown and Webster 2004) that is highly recognisable today: contemporary bodies are, as many commentators have pointed out, understood to be biomedically malleable and potentially open to multiple 'enhancement' technologies (Hogle 2005). In the case of 'pathological' puberty, children's bodies are assessed by biomedical technologies such as X-rays and MRIs and reordered with drugs injections, implants or pills. The human actors involved in such reorderings are multiple and include endocrinologists, psychiatrists, parents, support groups, pediatricians, pharmacists, pharmaceutical company representatives, peers, teachers and the children themselves.

But these cases also demonstrate that pathological puberty is not just about blood, guts and machines but about the social, experiential living of particular kinds of bodies. The actors defining these bodies are much more diverse than the drugs and humans listed above. We learn from the examples of pathological puberty that the hormonal processes of sexual development are opened onto social and environmental actors in ways that profoundly challenge models of internal, genetic or hormonal causation – indeed, that constitute puberty as a biomedical 'mystery'. From these examples, it becomes evident that puberty is not 'simply' biological, but is affected by a range of conditions, many of which are external to the child's body (sunlight, food, 'race', toxins, television, shampoo and obesity, for example). All of these are arguably linked to biological factors (genes in the case of 'race', hormones in the case of toxins, TV, sunlight or shampoo), but such links are neither simple nor direct. All of these factors, I suggest, trouble conventional social/biological distinctions.

Studies of precocious puberty show that other factors even less directly linked to biology affect pubertal timing (for example, migration, emotional deprivation and stress). Questions around the contribution of such factors to the ordering of pubescent bodies demonstrate the difficulties in making biological/ social distinctions when talking about the actors involved in defining bodies in biomedical settings and discourses. These difficulties are even further expanded in the case of transgender or Gender Identity Disorder experiences, in which the social demands of the child and family are pre-eminent and are, in some clinical and national contexts, translated via rigorous psychiatric technologies of assessment into biomedical procedures. Such translations raise complex issues about consent and the long-term effects of such intervention, but they are nonetheless understood by some to provide much needed opportunities for some children to have time to consider body-changing decisions. Although, as Hird argued, discourses of Gender Identity Disorder are often conservative in relation to sex, gender and sexuality, stories about children wanting to perform different kinds of gender demonstrate that puberty is never simply a natural or inevitable consequence of genetic and hormonal cascades. Puberty is a lived, social experience that has profound consequences for who we think we are and how others think we should behave. The experience of this particular group of children highlights the complex bio-social negotiations going on for all children undergoing this period of change

When bodies meet pharmaceutical machines in clinical practice, they do so as complex, lived entities. Contemporary bodies are not only constituted by blood and guts, but are always articulated with machines, at both metaphoric and practice levels. They are also always lived: psychologically, emotionally, environmentally, historically, geographically. The actors articulating pubescent bodies are not just 'biological': instead, puberty is configured and lived through interactions between a range of actors that confound attempts to arrange hierarchical circles of significance or to establish centres and peripheries. To approach puberty more fruitfully, I suggest, we need to experiment with different models of understanding bodily experiences and contemporary articulations of blood, guts and machines. One way of doing this would be to shift critical attention away from pathologized bodies and focus instead on opening up the experience of 'normal' puberty to investigation and/or experiment. Such an approach would avoid reinforcing the model I have described in this chapter in which 'normal' puberty is understood as 'simply' biological (genetic and hormonal) and pathological puberty figured as either too biological (as in the case of delayed puberty) or overly open to the social (as in the cases of early puberty and un-desired puberty). The consequences for children diagnosed with pathological puberty are profound, and as this group increases in size, we need to be ever-more vigilant about how treatment rationales and protocols are established and materialized. Critical research on puberty, I suggest, should refrain from making *a priori* judgements about normality and abnormality and focus instead on exploring how we might facilitate health and happiness for all children in their transition to adulthood.

References

Alonso, L.C. and Rosenfield, R. L. 2002. Oestrogens and puberty. *Best Practice in Research in Clinical Endocrinology and Metabolism* 16(1), 13–30.

Brown, N. and Webster, A. 2004. *New Medical Technologies and Society: Reordering life*. Cambridge and Malden MA: Polity Press.

Canguilhem, G. [1978] 1991. *The Normal and the Pathological*. Translated by Carolyn R. Fawcett in collaboration with Robert S. Cohen. New York: Zone Books.

Chase, C. 1998. Surgical progress is not the answer to intersexuality. *Journal of Clinical Ethics,* 9(4), 385–392.

Ebling, F.J.P. 2005. The neuroendocrine timing of puberty. *Reproduction,* 129, 675–683.

Ellis, B. 2004. Timing of pubertal maturation in girls: An integrated life history approach. *Psychological Bulletin,* 130(6), 920–958.

Fausto-Sterling, A. 2000. *Sexing the Body: Gender politics and the construction of sexuality.* New York: Basic Books.

Fox Keller, E. 2001. *The Century of the Gene.* Cambridge MA: Harvard University Press.

Gender Identity Research and Education Society. Undated. *Early Medical Treatment for Transsexual People.* [Online]. Available at: http://www.gires. org.uk/Text_Assets/GIRES%20-%20ARTICLE%20-%20Early%20Medical% 20Treatment.pdf [accessed: 2 August 2007].

Giordano, S. 2008. Ethics of management of gender atypical organisation in children and adolescents. *International Public Health Policy and Ethics,* 42, 249–272.

Herman-Giddens, M. E., Kaplowitz, P. B. and Wasserman, R. 2004. Navigating the recent articles on girls' puberty in pediatrics: What do we know and where do we go from here? *Pediatrics,* 113, 911–917.

Hird, M. 2003. A typical gender identity conference? Some disturbing reports from the therapeutic front lines. *Feminism and Psychology,* 13(2), 181–199.

Hirsch, H.J., Gillis, D., Strich, D., Chertnin, B., Farkas, A., Lindenberg, T., Gelber, H. and Spitz, I.M. 2005. The Histrelin implant: A novel treatment for central precocious puberty. *Pediatrics,* 116, 798–802.

Hogle, L. 2005. Enhancement technologies and the body. *Annual Review of Anthropology,* 34, 695–716.

Holmes, M. 2000. Queer cut bodies, in *Queer Frontiers: Millennial geographies, genders and generations,* edited by Joseph A. Boone et al. Madison and London: University of Wisconsin Press, 84–110.

Kirk, J. 2004. *Shared Care Protocol for the Use of GnRH Agonists in Central Precocious Puberty (CPP).* London: British Society for Paediatric Endocrinology & Diabetes (BSPED). www.bsped.org.uk/professional/ guidelines/docs/GnrHagonistsharedcare.pdf.

Martin, E. [1987] 1992. *The Woman in the Body: A cultural analysis of reproduction.* Boston: Beacon Press.

O'Sullivan, E., O'Sullivan, M. and Mann, N. 2002. Precocious puberty: A parent's perspective. *Archives of Diseases of the Child,* 86, 320–321.

Oudshoorn, N. 1994. *Beyond the Natural Body: An archaeology of sex hormones.* New York and London: Routledge.

Oyama, S. 1985. *The Ontogeny of Information; Developmental systems and evolution.* Cambridge: Cambridge University Press.

Palmert, M.R. and Boepple, P.A. 2001. Variation in the timing of puberty: Clinical spectrum and genetic investigation. *Journal of Clinical Endocrinology and Metabolism,* 86(6), 2364–2368.

Parent, A.S.,Teilman, G., Juul, A., Skakkebæk, N.E., Toppari, J. and Bourguignon, J.P. 2003. The timing of normal puberty and the age limits of sexual precocity: Variations around the world, secular trends, and changes after migration. *Endocrine Reviews,* 24(5), 668–693.

Roberts, C. 2007. *Messengers of Sex: Hormones, biomedicine and feminism.* Cambridge: Cambridge University Press.

Sherwood, L. 1997. *Human Physiology: From cells to systems.* 2nd edition. St. Paul: West Publishing Company.

Sherwood, L. 2007. *Human Physiology: From cells to systems.* 6th edition. Belmont, California: Thomson, Brooks/Cole.

Smiley, L. 2007. Girl/boy interrupted. *SF Weekly.* July 11. www.sfweekly. com/2007-07-11/news/girl-boy-interrupted-/print.

Spanier, B.B. 1995. *Im/partial Science: Gender ideology in molecular biology.* Bloomington: Indiana University Press.

Stacey, J. 2000. The global within: Consuming nature, embodying health, in *Global Nature, Global Culture,* by S. Franklin, C. Lury and J. Stacey. London: Sage Publications, 97–145.

Throsby, K. and Roberts, C. Forthcoming. Getting bigger: Bodies, genes and environments, in *Nature After the Genome,* edited by S. Parry and J Dupré. London: Blackwell.

Traggiai, C. and Stanhope, R. 2003. Disorders of pubertal development *Best Practice and Research in Clinical Obstetrics and Gynaecology,* 17(1), 41–56.

Van de Waal, D. and Cohen-Kettenis, P.T. 2006. Clinical management of gender identity disorder in adolescents: A protocol on psychological and paediatric endocrinological aspects. *European Journal of Endocrinology,* 155, 131–137.

Virdis, R., Street, M.E., Radetti, G., Pezzini, B., Benelli, M., Ghizzoni, L. and Volta, C. 1998. Precocious puberty in girls adopted from developing countries. *Archives of Disease in Childhood,* 78, 152–154.

Waldby, C. 2000. *The Visible Human Project: Informatic bodies and posthuman medicine.* London and New York: Routledge.

Chapter 2

Learning to Produce, See and Say the (Ab)normal: Professional Vision in Ultrasound Scanning During Pregnancy

Kerstin Sandell

This chapter deals with midwives learning to do ultrasound scans in week 17 of pregnancy[1] and a central aspect of that learning: seeing and communicating the (ab)normal. It is an investigation into acquiring what Charles Goodwin refers to as a 'professional vision' (1994) and into what that vision entails. One of my starting points is Donna Haraway's insight that:

> Struggles over what will count as rational accounts of the world are struggles over *how* to see. (Haraway 1991:194)

The focus is on 'what we learn how to see' (Haraway 1991:190), or the structuring of seeing in a medical practice.

An ultrasound scan, as presented to me during fieldwork, has the medical purposes of dating the pregnancy through measuring the foetus' femur length, head and abdominal circumference, establishing how many foetuses[2] there are, locating the placenta and doing a full body malformation scan. There is also the more social/cultural purpose of seeing/meeting/presenting the baby. In Sweden, these ultrasound scans are done by specially trained midwives at ultrasound clinics. In the hospitals where I did fieldwork, the scan is usually scheduled to take 20 minutes, and another ten minutes is allotted for administration and record keeping. If the midwife discovers something irregular, the patient is referred to an obstetrician, preferably the same day, for another scan and hopefully a diagnosis.

---

1   The scan is preferably done in weeks 17–18, but can be done in weeks 16–20. Abortion at the woman's request can be performed in Sweden until 18 full weeks and until 22 full weeks with permission from the Abortion Committee under the National Board of Health and Welfare.

2   I will use 'foetus', unless for analytical purposes I want to show that the midwives use the term 'baby'. In the field, foetus was usually used between professionals, and 'baby' or 'it' when talking to parents in cases when everything seemed normal. For a feminist discussion of the implications of using the term 'baby' before birth in constructing the foetus as an individual, see, for example, Lorna Weir (1998).

This chapter focuses on the (ab)normal, the distinction between the normal and the pathological. I argue that negotiating that boundary and maintaining it (as objective) is one of the central activities in medicine, deciding what is inside the jurisdiction of medicine, what could and should be treated. This has vast consequences for patients forced or allowed in or out of medicine across this boundary (Sandell 2001, Sandell 2004). This distinction is central to what midwives must learn to become skilled in ultrasound scanning. It is not a contested distinction; drawing the boundary between normal and abnormal is a major reason for doing routine ultrasound scans. Earlier feminist research into pregnancy ultrasound (and prenatal diagnosis) has mainly focused on the aspect of meeting the baby and women's/parental feelings, reactions and choices (Mitchell 2001, Rapp 1991) and the costs and risks in a broader sense of pre-labour interventions (Casper 1998). Furthermore, the cultural meanings and spread of ultrasound images more generally and in relation to US abortion politics more specifically has also been researched; see, for example, Karen Newman (1996) and Janelle Taylor (1992, 2004). In this chapter I will instead analyse how seeing the distinction between the normal and the pathological is learned in practice.

For several reasons, ultrasound is an especially interesting technology to study. First, two professions are involved in interpreting its images, professions usually perceived as working on opposing sides of the pathological/normal boundary: obstetricians and midwives. Second, during routine scanning, images are both produced and interpreted by midwives, a situation differing from that of many other medical technologies, such as CT and X-ray imaging, in which technicians produce the images and doctors interpret them afterwards. Third, ultrasound is a method fully established as routine, yet there is still no scientific consensus as to whether routine scans really make a difference in measurable outcomes in relation to malformations. The 650-page systematic literature review on prenatal diagnostics by the Swedish Council on Technology Assessment in Health Care, for example, concludes that the impact of ultrasound on prognosis and survival is 'unclear'. The question is labelled 'a knowledge gap', where studies that would conclusively identify effects are 'practically impossible to realize' (322) (see also Ann Rudinow Saetnan's research on Norwegian consensus conferences on obstetric ultrasound (2002)). This makes it an interesting example of a routine healthcare policy open to investigation by STS scholars (see Joyce 2005: 456).

Ultrasound at around week 17 in pregnancy is routine practice in Sweden. Even though the scan is optional, it is fully incorporated into the maternity care programs provided free of charge to all citizens and permanent residents in Sweden, and an overwhelming majority of women undergo it. To maintain ultrasound as routine practice within maternity care programmes, prenatal care providing midwives are trained to administer ultrasound scans through an apprenticeship relationship, in which a senior midwife with extensive practical experience of ultrasound scans teaches the trainee midwife through demonstrating and supervising. After the supervised training, the trainee midwives I interviewed attended or were to attend a course in ultrasound, either for midwives only or for midwives and obstetricians together, organized by their professional organizations.

How such learning is organized provides a good example of the conceptualization of learning as situated, a theoretical perspective developed by Jean Lave and Etienne Wenger (1991). This perspective aims to grasp the situated and social nature of learning. Through stressing *practice*, it offers the possibility of analytically highlighting the resources offered and skills to be acquired in the process. The perspective conceptualizes the person learning as a *legitimate peripheral participant*, the goal of the learning process for this person being to gradually become a full participant. The context of learning is understood as a *community of practice*, a concept that conveys that knowledge and skills are always part of, reproduced in, and kept up in situated everyday practices by and within a specific group of practitioners.

My study is based on interviews with both supervising midwives and midwives who had recently finished their supervised training. Furthermore, I conducted participant observation of routine scans with more than half of the midwives interviewed, for one or two days with each midwife. I was unable to be present during the scanning sessions where one midwife teaches another to do scans. I also attended a week-long course for midwives and obstetricians and a world congress on ultrasound during pregnancy.[3]

Professional Vision

The theoretical framework of this paper is formed by the concept of *professional vision*, coined by Charles Goodwin (1994). Goodwin argues that the concept captures the discursive practices that become the sign of a profession's craft and 'the ability to build structures in the world that organize knowledge, shape perception, and structure future action' (1994: 628).

I will make use of Goodwin's three aspects, or discursive practices, involved in professional vision, namely, *coding, highlighting, and producing and articulating material representations*. Coding 'transforms phenomena observed in a specific setting into the objects of knowledge that animate the discourse of a profession', highlighting 'makes specific phenomenon in a complex perceptual field salient by marking them in some fashion' (1994: 606), and material representations can be, for example, graphic representations or maps. My starting point is Goodwin's statement that 'insofar as these practices are lodged within specific communities, they must be learned' (1994: 627).

Routine ultrasound scanning is done in a different context from the ones Goodwin explores in his 1994 paper 'Professional vision'. There, Goodwin

---

3   Organized by the *Svensk Förening för Obstetrik och Gynekologi* (SFOG; Swedish Society of Obstetrics and Gynaecology) and the 14th World Congress on Ultrasound in Obstetrics and Gynaecology, 31 August–4 September 2004, in Stockholm, respectively.

discusses how archaeologists learn how to analyse soil/dirt, and how the Rodney King video was used and interpreted in the court room. Of interest in these cases is how a specific tension is created between the actual object and the produced object of knowledge. Goodwin uses the term professional vision to denote how practitioners learn to see the material world in specific ways, simultaneously constructing themselves as professionals and what they see as (scientifically) relevant objects of knowledge. The object of knowledge in ultrasound is the (ab)normal foetus, seen with the professional vision that distinguishes deformities and pathologies. Specific for ultrasound is that the practice of seeing is not the locus of knowledge production. The scientific context for the debate and construction of knowledge about foetal deformities and pathologies is obstetric/medical research and publications. Routine scans performed by professional midwives are thus not a locus of knowledge production as much as a place of application.

I will start by exploring the shared development of the skill to produce images and the vision needed to see that they are the right ones. I will then analytically reveal how midwives gradually learn to recognize and know the normal, to be able to react to the abnormal through highlighting and partly coding the pathological. Finally, I will discuss how midwives learn how to tell patients/parents-to-be about the results of the ultrasound, which articulates the difference between reading an ultrasound image as an expert or a witness.

Integrating Doing and Seeing

Ultrasound has a specific quality in relation to Goodwin's understanding of professional vision – there is nothing to see if the ultrasound image is not produced. Goodwin distinguishes between *a domain of scrutiny* (e.g., the soil for archaeologists) and the *discursive practices* being deployed in this domain to produce objects of knowledge, where material representation is one discursive practice. I would argue that the ultrasound image in the specific activity of scanning is both a domain of scrutiny *and* a material representation *at the same time*. Thus, there is no pre-existing or independent domain of scrutiny. The ultrasound image is a representation of the foetus without the real/the original being independently available. In this section, I focus how producing that image is learned through what I conceptualize as processes of integration and orientation.

The starting point for learning ultrasound is the assumption that 'everyone' has a basic understanding of what can be seen on the screen: to know that it is a foetus does not require learning. This is taken as given.

> *KS*: Is it obvious that you understand what you see?
> *Supervisor*: When using today's ultrasound machines with their high resolution, I think that most people become very fascinated when, almost the first time you use the transducer, suddenly, if you are lucky and the child is cooperative and lies in a good position, it's like, 'My God, I can see the profile and the lips!'

Then a hand comes up with five fingers. So, yes, I think so. If you have a good machine, the pregnancy is of sufficient duration, and the mother depicts well, then I think it is really easy today.

The senior midwives report that the quality and resolution of ultrasound images have improved dramatically. Previously, images were more of a grey blur, and even if the midwives tried to show parents-to-be central structures, the midwives expressed great doubt as to what the parents could actually discern. Now the understanding is that 'everyone' can, almost instantly, recognize that the imaged object is a foetus; including distinguishing major structures, such as the spine, head, heart, arms and legs, though how much parents-to-be actually see and understand still varies greatly (see also Mitchell 2001).

If knowing that the image on the screen is a foetus is easy, the ability to produce the desired images and to understand the images produced is considered very difficult to learn. This practice calls for what I call integration, the ability to effortlessly shift between the images desired and produced, and to associate this with the movement over the abdomen of the hand holding the transducer. One midwife described it like this:

> *Trainee*: It is difficult to combine myself, my body, with what I see on the screen, how I move my arm, and what happens on the screen. … To make it become a unit.

The supervisor can help the trainee learn such integration through hands-on guiding, such as putting her hand on the trainee's and showing her how to move the transducer. This hands-on instruction was described by one midwife as what 'made the penny drop' during the learning process.

The unity of hand movements and image is further articulated as learning how the foetus is positioned in relation to how the transducer is placed on the abdomen. The foetus moves freely, with no fixed orientation in relation to the woman's body onto which the transducer is placed. This is different from the production of other medical images. For example, in vaginal ultrasound the uterus and fallopian tubes are always located in the same position in relation to the outside of the body.

> *Supervisor*: That's what is difficult to translate [between hand movement and image], how to think three dimensionally. You have the mother in one plane, and that is what you see, but then the foetus is in another plane, there. So you have to … it has to settle in the hand, so to speak, how to move the hand in order to find the foetus.

Since the foetus is invisible without the transducer, trainees try other ways to visualize the foetus and its relationship with the transducer and the images that can be produced.

> *Trainee*: Sometimes, I try to think I have a doll (or whatever). And then I imagine that I'm moving a thing over it, and then I think that if I hold it like this, I see that.

In this attempt to combine the movements of the transducer over the abdomen with the images produced and the position of the foetus, it is necessary to grasp how the image is the result of ultrasound waves sent into the body and immediately reflected back. I want to highlight two aspects of this phenomenon, conceptualized by myself as a beam – but with a 'twist'. One senior midwife explained the combination of transducer and image to her students using the image of using a torch shining a beam of light into the forest at night.

> *Supervisor*: Depending on how you direct it, you can bring out what you want to see. You can look at the treetops or the ground.

With this she tried to convey that what is seen is only what the ultrasound waves are directed toward and reflected from. Another aspect of what is seen in relation to the transducer and the position of the foetus, the 'twist', is arguably more counter-intuitive: the image is of cross sections of the foetus, as if the body were cut by the waves from the transducer like the end of a log, showing the rings of a tree.

What is counter-intuitive is that the ultrasound scan does not produce an image from the front, as photos or X-rays do. The presentation of the image in relation to the position of the transducer is therefore at first experienced as rotated 90 degrees in the 'wrong' direction.

> *Trainee*: Yes, it is that twist in the image that you have to handle here [i.e., process mentally], and it isn't that easy every time.

This difficulty is also evident in the way midwives often explain to the parents-to-be that the image they are seeing is of the head of the foetus 'from above', although it is actually a cross section from the side.

Another counter-intuitive aspect concerns the range of movement required to produce the desired image. That the image is a cross section means that to produce the image of the skull, the transducer (the waves) could come from any direction, as long as it is directed in the same plane. It does not matter whether the transducer is closest to the front or the back of the head or to either ear. This means that the same image can be produced from very different positions of the transducer on the abdomen.

> *Supervisor*: Many say, 'I feel the child kicking here, and yet I am over here with the transducer!' To get that, if the child is lying downward with the head and the back facing up, then you have to put the transducer here [indicating the position on her own body]. But if I do not get a good image, I might have to be up here or

down here ... and also to avoid shadows from an arm, or if they lie folded, you
have to try to go around.

That such a large range of movement is needed to produce an image of one part
of the foetus is not self-evident; neither is the fact that very small movements of
the transducer can result in images of entirely new things. With small movements,
the trick is to learn not only that the movements are small, but that tilting the
transducer, using only parts of it, and easing or increasing the pressure also have
effects. To learn this, hands-on instruction is central; in the end, however, the
trainee has to learn to do it on her own.

> *Supervisor*: You can help them manoeuvre a little, but then you have to let go.
> They have to tilt and direct [the transducer] on their own. They have to decide on
> their own that 'if I want to look in that direction, I move the hand like this'.

Even if instructions, both verbal and hands-on, are central to learning, repetitive
practice has to be added as well. All the midwives repeatedly stressed that the
number of scans, the amount of practice, is what produces skilled scanners. This
is also why the required training under supervision is often quantified; several
midwives mentioned that the supervised period should encompass at least 200
scans.

The desired results, i.e., knowing where the transducer and the foetus are in
relation to what is seen on the screen, is expressed by one midwife as 'letting it
settle in the medulla oblongata, or wherever it settles'. Another said it was like
learning to drive a car: you have to know what to do, and when you truly know
it, you just do it reflexively. Yet another compared it with the feeling of doing a
vaginal exam, where an instructor can explain how it should feel, but you can
never know how it feels until you have done it yourself.

A result of the learning process is that the meaning of 'where you are' changes.
At the beginning, the attention of the midwife is focused on where she is on the
abdomen with the transducer, and where the foetus is in relation to the body of the
mother-to-be. When this orientation aspect of the integration skill is learned, the
meaning of 'I am here and want to go there' changes and is entirely in relation to
the body of the foetus. The skill learned can thus also be framed as the midwife
effortlessly knowing where she is and how to get to where she wants *in the body
of the foetus*. The collapse of the domain of scrutiny and the representation is
tangible: through the image, the midwife is *in* the body of the foetus, where she
obviously could never be physically.

The practical, tacit, embodied knowledge needed to be able to produce the
images is the prerequisite for seeing anything at all, to have something onto/into
which the professional vision can be placed (cf. Goodwin 1994: 614). Since what
has to be learned is embodied, the supervisor evaluates the skill and comprehension
of the trainee through watching her movements, and teaches through correcting
and instructing hands-on in the scanning situation. If the image is not produced

correctly, if the midwife is not *in* the body of the foetus, comprehension and knowledge will be lacking, and vice versa.

Knowing the Normal and How the Abnormal is Highlighted

One purpose of the ultrasound scan is to see whether there are any malformations, the task of the midwife being to know the normal in order to react when the image is *not* normal, when something is not as it usually is.

> *Supervisor*: But as a midwife, it's not your job to make a diagnosis or to say what the consequences are. Instead, it's actually only to [say] this falls outside the normal, that most don't look like this.

The midwives used the following expressions to describe how they perceived the abnormal in an ultrasound image: 'It burns itself into your consciousness, it's strange' (trainee); 'It catches your eye, directly' (supervisor); 'Often, at first glance you see that this does not add up' (supervisor). What I, following Goodwin, will call the 'highlighting' of the abnormal, is thus described as immediately produced – almost as soon as the midwives put the transducer on the abdomen, they recognize the abnormal. The midwives understand the ability to immediately recognize the abnormal as primarily acquired through observing many normals.

> *Supervisor*: If you have seen thousands of normals, then you see that this is not normal.

Even a newly trained midwife now doing scans on her own, and who had yet to see any deviances, was convinced that she would be able to react to an abnormal scan through having seen many normals. Again, the number of scans is stressed, in order to 'put the normal images in your head'. Learning to know the normal in ultrasound scanning is thus achieved through exposure to many real foetuses. This is embodied, experienced, and cumulative knowledge acquired through multitudes of visual impressions. It stands in contrast to the standardized bodies often used in teaching anatomy and depicted in textbooks and other similar pedagogical material (see also Waldby 2000).

On closer examination, however, the seemingly automatic progression from observing many normals to reacting to the abnormal becomes somewhat indistinct. Instead, highlighting of the abnormal seems to be a product of learning in a community of practice, through constantly discussing with colleagues how to interpret the images in terms of where to locate the boundary between the normal and the abnormal. Highlighting, thereby, is partly learned through being told to look for specific things in the images: where to look, what to see and what to react to. One example of this is the cross section of the head, where the diameter of the skull is to be measured.

> *Supervisor*: The head – it's easy since it does not change shape, but you have to be at the right level and have the right angle anyway. Then the image appears in a specific way and you have markers there. You should see the midline structure and septum – a slight notch in the midline structure, then you are at the right level. And of course the midline should be in the middle, to indicate that you are not slanting. So you have to learn that: how the image should appear there, exactly.

This is only part of what the midwives have to see in the image and only one of the many images that midwives must learn how to produce. Learning such markers creates the ability to react when something that should be seen in the image is not there, or is different. Through the use of markers and their production during supervised training, midwives are exposed to a large number of specific images. Creating and seeing visible markers in the images was described by the midwives as being able to produce *good images*.

> *KS*: When you are a supervisor, what is the most difficult thing to convey?

> *Supervisor*: It is how to get a good image. That's the alpha and omega, getting a good image, otherwise you cannot judge anything at all.

Learning to perform an ultrasound scan thus at the same time entails being able to produce good images and to see specific markers in them; these two aspects are inseparable in practice. The markers are signs both of possible abnormalities and that one has obtained a good image.

Central to what is *correct* in good images is being in the right plane and having the right angle; which are stressed because of the risk of misrepresentation, and hence of misinterpretation.

> *Supervisor*: What section I am in is very important. You can almost make a deformity look normal if you see it from a certain angle. And the same goes for the heart: you can make almost any heart look normal, and vice versa. If I am slanting [the transducer] in a given cross section, a heart can look very strange.

Images in other planes and from other angles may not be wrong, *per se*, but trainee midwives have not learned what to recognize as normal in them or to react to the abnormal in them. Scanning thus involves producing a series of standard images for which midwives have learned the signs and markers that should be there, as a way of knowing that the image is both 'good' *and* normal.

Midwives constantly told me that being systematic was important when doing a scan. One midwife explained that being systematic meant always doing the scan in exactly the same way. This meant that one should first get an overview of the uterus, scanning up and down, side to side, and then scan the body of the foetus, at a perpendicular angle, from head to toe, moving through the body vertically to see the spinal cord from all angles. That the position of the foetus could cause problems was pointed out to me in this context; in which case the order of the scan could be changed, since the midwife may have to wait for the foetus to move or try some tricks to make it move. Being systematic seemed important for several reasons. First, it is part of learning how to see specific images; a senior midwife talked about learning to do detailed scans of the heart:[4]

> *Supervisor*: [Scanning the heart] is the most difficult but also the most fun. We brought in a doctor, a heart specialist, from London for four days. Hands on, really. And I think it dawned on us all then, that wow, we got a structure – this is how to do it. Then it was much easier.

> *KS*: What did she teach you?

> *Supervisor*: She taught us exactly in what planes to see, how to see, how it should look. One, two, three, four [indicating the movements of the transducer], this is what you should see.

What is important here is her emphasis on having a structure when learning to do the scan – one, two, three, four, specific moves – to cover systematically what should be seen. Previously, she told me, they had difficulties finding what they needed to see and thus also in perceiving the desired signs and markers. As the practitioner saying this was a senior midwife (she was the head ultrasound midwife at a university hospital and had worked with ultrasound for over 20 years), this comment indicates that learning through hands-on and embodied instruction is a central element throughout a midwife's career.

Second, a systematic approach ensures that the midwives produce *all* the images required, that they do not miss anything.

> *Supervisor*: That you [know] you have checked this. Then, maybe you did not see what you should, but I know that I did check, to the best of my ability, I did check. You see, when the kid is born 20 weeks later, and then they [i.e., the parents] come to you and ask why you did not see this. And apparently I did not, but I did check, I did try and I did check. At the time nothing was visible – at least I did not see anything. And it is important to be able to say that – for your own sake if for nothing else.

Being systematic is important given that the only documentation of a scan in which nothing abnormal is found is a note in the patient record that the scan was normal,

---

4   In most clinics, what is required is an image in which the four chambers of the heart can be seen, an image produced perpendicular to the spine, in which the location and size of the heart can also be evaluated. In this case, the midwives also learned to look at the large vessels leaving the heart.

that there was nothing to record. There is nothing to turn back to, no possibility of re-checking images classified as normal.

Third, being systematic is also a way of practically and perceptually making all the different images comprising the scan cohere into a process and a whole. One reason midwives gave for doing the scan systematically was that they would then always know where they were in the body of the foetus. A midwife pointed out to me that even a skilled midwife cannot interpret a snapshot image out of context: to interpret an image correctly, she must know how she got that particular image, what she had seen before and what remained to see. The scan also has a temporal element in terms of the sequence of what should be seen, which makes it into a process. During the scan, midwives look for the movements of the foetus, how it breathes and whether it swallows over time. The scan becomes a coherent whole when all the requested images are evaluated together. Then, a combination of 'small' observations, which in isolation are not worth noting, could mean something and be a reason to react. For a trained midwife, quickly integrating these disparate impressions into a whole is central to forming an immediate impression at the beginning of a scanning session.

Learning to know the normal and what to react to is thus learned through producing specific images systematically, and integrating them in relation to a whole and a process. The midwives have to learn to be meticulous in terms of the intimately linked aspects of images and movements. Learning to know the normal has, as in learning to produce the images discussed in the previous section, the same nature of embodiment, where the supervisor can evaluate and correct the trainee's knowledge through her practice.

Knowing the right images and what to see, however, is not enough for the abnormal to highlight itself. The boundary between the normal and the abnormal must also be consistently learned through discussing how to interpret images. These discussions are most common when the trainee midwife is gradually expected to do scans and interpret them on her own. This process was intensively supported by the senior midwife, first by looking over the shoulder of the trainee, always ready to intervene, and later by always being available to answer questions.

> *Trainee*: I asked her a lot in the beginning: is this how it should look, and is this part of what is normal?

Although practice is important, being able to ask when one is unsure is *decisive*. If the trainee does not get answers about how to properly interpret an image, then she does not learn if and when to react – she does not learn what should highlight itself. This development of the midwives' professional vision was described by the trainee midwives as gradually learning to trust what they see. They described an initial insecurity, when they asked themselves whether they would be able to see any deviancy that might be present. They described their reactions when first seeing something abnormal in terms of disbelief, not trusting their vision and/or the images they had produced.

> *Trainee*: In the beginning, I was unsure, even of things that really were diseased. I did not trust myself. I thought that maybe I had not managed to produce the right image, that's why the skull was empty. Because I actually saw one of those where the skull really was empty – only the cranium and liquid and nothing else. Then I thought this cannot be, the head cannot be entirely empty. But it was.

If the senior midwife, when asked, confirms that it is indeed a correct interpretation, it becomes a learning experience of this particular deviance ('It *can* be this way'), producing trust in one's professional vision – I did react, it was right to react, I can trust what I see.

Asking colleagues when in doubt was integral to forming the community of practice, even for experienced midwives; colleagues were expected to be generous and helpful. Scanning is a process, and the colleague called to help always took the transducer to see for herself; the one calling for help, however, can and does look over her shoulder. As one trainee explained it, she learned from seeing whether the senior midwife saw the same thing.

> *Trainee*: Then [I see] if the other person can produce the same image, or if I used the wrong angle or was unable to obtain the image. ... I try to be present, so I can learn from what others see in relation to what I saw.

Asking the supervisor or another experienced colleague for advice contributed in everyday practice to the formation of professional vision, something that the descriptions of the 'almost automatically highlighted abnormal' and the stress on practice obscures. Learning to trust one's professional vision, to distinguish the normal from the abnormal and to react accordingly, is thus achieved in a community of practice. The result is described by a midwife as follows:

> *Trainee*: Now I feel secure in what I see. Even if I have not seen something before, I know that it is not the way it is supposed to look.

Knowing the normal is a skill that must be maintained, even for experienced midwives.

> *Trainee*: It has to do with your memory for images. You have to reinforce it; it has to be constantly maintained.

The professional organizations make recommendations as to how many scans a midwife should do every year.[5] Some clinics also worked with what could be

---

5   This recommendation was criticized by some midwives at smaller units, where the total number of scans per year did not reach the minimum load for two midwives, but where they claimed at least two midwives were nevertheless needed to cover for illness and vacations.

called internal supervision. Colleagues could double-check each others' scans to make sure they kept to the right angles and planes. A midwife especially adept at a specific skill, or who had just learned something new at a course, could function as a supervisor to help develop and enhance her colleagues' skills.

The professional vision is shaped so as to highlight the abnormal as an automatic reaction. It is clear that what Goodwin calls 'highlighting' makes overt those factors, in this case the pathological, that contain information relevant to a field. It is the abnormal, the deviant, the (possibly) pathological that gets highlighted. The perception of the abnormal highlighting itself is acquired through supervised learning, wherein the trainee moves from being a peripheral participant to full participation, and learns through embodied knowledge to produce the right images. This is a process in which what to see and how to produce the images are intimately linked. This learning is accomplished through constantly discussing where the boundary between the normal and abnormal lies in interpreting images. The outcome is described by the midwives as the ability to trust what they see, i.e., professional vision. Discussing and interpreting images is also how the skills are maintained and developed, something that even experienced midwives must do continually.

Goodwin identifies coding as a discursive practice, but I would not say that reacting to the abnormal qualifies as coding, at least not fully. It is rather screening work, selectively done so that obstetricians will be able to do their jobs. Neither would I say that letting a patient with a normal scan leave is coding; a better term for that is 'passing', since what is happening is that nothing is deemed noteworthy. I base this analysis on the lack of material representations, as the only representation after a scan in which nothing abnormal is noted is a standard note in the record and the image that the parents bring home. This snapshot is, when possible, a specific image, namely, the whole body from the side in which the profile, spine, arms and legs can be seen; an image that midwives think parents expected and knew how to read. Furthermore, it is technically complicated to save reasonable representations of the scan for normal cases, since the normal is based on the whole scan, all of the images and processes observed during the course of the procedure. There are just too many images to save, as the normal is neither specific nor localized enough to qualify as coding and cannot be saved as materialized representations.

Learning Coding, Learning to See More

> *Trainee*: It is super if you are well educated and know a lot, but the responsibility of the midwife is to distinguish the normal from the pathological. It is not to diagnose.

In this section, I will focus on the 'super' in the above quotation. Even though midwives' 'only' task is to react when something is not normal, the pathological being the object of study and field of knowledge of obstetricians, midwives learn to see and know more than the division of labour would indicate, especially with time and experience. On one hand, they learn to code the pathological; on the other, they learn how to see more and more.

Midwives learn to classify what is not as it usually is in three ways: through actually seeing abnormalities and learning the associated diagnoses of the obstetrician; through seeing abnormalities in snap images and videos in professional settings; and through getting feedback regarding false negatives and positives.

First, since abnormalities are rare, midwives must conduct many scans over the years to see a sufficient number of repeated abnormalities to learn to diagnose what they have seen. This improves and expands their professional vision into the realm of obstetricians, that is knowing the pathological. Learning to diagnose thus partly occurs by seeing the deviances coded by obstetricians. Even if the link between what to look for and what may be deviant is intimate, the midwives claimed that there is a qualitative difference between looking for it and actually having seen it. Having actually seen the abnormal creates the knowledge, on next seeing it, that 'I have seen this before, and this is what it is.'

Learning to see more in a scan expands and develops the professional vision of midwives more than does learning to code the pathological. Midwives learn to see richer images both by becoming more experienced and because the machines are getting better. When being newly trained, however, learning to see more is mainly a function of simply doing more scans.

> *Trainee*: I know exactly what we are supposed to see, what we should look for. But then, as I get more skilled, I see more than we are obliged to see. You learn to look for the vessels from the heart, and then there is the cleft lip and palate, club foot, and other instances where you realize that this must be what I'm seeing.

When a midwife is more experienced, a combination of curiosity about what can be seen and better machines are factors contributing to the richer images they read.

> *Supervisor*: Yes, we come to see more and more. I can now find the uterus in the girls. I hadn't seen it before, though I'd looked for it many times, but now I can see it.

Being able to see more has implications for the routine scan. If something can be seen, it could possibly be deviant, leading to questions such as: When is something deviant and should midwives report it? Should this new aspect be on the check-list,[6] and should midwives from now on try look for this in all foetuses? Can a

---

6   What midwives should be able to see is often compiled in checklists, and 31 of the 45 clinics doing routine malformation scans used checklists in 2004 (Statens beredning för medicinsk utvärdering 2006). The checklists are developed locally and thus vary: I came

midwife choose *not* to see something once she has started to see it? Seeing more and more thus creates grey areas in relation to what to see and what to react to.

Improving the ability to see more and more also actualizes the link between seeing and knowing. There was tension in how midwives understood the future of ultrasound. On one hand, I could discern a desire in which seeing more was equivalent to knowing more and being able to do more, a desire in which there was an automatic link between seeing, diagnosis and treatment. It was as if today's uncertainty about what is seen and what that means could be resolved by seeing still more, as if there was, or at least could be, a link in medicine between making a diagnosis and offering a (curative) treatment. On the other hand, some midwives expressed apprehension. They thought that better machines would mean seeing more details that could indicate deviations. This would mean a proliferation of deviances, in terms of 'this does not look the way it usually does', where in many cases they would never know what the deviances meant in the long run. This latter view takes into account the extensive work being done in research and evident in the literature, where efforts proliferate at least tentatively and through probabilities to establish a link between what is seen in images and risks for specific abnormalities. This work could create more specifications the midwives could or should take into account when conducting a scan.

Secondly, the pathological can also be learned through seeing video and snap images of deviant 'cases'.

> *KS*: Does it help to see images of deformities?
>
> *Trainee*: It does, because you do not encounter many of them. Many such deviances you will never see in your lifetime. But the images give you a feeling, and when you see something deviant you have a sense of recognition, of having seen this before.

Deviant images are displayed in an organized form in published work, at conferences, in courses of the type I attended, at various kinds of meetings involving case discussions for educational purposes, and not least during rounds at the clinics. Rounds were requested by the midwives when they did not exist, and were very appreciated when they did. Here, the differences between hospitals were significant. The midwives working at university hospitals said that rounds were institutionalized, and that both obstetricians and midwives participated in them. At other hospitals, rounds did not exist. During case discussions, an obstetrician often not only displayed and explained (highlighted) images of the abnormal, but also discussed the etiology of the deformity, its prevalence, other conditions linked to it, and treatment and prognosis if relevant. When rounds existed, they gave the midwives the advantage of 'learning to recognize deviances' (supervisor), that is, learning to code.

---

across cleft lips and vessels from the heart on some checklists, for example, but not on others.

It is worth noting a tension between seeing and knowing. The abnormal is discernable because foetuses at this stage of pregnancy are uniform, so the normals should all look the same. Despite this, the normal cannot be learned through looking at standardized images nor can it be represented in images. The pathological, on the other hand, is understood as anything seen in an image that varies or deviates. At the same time, these deviances are localized and thus can be represented in ultrasound images, both snap images and short video clips.

A third aspect of scanning practices that the midwives cited as relevant to learning was getting feedback regarding false negatives and positives. This, however, seemed difficult to organize. Only one midwife could say that her clinic had a fully functioning feedback loop encompassing delivery, neonatal and paediatrics, which was accomplished by entrusting one midwife at the ultrasound clinic with the task of looking through the newborns' records. Even when this feedback loop worked, the ultrasound midwives could only follow up the newborns, but did not know what happened to these children as they grew up. The feedback was mainly seen as useful when there were false negatives, as a way of learning what needed to be better observed. Since there is no visual documentation of scans classified as normal, however, the results cannot be referred back to individual patient scans. Such feedback instead builds general awareness of what midwives at the clinic might miss, or should look out for. Missing something is a definite fear, as discussed above, and one that is expressed through an emphasis on being systematic, so as not to miss or forget anything. At the same time, for midwives, part of learning ultrasound scanning is realizing that they will inevitably miss some abnormalities. One midwife described this in relation to what she got out of the theoretical course that I also attended.

> *KS*: What do you think about the possibility that you might miss something?

> *Trainee*: It is very tough. At the same time, it was very good to meet experienced lecturers who said that you can expect to find 80%. So 20% you do not find, and *they* say that. That actually felt reassuring; it was good to hear that.

Midwives thus learn not only to react to deviances, but also, through experience and rounds, to code the pathological, even though this is not their task. I think one can see 'the pervasive power of coding schemes to organize apprehension of the world' (Goodwin 1994: 608) at work here, in that it is precisely the deviant that is interesting, that everyone wants to see, and that can expand one's professional knowledge. In relation to initial disbelief at seeing something deviant, the development of professional vision increasingly entails a fascination with and focus on the deviant, where in addition the tendency is that the more unusual a deviance is and the more difficult it is to code, the more interesting it is perceived to be.

Goodwin identifies the importance of producing graphic representations in science, and how this, in the case of archaeologists in particular, is central to learning the trade. In this sense, ultrasound images are graphic representations primarily in case discussions, in the form of snaps and video clips, accompanied by explanations of what they depict and signify. In the patient record, the diagnosis, the code, seems to be the major material representation; notes in the record about what was seen in the scan, some snaps, and maybe the results of other diagnostic tools (e.g., amniocentesis) are supporting elements.

Telling What is Seen – Telling Everything/the Truth

How do midwives learn what they should tell the parents-to-be about what is seen in the scan? Results are presented by the midwife during the scanning process, and one of the important things midwives learn is not only to see the right things, but also to say the right, and the same, things. Midwives working together develop a common practice as to what to say and how to say it, which is conveyed via supervision. Although how to approach patients was seen as justifiably variable, depending on midwives' personalities and styles, it was regarded as very important that different midwives give out the same information.

The scan is described by many midwives as a high-tension zone between the extremes resulting from the two purposes of the scan: detecting malformations and seeing the baby.

> *Trainee*: But many come anyway, with the expectation that it'll be fun and that you'll get a cute picture of the child. Or they are so incredibly scared that they don't even dare look at the screen.

It is in this high-tension zone the midwives do the scan and communicate the results, within their professional limits. The policy that midwives return to, as a credo, is that they (here including both midwives and obstetricians) are obliged to communicate everything they see.

> *Supervisor*: At the beginning, for example, we had a discussion of whether we should say that we had seen a cleft palate in week 18. Should we bother the pregnant women, should they have to think about this? Some might opt for abortion. These things emerge. But we came to the conclusion that it is best to say everything.

'Telling everything' is done in two very different situations: by far the most common one is when nothing abnormal is found; the other occurs when something is found. When nothing abnormal is evident, the results are always communicated in carefully worded, guarded terms. Midwives learn to take into account the limitations of the images, that not everything can be seen, and that some abnormalities develop after weeks 17–18.

KS: The patients often ask: does it look ok, is it normal? Do you discuss how to handle that?

Supervisor: Yes, we have talked about what we should [say]. Then you can say, 'It looks good, as far as I can see.' You always have to add that – from what can be seen here and now, with ultrasound right now, it looks normal. We try to say similar things, like 'It looks like it usually does at this time', expressions like that.

These tentative expressions were used again and again, in every scan I attended, with very little variation. The normal is thus never definitive: statements about it are always conditional.

The other situation is when something is seen as deviant, or unclear. Here the immediacy of the situation is acutely felt: the parents-to-be are looking at the screen. The strategy midwives develop to handle this situation is to reserve some time at the very beginning of the scan for themselves, giving them time for a quick preliminary look. They say something like, 'I will first take a look, and then I will show you.' For me, that period of time seemed very short, but as I have described earlier, midwives claim to see almost immediately if something more serious is wrong. Even this brief time gives them some advantage in the immediate situation.

Supervisor: I can sit and ponder a little, because they have not noticed that something is amiss. If you mind your Ps and Qs a little, they will not realize that something is wrong and you get some time to think. Then you have to tell, but you get some lead time.

Although the midwives can gain some time through this manoeuvre, they are aware that the patients are very observant. Even though the parents-to-be may not understand the image, they do notice the midwife's body language, facial expressions, even breathing, if and when the midwife stops at something, or takes many pictures. Many midwives expressed a concern that, when finding something unusual, they may create unnecessary worry.

Supervisor: That's what's difficult. You have to compose your features and mind the pitch of your voice, before you say anything. You cannot think out loud; you have to think quietly by yourself, so as not to create too much worry. Because that's what we do, with prenatal diagnosis, most of the time.

Wording is central here, and shared in the community of practice. Its function is to avoid causing unnecessary worry and to stay on the right side of the professional boundary by not giving a diagnosis. Midwives told me that they use expressions like the following: 'Here I see something I usually don't see' (trainee); 'This doesn't look like the image I normally see' (trainee); 'This doesn't look as I expected it to' (trainee), and 'This deviates from what I have seen before' (supervisor).

The normal resurfaces here as the referent for midwives. The most difficult cases, in terms of knowing what to say, concerned what some midwives referred to as 'small' deviances, meaning both clearly visible and identifiable deviances, such as a missing finger, understood to be minor, and cases when the midwives are unsure as to what a deviance means, but when it probably does not signify anything pathological or clinically relevant.

> *Trainee*: It's those small deviances that you don't really want them to bother about. Because I do not think myself that it's anything. Then it's difficult to know how to put things, I think, because they will be sad anyway. That's just the way it is.

The 'big' deviances are understood as serious, but in such instances it is not that difficult to know what to say and do.

> *Trainee*: When you see serious deviances, it's not really difficult for us or for the parents, to decide or to give information. Most don't find it difficult to reach a decision.

When serious and visibly obvious deviances occur, the professional boundary is not always strictly kept. For example, one central moment early in the scan is to show the beating heart. One midwife said that it was meaningless to talk to the parents unless you first showed them that the foetus/baby was alive. If there are no heartbeats, this is seen as something the midwife can and maybe should tell the parents-to-be, even though the doctor may later also do a scan and talk to them.

When presenting the results to the parents-to-be, the parents are made into witnesses of the midwives' professional vision. It seems very difficult, perhaps impossible, for the parents to argue for another interpretive framework than that presented by the midwives. Goodwin, in writing about the power to speak as a profession, states that there is 'a tremendous asymmetry about who can speak as an expert about the events on the tape [of the Rodney King beating] and thus structure interpretation of it' (1994: 624). It is the same in the case of ultrasound images: obstetricians can speak as experts, midwives can learn to see as experts, but parents-to-be/patients can only witness. Goodwin states that victims in a courtroom do not constitute a profession (Goodwin 1994: 625), nor do the users of health care. Their bodies, or the bodies inside them, are the object of scrutiny, and the patient only has a voice outside, and only after the professional vision has been articulated. For my analysis here, the important aspect is that, in presenting the parents with the scan results, the object constructed and coded by the professional vision is made into a fact, or the truth about the (ab)normal foetus. When this fact has been presented to the parents-to-be, they are left with the choice of what to do about that fact, generally choosing between an abortion or preparing psychologically during pregnancy for having a child with a deformity and then giving birth.

Conclusions

In this chapter, I have investigated how professional vision in routine ultrasound scanning during pregnancy is attained, with a focus on how midwives learn to see the (ab)normal.

What is learned is largely identifiable, using Goodwin's notions of coding and highlighting, as part of the professional vision. The task of the midwives is to learn to know the normal and to be able to react to the abnormal. The end result of such learning is that the abnormal highlights itself, and that the midwife trusts her professional vision to produce that highlighting. Coding is a way of saying what the abnormal is, of giving a diagnosis, of identifying the pathology. Merely distinguishing that something is abnormal through reaction is not, I would argue, coding. For midwives, coding is excess knowledge, being part of the obstetrician's field of knowledge; midwives, however, learn through experience and case discussions led by obstetricians, and are usually interested in learning, as a way of developing their professional vision. In this way, they also become part of the practices that sustain the focus on the object of study – the pathological – and thus contribute to maintaining the fascination and curiosity with and visual focus on the deviant. The normal, even though it is the major constituent of the midwives' work, tends to disappear, or just pass, with a tentative and cautious stamp of 'ok for now' or 'ok as far as we can see.'

The skills learned are embodied and maintained in a community of practice. The training is imparted by the supervisor's hands, guiding the trainee in how to produce images, and then also evaluating and correcting the trainee in an embodied way, accompanied by ongoing discussion of how to interpret images as normal or abnormal. Despite the midwives' own description of highlighting as automatic, I have found that it is learned through intensive interaction in the community of practice, where producing and interpreting the images are intimately linked: seeing the right thing is thus doing the right thing.

In relation to the third discursive skill noted by Goodwin, producing material representations, the ultrasound images are ambiguous in that they are *both* a representation *and* the field of scrutiny. The midwife must learn how to produce the 'right' image as measured against other possible ultrasound images, not against 'the real'. There are not as many visual, material representations in existence as one might expect: normal scans are not visually documented. Ultrasound images, especially from normal scans, are material representations existing only in the present, during the scanning itself. Even when something is deviant, and snaps are saved in the patient record, the image is less relevant than the diagnosis itself (sometimes together with results from other diagnostic tools). I would even claim that the diagnosis itself becomes the material representation. The snapshots thus do not stand on their own, as most medical images do, not even for trained midwives and obstetricians.

Finally, I want to reflect on ultrasound scanning as application and as routine medical practice. Goodwin writes that the members of a community of practice or profession expect each other to code observations correctly or at least well enough (1994: 615) when they are transformed into knowledge/data; by this, the community members become accountable to each other and create an arena where findings can be contested. How does this work in the case of ultrasound? To whom are scanners accountable? Are interpretations ever contested, and, if so, how? I would argue that interpretations of images, the professional vision, are not contested in everyday practice in ultrasound scanning. Instead, ultrasound is used as an objective medical examination, as if it were a quality control or diagnostic tool. Here parents-to-be/patients play an important role in witnessing the results, where their trust in the community of practice and medicine is strong and relied upon. At the same time, local variation in the scanning practices is significant, in both what is looked for and how scans are followed up on. Yet, there is a lack of struggle concerning what to see. For parents, midwives and ultimately policy makers, the midwives' professional vision is taken as a rational account of the world. Perhaps because of this, learning to do ultrasound, to acquire the professional vision, is ultimately learning to see and accept the boundary between the normal and the abnormal.

References

Casper, M.J. 1998. *The Making of the Unborn Patient: A social anatomy of fetal surgery*. New Brunswick: Rutgers University Press.

Goodwin, C. 1994. Professional vision. *American Anthropologist*, 96(3), 606–633.

Haraway, D.J. 1991. Situated knowledges: The science question in feminism and the privilege of partial perspectives. In *Simians, Cyborgs, and Women: The reinvention of nature*, edited by D. Haraway. New York: Routledge, 183–201.

Joyce, K. 2005. Appealing images: Magnetic Resonance imaging and the production of authoritative knowledge. *Social Studies of Science,* 35(3), 437–462.

Lave, J. and Wenger, E. 1991. *Situated Learning: Legitimate peripheral participation*. Cambridge: Cambridge University Press.

Mitchell, L.M. 2001. *Baby's First Picture: Ultrasound and the politics of fetal subjectivity*. Toronto: University of Toronto Press.

Newman, K. 1996. *Fetal Positions: Individualism, science, visuality*. Stanford: Stanford University Press.

Rapp, R. 1991. Moral pioneers: Women, men, and fetuses on a frontier of reproduction technology. In *Gender at the Crossroads*, edited by M. Di Leonardi. Los Angeles: California University Press, 383–395.

Saetnan, A.R. 2002. Scientific? Democratic? Effective? Towards an evaluation of Norway's first medical consensus conference. *Science and Public Policy,* 29(3), 201–220.

Sandell, K. 2001. *Att (Åter)Skapa 'Det Normala': Bröstoperationer Och Brännskador I Plastikkirurgisk Praktik*, Pandora Serien. Lund: Arkiv.

Sandell, K. 2004. The normal and the pathological in medicine: With a focus on plastic surgery and reproduction of injustice. In *Medicinsk Genusforskning : Teori och Begreppsutveckling*. Stockholm: Vetenskapsrådet, 62–69.

Statens beredning för medicinsk utvärdering. 2006. *Metoder För Tidig Fosterdiagnostik: En Systematisk Litteraturöversikt*. Stockholm: Statens beredning för medicinsk utvärdering.

Taylor, J.S. 1992. The public fetus and the family car: From abortion politics to a Volvo advertisement. *Public Culture,* 4(2), 67–80.

Taylor, J.S. 2004. A fetish is born: Sonographers and the making of the public fetus. In *Consuming Motherhood*, edited by J.S. Taylor, L.L. Layne and D.F. Wozniak. New Brunswick: Rutgers University Press, 187–210.

Waldby, C. 2000. *The Visible Human Project: Informatic bodies and posthuman medicine*. London: Routledge.

Weir, L. 1998. Pregnancy ultrasound in maternal discourse. In *Vital Signs: Feminist reconfigurations of the bio/logical body*, edited by M. Shildrick and J. Price. Edinburgh: Edinburgh University Press, 78–101.

Chapter 3
Accounting for Incoherent Bodies[1]

Dawn Goodwin and Maggie Mort

Frequently, in medical practice, there will be multiple, incompatible explanations of a patient's condition, prompting numerous and different possible courses of action. Decision making, in these circumstances, has been analysed as a process of alignment – by bringing together various sources of knowledge, and weighing one against the other, a narrative is produced which explains the majority of the patient's signs, symptoms, readings and measurements. Constructing a coherent story simultaneously organizes prospective actions; the story contains an appropriate response on the part of the practitioner.

More recently in Science and Technology Studies (STS), attention has turned from looking at methods of closure – how, of all the paths that might possibly be taken, options are reduced and a single path emerges – to exploring the *multiplicities, disunities and incoherences* of bodies, objects and knowledges. Here, analyses have highlighted how, despite there being tensions, *differences* are not necessarily resolved, they endure. However, in healthcare settings the notion of professional accountability has become increasingly significant, consequently, the existence of unresolved differences can sometimes be deeply problematic. Health care practitioners work in cultures where certainty – of knowledge, diagnoses and actions – is highly valued and, on one level, enacted as a prerequisite for interventions, and yet on another level, it is frequently, if implicitly, enacted as an unattainable *ideal*.

In this chapter we explore how accountability can be achieved both in circumstances where a coherent narrative may be drawn and where, despite concerted efforts at alignment, the disunity of the patient's body persists. First we discuss the role of routines and 'norms' of a clinical setting, and how these come to signify accountable practice. However, even in routine situations, bodies aren't entirely unified. Then in the next section we explore how incoherences are addressed in situations where an organizing script – a routine – is missing, so that a course of action must be pieced together and clinicians must work overtly to make each step, action or intervention accountable.

The implications of this analysis lead us to suggest an exchange of understandings between different 'accountability communities'. Policy-makers

---

1   This chapter was originally published in Goodwin, D. 2009. *Acting in Anaesthesia: Ethnographic encounters with patients, practitioners and medical technologies*. Cambridge: Cambridge University Press. Reprinted with permission.

and practitioners might be encouraged to engage with an ethnomethodological notion of accountability; then ethnomethodologists and science studies researchers might engage more deeply with a professional notion of accountability. In this way, in order to accommodate the fluidity and multiplicity of clinical practice, professional codes of practice might move away from a notion of accountability that is tethered to individuals and distinct actions. And then, in order to accommodate the constraints faced by clinicians, social scientists could give more prominence to the exemplary (and critical) nature of practice outcomes.

More or Less Coherent Bodies

It is Saturday morning, an 8-year-old child is having an 'Open reduction and internal fixation' of his broken arm under general anaesthetic. This involves surgically exposing the fracture, realigning the bones, bridging the fracture with a metal plate secured by metal screws, and then closing the wound. The anaesthetist, (a medically qualified doctor undertaking a seven year training programme in anaesthesia) Dr Wilkins, is relatively new to the specialty – he has been practising anaesthesia for six months, mostly under supervision, and this is one of the first occasions he has worked independently. The action begins in the operating theatre with the surgery already under way.

> The pulse rate, displayed on the monitor, goes back up to 130. Dr Wilkins peels back the tape covering the patient's eyes, lifts the eyelid and looks at the pupil, he then administers more morphine. He has given 5mls so far. Pulse 147, blood pressure 147/51.

> Dr Wilkins turns to me, he says he had given five of morphine and the patient's pupils were pinpoint, now the pupils are really wide again and the patient is also taking on a lot of isoflurane. *(This indicates that the patient is responding to pain as he has insufficient analgesia to counter the effects of surgery.)*

> Pulse slowing to 103. Dr Wilkins records on the anaesthetic chart some measurements from the list on the screen. Pulse 86. He stands leaning on the drip stand, watching the monitor. Blood pressure 120/44. He turns the volume down on the pulse oximeter. 'High end tidal CO2' *(measurement of expired carbon dioxide)* flashing on the screen, the numbers in white read '8.7'. Dr Wilkins presses some buttons on the monitor and scrolls through some screens. (I think he is changing the alarm limits on the end tidal carbon dioxide measurements as one of the screens he scrolled onto was called 'Airway Gases', and following this the number stops flashing.)

> Dr Wilkins feels the patient's forehead. An ODP enters with the controlled drug book. Dr Wilkins asks the ODP for 50 mgs of voltarol *(a pain killer)*. End tidal

carbon dioxide now reading 9.2 and not flashing. The ODP enters, hands Dr Wilkins a glove and a voltarol suppository. Dr Wilkins administers the voltarol suppository, then looks at the pupils again and gives more morphine (about eight mls given in total).

I ask about the end tidal carbon dioxide readings, he says he did change the limits. He says: 'its probably because he is hypoventilating, it's quite high but it's all right'.

End tidal CO_2 now flashing again and reading 10, pulse 80, blood pressure 108/48. Dr Wilkins watches the surgery.

These fieldnotes were taken by the first author, formerly an anaesthetic nurse, during a one-year period of fieldwork at two hospitals in the UK. Accordingly, the notes reflect a certain degree of detail, familiarity and understanding of anaesthetic practice. This scene tells of an inexperienced anaesthetist learning to distinguish the boundaries of routine practice. He takes the raised pulse rate as a sign that the patient is experiencing pain, the appearance of the patient's pupils, going from pinpoint to wide, and the raised blood pressure (147/51 is high for an eight year old) adds weight to this account. Further affirmation is provided by the amount of isoflurane, an anaesthetic vapour, the patient inhales. Not all patients undergoing general anaesthesia are paralyse and their breathing regulated by a ventilator, and as this patient still regulates his own breathing he can 'take on' more isoflurane by increasing the depth and rate of inhalation. The more anaesthetic inhaled, the deeper the level of anaesthesia thus countering the painful effects of surgery.

Drawing together these measurements and signs with situational details such as the surgical manipulation of the fracture, produces a relatively coherent account of a body in pain. In weaving together information from different sources and of different types, the anaesthetist creates 'a single, more-or-less coherent account, through which events themselves unfold' (Atkinson 1995: 95). Events unfold through this narrative, as it simultaneously constructs the appropriate medical practices, treatments and interventions. Berg (1992: 156) explains:

> [W]hat matters is that the physician makes a patient problem solvable by reducing the infinite array of possible actions to just one disposal.

A solvable problem inherently contains a disposal. Physicians do not diagnose first, then decide upon a therapy (although this staging may be applied in retrospect), rather, accounts and disposals are constructed together (Berg 1992): a patient in pain requires analgesia. Here, the anaesthetist administers morphine for immediate effect and voltarol to cover the next few hours. Subsequent signals from the patient, the pulse slowing to 86 and the blood pressure reading falling to 120/44, suggest that the analgesia has had the desired effect of counteracting the pain of surgery, and thus confirms that the problem was indeed pain.

Nevertheless, even in this most straightforward of cases, the patient's body is not entirely coherent. The carbon dioxide readings, for instance, do not fit within this explanation and suggest a slightly different bodily state – one that has been *over*-analgesed. Exhaled carbon dioxide is primarily measured as an indication of the adequacy of ventilation. However, given that one characteristic of morphine is to act as a respiratory depressant, if the anaesthetist overestimates the amount of morphine required this will result in insufficient ventilation (in a patient regulating their own breathing) and a corresponding rise in the amount of exhaled carbon dioxide. Therefore, the end tidal carbon dioxide reading can also serve as an indirect measure of the sufficiency of analgesia. The anaesthetist's actions may have not only relieved the pain, but also depressed the patient's ability to breathe.

So the anaesthetist seeks to ascertain whether he has given the appropriate amount of analgesia. After giving the first 5ml of morphine, he feels the patient's forehead, since a clammy or sweaty forehead serves as another indication that the patient is experiencing pain. However, this appears to discredit the possibility of an over-analgesed patient, as the anaesthetist continues to administer more analgesia: first, a voltarol suppository and, on checking the pupils again, some more morphine.

Even in routine situations such as this, bodies aren't entirely unified; here, producing a coherent body means disregarding the carbon dioxide measurements. This is not to say that the carbon dioxide readings are incorrect, the anaesthetist clearly accepts the veracity of the readings, acknowledging that the patient is 'hypoventilating'. Rather, it is that the practitioner needs to be confident that his actions are warranted, and the more the signs align – the more coherent the account – the more secure he is in his reading of the patient's body. Coherent bodies provide a good basis for action.

Connecting Coherent Bodies, Certainty and Accountability

However, the 'evidence' of the readings and measurements cannot be disregarded lightly. There are cultural expectations in medicine that doctors must achieve some degree of certainty in their practice (Atkinson 1984, Adamson 1997). In this respect, Adamson (1997: 135) points to the role played by hospital rules, regulations, rituals and routines:

> Certainty is a moral ideal to be achieved through measures such as routinely checking patient's arm bracelets before administering drugs, regularly monitoring their vital signs, their IV drips, and the machines to which they are attached, continuously forming images of their bodies, and constantly analysing their bodily fluids and tissues. In many situations, expressions of uncertainty by medical professionals would violate norms and invite punitive sanctions.

The routine checking, and the need for certainty, draws attention to the context of accountability in which 21st century Western medicine is practised. Adamson adds that when a clinical picture is unclear, physicians will typically resolve the problem of 'what to do' in favour of the norm or routine. The scene above shows the anaesthetist tentatively constructing the carbon dioxide readings as within, albeit perhaps marginally so, the limits of normal: 'it's quite high, but it's all right'. This view is supported by the checking – of the pupils, the feel of the skin, and the continual monitoring of the vital signs – these activities perform accountable medical practice and bolster the anaesthetist's confidence in his understanding of the situation.

In ethnomethodology, accountability is considered to be an ever-present background feature of all social and practical action. Accountability refers to 'the ways in which actions are organized: that is, put together as publicly observable reportable occurrences. They are not only done, '*they are done so that they can be seen to have been done*' (Button and Sharrock 1998: 75, our emphasis). This draws attention to the ways in which participants might 'have in mind' the possibility that their actions can be inspected and hence held to account (Neyland and Woolgar 2002). Not only are these routine checks publicly observable procedures that serve to establish, amongst those present, a degree of certainty that the patient is in pain and further analgesia is warranted, but further, these checks may also indicate the doctor's awareness that his actions may be questioned subsequently by unspecified 'others'.

Moreover, a *routine* situation, itself, confers some security: 'the safety of the norm' (Konner 1988: 366). A routine situation constitutes a frame of reference that delineates what are appropriate actions and what are not. Within this frame of reference, sets of actions are repetitively and habitually carried out without explicitly needing to reflect on or legitimate the actions involved (Berg 1992). If the carbon dioxide readings can be regarded as within normal limits, then administering more analgesia to a patient in pain is an appropriate and legitimate action.

On the one hand then, the checks and monitoring are just part of routine practice, not necessarily significant in legitimating diagnoses and interventions, and on the other, the checks and monitoring activities can be read as an effect of the culture of certainty in which doctors practise, wherein the checks constitute accountable action. This apparent paradox can be resolved if one accepts that the routine practices incorporate sets of accountable actions, they build into 'normal' practice activities that support and confirm the ongoing action. So learning the routines, and learning what constitutes 'normal', means learning to practise accountably. In this scenario, the anaesthetist is learning to define the boundaries of normal practice, and given that he had to change the limits on the anaesthetic machine to prevent it from alarming, this indicates that the patient's carbon dioxide readings fall outside at least one (narrow) construction of 'normal'. So the anaesthetist's checking is cautious and explicit, and his articulation of 'normal' perhaps provisional pending the outcome of this episode: the phrase 'it's quite high, but it's all right' implicitly carries with it the proviso 'for now'. 'It's all right' insofar as it resolves shortly, once the need for such a degree of pain relief has passed and the effects of the analgesia have begun to wane.

More or *Less* Coherent Bodies

The scenario below takes place in the intensive care unit. It describes a critical period of a patient's care. The patient is reviewed during the morning ward round in which a consultant anaesthetist, two junior doctors and several nurses discuss his condition. The staff are aware that the patient's condition is deteriorating but are unable to identify precisely why. The scenario spans approximately two hours necessitating some fieldnote editing and this is indicated in italics, as are the explanations we have added. After intense work to isolate and address the problems, and to stabilize the patient's condition, the consultant conveys the course of events to the family. These scenes show how a team of practitioners work to align the patient's signs, symptoms, histories, and measurements into a convincing and coherent story, and it also shows the patient's body resisting such unifying logics.

The first scene begins with the nurses, student nurses, two junior doctors (one surgical trainee and one anaesthetic trainee) and a consultant anaesthetist, all scrutinising the patient's chest X-ray before reviewing the patient himself. They discuss whether he might have a pneumothorax, a term used to describe a leak in the lungs through which air escapes but remains trapped within the chest cavity, compressing the lung and preventing proper inhalation.

> Dr Williams *(consultant anaesthetist)* puts up some 'chest films' and discusses with the two junior doctors whether it shows a pneumothorax – they conclude it does. Dr Davis *(surgical trainee)* hands them another X-ray that they look at. A further two nurses and one student nurse also gather around the X-rays. The consultant questions the nurses: 'If you saw this what would you think?' One of the nurses mentions that the 'trachy' *(tracheostomy – a surgical opening in the throat through which the patient is intubated and ventilated)* tube is pointing the wrong way.
>
> Dr Williams: 'The trachy looks like it is in the wrong place… Is there anything we need to do in a rush because of this X-ray?'
>
> Dr Chatterji *(anaesthetic trainee)*: 'No.'

When first appraising the X-rays, two explanations for the patient's condition are discussed: is the tracheostomy tube wrongly positioned and is there a pneumothorax present? Crucially, however, whilst the X-ray may hint at these possibilities, the X-ray alone is not considered definitive enough to warrant such invasive action. In a study about medical imaging, Joyce (2005) explains that physicians integrate information from a variety of sources, seldom relying on a single source to warrant action. To do so means that they might treat a patient for a disease that exists only in that particular source – in the case above, the doctors might treat the patient for a pneumothorax that only exists in the X-ray. Attention, therefore, turns from the X-ray to the patient himself. The more elements that can be aligned, the more persuasive the account.

At the patient's bedside:

Dr Williams briefly recounts the patient's history of care in the ICU: '... attempted tracheostomy... bleeding ... Charlie *(Dr Davis – surgical trainee)* saved the day...'

The nurse who answered the question about the trachy (I see from her name badge she is called Lucy) gives a history of the last day's care: '... CO_2 keeps going up and up, it doesn't seem to matter what you do to the ventilator... tachycardic *(raised heart rate)* ...'

Dr Williams: 'Why?'

Lucy: 'He's struggling.' She continues with the history mentioning the patient's urine output, potassium levels, on TPN feeds *(liquid nutrition administered intravenously)*, no bowel sounds...

Dr Williams: '... Anyone examined him?'

Dr Davis *(surgical trainee)* responds: 'Very quiet breath sounds, CO_2 retaining. I don't think he's getting rid of... *(he turns to the ventilator and points to the trace)*... little notch there.'

Dr Williams: 'Why is he... quick listen to his chest.' He puts the stethoscope to the patient's chest then disconnects the ventilator.

Lucy: 'Did you mean to do that?'

Dr Williams: 'Yes. What can you hear? (He listens by the tracheostomy.) ... Big wheeze... basically his chest is full of gas... chest is so full, can't get... (he feels the patient's tummy)... distended but... don't want any air trapping *(in which the expiratory phase of respiration is not completed before the ventilator delivers another breath, consequently air is 'trapped' within the lungs)*... 200 mls plus... chest getting bigger and bigger no matter what pressures... expiratory wheeze...blood cultures...'

Dr Williams and the two junior doctors discuss various aspects of the patient's condition and decide they need to change the pattern of ventilation.

In the scene above, the team quickly focus on a problem with the ventilation: high and climbing levels of carbon dioxide is the first element mentioned both by the nurse and the junior doctor. Aligning the carbon dioxide levels with an expiratory wheeze and an expanded chest, Dr Williams, the consultant anaesthetist, suggests 'air trapping' may be the problem. 'Air trapping' is a common problem for ventilated intensive care patients. Accordingly, it seems the nurse has already considered this, pointing out that the carbon dioxide levels remained high in spite of adjustments to the ventilator. In the first instance, then, uncertainty over the patient's condition is resolved in favour of a problem routinely encountered. Practical and epistemological reasons for this are entwined. As Atkinson (1984) points out, medical education promotes the conceptualization of diagnosis as 'puzzles' with definitive solutions, a notion supported by the concentration, during the training of student doctors, on hospital medicine in which the ambiguity and diffuseness of health and illness in general practice has already been filtered out. Consequently, the nature of medical inference is often 'reductionist':

> Whether the patients on the wards have a common complaint or an unusual one, the chances are that they have got some well-established observable and relatively discrete pathology. (Atkinson 1984: 952)

In this, Atkinson also points to an intrinsically straightforward, practical reason for focussing on a common problem – that is, as 'air trapping' routinely affects many ventilated patients in intensive care, it is highly probable that it will also be a problem for this patient.

First, they increase the expiratory period on the ventilator settings then discuss what to do if this doesn't improve the situation.

Dr Williams interrupts: 'I wouldn't get him to breathe himself… air trapping…'

Dr Chatterji *(anaesthetic trainee)*: 'You mean paralyse him?'

Dr Williams: 'Yes. Give some atracurium *(muscle relaxant drug)* now, just see if it works…'

Dr Williams alters something on the ventilator. Lucy returns with some ampoules of atracurium.

Lucy: '50 George *(Dr Williams – consultant anaesthetist)*?' *She injects.*

Dr Williams: '… if paralysed, well sedated, I think he's well sedated… infected element, don't know what it is… paralyse and ventilate… Why is that going up and down? (He points to the screen)'

Lucy: 'Not a smooth expiration.'

Dr Williams: '… just bag him. (He disconnects the ventilator and connects a manual ventilation circuit.) Suction catheter.'

Lucy feeds a catheter down the tracheostomy. Dr Williams disconnects the manual ventilation circuit and listens, head by the patient's throat. He presses with both hands on the patient's chest.

Dr Williams: 'What can you hear?'

Lucy: 'Nothing.' She listens, her head by the patient's throat.

Dr Williams: 'He's still exhaling. (He reconnects the ventilator.) Are we ventilating?'

Dr Chatterji: 'No.'

Dr Williams switches back to the manual ventilation circuit, Dr Davis ventilates. Dr Williams moves round to the head of the patient and removes a pillow. He lifts the patient's chin up and holds the tracheostomy tube and takes over ventilating.

Dr Williams: 'Quite high pressure… do about 6 a minute.' He hands the bag back to Dr Davis who turns the valve on the circuit and squeezes the bag with both hands.

Dr Williams: 'Air entry very quiet… give a nebulizer now.'

Lucy: 'Salbutamol.' *(A drug inhaled to dilate the airways.)*

Dr Williams: '10 mls of 1 in 10 000 adrenaline. Bronchoscope … Let's have another look at the X-ray, check we are not missing anything.' We all go back to the viewing box.

They decide to paralyse the patient, simplifying the situation by bringing the patient's breathing completely under mechanical control, but still ventilation is problematic. They change the circuit and ventilate manually, thereby excluding the machine from the equation, but the pressure required to transfer oxygen from the reservoir bag to the patient's lungs remains high suggesting that the difficulty is to be located within the patient's body.

Disconnecting the circuit from the tracheostomy, the consultant and the nurse listen. The consultant suggests the patient is 'still exhaling', again performing a link between prolonged and difficult expiration and high carbon dioxide levels. That the intensive care nurse is unable to hear anything suggests that 'air-trapping' – although a common problem – is not self-evidently present, rather, 'air-trapping' is a diagnosis that has to be constructed and legitimated out of somewhat ambiguous signs and symptoms.

This process of legitimation in the presence of ambiguity is explored by Singleton (1998) in her study of the cervical screening programme. Taking a science studies perspective, she highlights how negotiating such ambiguities forms an integral part of diagnostic work: looking at the laboratory practices involved in the diagnosis of cervical cell samples, Singleton identifies how, not only do the cells change in ways that do not easily fit the categories on the report card, but that even where cell changes are clear, the significance of the changes (whether the changes relate to malignancy or not) is contentious. Furthermore, the diagnosis is not solely made on the appearance of the cells, instead, the appearance of the cells is interpreted differently depending on the age and marital status of the woman and on the number of children she has born. Singleton suggests that 'the ability of the laboratory to detect precancerous changes *depends* on its ability to accommodate instability and ambiguity' (1998: 102, our emphasis).

This insight, that diagnostic work in the laboratory demands engagement with uncertainties and instabilities can also be applied to the process of *clinical* diagnosis:

> Diagnosis is never complete or definitive; it is a process of discovery which unfolds over time. (Adamson 1997: 142)

Whilst the notion of 'discovery' might be problematic for a science studies readership, this quotation does at least emphasize the way that a diagnosis does not irrevocably determine the ontology of the patient's body. Although diagnoses might, in part, organize actions and care, diagnoses are 'done' in ongoing contingent performances that are always susceptible to change:

> Initial diagnosis is regularly falsified by new clinical results or the appearance of new symptoms. (Adamson 1997: 149)

Going back to the scenario above, the staff are unable to make a diagnosis of 'air trapping' convincing and so work intensively to legitimate their interventions. Without a diagnosis, there is no clear organizing routine, and working outside a routine invokes vulnerability, it 'implies that the correctness of the action needs to be explicitly renegotiated: the legitimacy which comes as a matter of course with a routine articulation is now absent' (Berg 1992: 171–172). This, in turn, promotes the visibility and prominence of the ways in which practices are legitimated: reasons for requested drugs are verbalized, the bronchoscope, through which the lungs may be visualized, is requested and the consultant returns to recheck the X-ray:

> Dr Williams: 'Is there a pneumothorax there?' He takes his glasses off and peers very closely at the X-ray. He follows lines on the X-ray with his finger.

> Dr Davis: 'You can see a line superimposed... I can't see a pneumothorax.' He points to the X-ray.

> Dr Williams: 'If we can't ventilate him we are going to have to stick drains in... this looks suspicious...' He compares today's X-ray to yesterday's. (At one point Dr Williams gets today's and yesterday's X-rays the wrong way round, Dr Davis corrects him.)

> Dr Williams: 'The lung is much more hyperinflated today.'

> We all follow Dr Williams back to the patient.

The X-ray suggests, but cannot definitively confirm, a pneumothorax. The team are still, at this stage, unable to couple the possibilities the X-ray suggests and the symptoms the patient exhibits tightly together; the mispositioned tracheostomy tube, the pneumothorax, and the hyperinflated lungs all remain separate and dissociated entities.

The Problem with Incoherent Bodies: How to Act?

Possibly, this search for a singular patient ontology is misguided. Mol (2002) asserts that the body is *multiple*. She explains how a disease – atherosclerosis – is different in different locations and practices. In the out-patient clinic, atherosclerosis is a complaint of pain on walking. In the operating theatre, atherosclerosis is the accumulated debris – atherosclerotic plaques – inside a vessel to be stripped out and discarded. And in the pathology laboratory, atherosclerosis is something seen under a microscope – a thickened intima, the lining of the vessel wall. These different atheroscleroses may cohere – pain on walking is caused by reduced blood flow to the lower limbs because of the build up of atherosclerotic plaques. However, this is not necessarily the case. Mol insists that 'bodies aren't always coherent'.

Mol does acknowledge, however, that the 'disease to be treated' is a composite object made up of such elements as the numbers that come out of the vascular laboratory, the complaints of the patient, and the body's supporting evidence ascertained on clinical examination:

> [T]he various realities of atherosclerosis are balanced, added up, subtracted. That,
> in one way or another, they are fused into a composite whole (Mol 2002: 70).

Mol suggests that a body's lack of cohesion is unremarkable; if coordination of apparent incompatibilities is not possible then differences may be distributed. Atherosclerosis may well be both pain and a clogged up artery but not both in the same site. It is pain in diagnosis and a clogged up artery in treatment. In this way, the possible tensions between variants of a disease disappear into the background when distributed over different sites.

However, the body in this scenario resists such coordination, refusing to be drawn into a 'composite whole', and neither is distribution an option. Here, incompatibilities are not dispersed between different sites, practices and times, but collected together in one location, at one time, when treatment decisions must be made urgently. Accordingly, the uncertainty is such that the staff are still unwilling to act on these possibilities: they do not want to risk inserting chest drains into a patient for a pneumothorax that exists only in the X-ray. However, ventilation is now so difficult it may be necessary to take such actions in spite of these misgivings: 'If we can't ventilate him we are going to have to stick drains in…'. In this instance, certainty of knowledge and in actions, is invoked as something of a luxury – an ideal – with the deteriorating condition of the patient forcing the hand of the medical staff.

> Dr Williams taps the patient's chest, he asks for a stethoscope, someone hands
> him one, and he listens to patient's chest.
>
> Dr Williams: '100% oxygen please… adrenaline, that's the concentrated stuff.'
> The intensive care sister has just handed him a syringe, he hands it back.
>
> Sister: 'What did you ask for?'
>
> Dr Williams: '1: 10 000.'
>
> The ICU Sister returns with the prepacked syringe of adrenaline and hands it to
> Dr Williams. He opens the blue plastic packet and squirts about 1 ml down the
> tracheostomy tube. Dr Williams watches the patient.
>
> Lucy: 'What is that for?'
>
> Dr Williams: 'Severe bronchospasm… it acts directly to break bronchospasm.'

Another diagnosis – bronchospasm – is briefly considered for which adrenaline is promptly administered. This is surprising perhaps given doctors' proclivity for acting on a number of integrated sources, however, this intervention is easily implemented and carries little risk and seems to be carried out more in an attempt to eliminate bronchospasm from the frame rather than in a serious effort to resolve the situation. Diagnosis, therefore, can be seen as a process of 'delimiting a field of alternatives' (Suchman 2000: 318) rather than simply selecting and confirming a favoured explanation. For this intervention, accountability, in the ethnomethodological sense of demand for, and giving of, reasons for conduct (Garfinkel 1967) is readily established. The purpose of adrenaline in this situation is questioned by the nurse and quickly answered by Dr Williams. Unfortunately, this course of action proves fruitless and Dr Williams comes back to consider the insertion of chest drains.

> Dr Williams listens again to the patient's chest. He feeds the suction catheter down and back again. He ventilates using the manual ventilation circuit, squeezing hard to empty the whole of the bag.

> Dr Davis brings in a foil tray containing some cannulae and puts a pair of gloves on. (I think I heard Dr Williams mention cannulae earlier.)

> Dr Williams: 'Hyperinflated lungs... chance to exhale... if in doubt do it.'

> Dr Davis inserts a cannula into the right side of the patient's chest. He removes the needle.

> Dr Williams: 'Lovely hiss.'
> Lucy: 'Setting up for a chest drain...'

> Dr Williams leaves, returning moments later with a syringe of water, he attaches it to the cannula and removes the plunger – I can now see air bubbling furiously through the water.

Given the considerable ambiguity as to the source of the ventilation problems and the persistence of doubt as to the presence of a pneumothorax, some further warrant is necessary for the insertion of chest drains. The increasing difficulty in ventilation means that this warrant is urgently required, consequently, a cannula is inserted into the patient's chest. The cannula is a quick and temporary measure, only to determine the presence of a pneumothorax. The comment: 'lovely hiss' confirms the assumption of a pneumothorax, and is visually reinforced by the sight of air, which had been trapped within the chest cavity, bubbling through the water in the syringe. With these events and interactions it is obvious to all present that the insertion of chest drains is a necessary intervention as signified by the nurse's comment: 'setting up for a chest drain'.

> *A cannula inserted into the left side of the patient's chest confirms the presence of a further pneumothorax and, under the supervision of Dr Williams, Dr*

Davis and Dr Chatterji insert a chest drain in each side. Following this the bronchoscope arrives:

Dr Williams feeds the bronchoscope down the tracheostomy: 'No obstruction in the right main bronchus... end of the tube stuck up against the wall... try ventilating now... any easier?'

Lucy: 'No.'

Dr Williams offers the eyepiece of the bronchoscope to Lucy who looks down it.

Dr Williams: 'You're ventilating against that .... Having a bit of a problem... get a tube handy...'

Dr Davis leaves. Dr Hargreaves *(another consultant anaesthetist)* enters.

Lucy: 'Crash trolley please!' She says this loudly, directed outside curtains. *('Crash trolley' contains resuscitation equipment.)*

Dr Williams briefs Dr Hargreaves on their actions this morning regarding this patient.

Crash trolley wheeled in by the intensive care sister.

Dr Williams: 'Take the trachy right out...'

Dr Hargreaves: 'When the bronchoscope was down what did you see...' He continues questioning Dr Williams.

Dr Williams: 'Ventilation very, very difficult... bronchoscope... against the posterior wall...'

Lucy ventilates. Dr Chatterji stitches in the chest drain.

Dr Hargreaves: 'Would a tube be easier?'

Dr Williams: 'You would know the tube would be pointing straight down... basically disconnect from the ventilator... long, long expiratory...'

Dr Hargreaves: 'Not paralysed?'

Dr Williams: 'We paralysed about 40 minutes ago... I think change the tube ... just see...'

Dr Hargreaves: 'I'd be surprised if it makes a difference…'

Dr Williams stands at the head, holding the patient's chin up and looking down at the patient's chest, frowning.

The arrival of the bronchoscope – a device that allows internal visualization of the lungs – enables Dr Williams to see that the end of the tracheostomy tube is pressed against the wall of the trachea thereby preventing exhalation. Finally, the X-ray no longer stands alone in suggesting a mispositioned tracheostomy, the bronchoscope provides visual affirmation of *how* it is mispositioned which explains *why* it is causing a problem: under positive pressure, air could be forced into the lungs, but with the end of the tracheostomy tube abutting the wall of the trachea, air couldn't escape. For Dr Williams this sight provides sufficient evidence to convince him to change the tracheostomy tube to an endotracheal tube. Not being privy to all the previous checks and attempts to elucidate this situation, some doubt still exists for the second consultant, Dr Hargreaves. This suggests something of a tension between how accountability is interactionally achieved amongst co-participants, and accountability in the sense of giving an abbreviated, somewhat decontextualized, 'account' for the judgement of others.

After further discussion with Dr Hargreaves over the type of tube to be used, Dr Williams decides to change the tracheostomy tube for a normal endotracheal tube. Before they can do so the X-ray team arrive and take a chest X-ray of the patient.

We all move back over to the bedside. Dr Chatterji listens to the patient's chest with a stethoscope. Dr Williams moves up to the head of the patient and takes over ventilating, he lays the patient flat.

Dr Williams: 'Let's just put down a normal tube first of all.'

Dr Davis: 'Do you want sux going in now?' *(Suxamethonium – a paralysing drug to allow intubation.)*

Dr Williams: 'Yes please.' He inserts the laryngoscope, then the tube into the patient's mouth but does not yet advance the tube down to the trachea. 'Ready to take the trachy out in a minute?'

Sister: 'Tell me when to deflate.'

Dr Williams: 'Is it stitched in?'

Sister: 'Shit.'

Dr Williams: 'Stitch cutter.' (Loudly, directed outside the curtains.)

The sister cuts the stitches holding the tracheostomy tube in place.

I look at the monitor – oxygen saturation reading 75%.

Dr Williams intubates then connects the manual circuit and ventilates: 'That feels better… Aspirate on the NG *(nasogastric tube).*'

Dr Hargreaves: 'Saturation coming up nicely.' Oxygen saturation is now 86%.

The sister directs Dr Chatterji on how to tape the chest drain down. (Patient looks pink again now.)

Dr Hargreaves: '89%…'

Dr Williams: 'Charlie *(Dr Davis – surgical trainee)*, try and ventilate.'

Dr Hargreaves: 'Everything under control from the monitor.' He stands next to me at the bottom end of the bed.

Dr Williams: 'See what the X-ray shows…'

Dr Hargreaves: 'I'll go down *(to the X-ray department)* and have a look.'

Dr Williams bronchoscopes again, down the tube this time. Three nurses work at securing everything – the endotracheal tube, chest drains, etc. (The atmosphere is calmer now, around the time of intubation it felt tense).

Whilst this securing work continues Dr Hargreaves (the second consultant anaesthetist) returns to report that the X-ray shows two pneumothoraces requiring a further two chest drains. These are inserted by Dr Davis and Dr Chatterji under Dr Williams' supervision. Dr Williams says that he needs to talk to the patient's family and asks Lucy to accompany him.

The critical situation begins to resolve as a result of exchanging the tracheostomy tube for an endotracheal tube. In a study about how radiologists construct accountability, Yakel (2001) refers to the sense in which accountability is commonly taken as something accomplished in, and represented by, a written record. Instead, and in line with the ethnomethodological sense of accountability, she suggests that accountability is achieved through a process of interactions between people and artefacts. The scene above shows the process of accounting for the exchange of tubes as the correct and appropriate action. Dr Williams comments immediately that ventilation 'feels better' and he invites Dr Davis to share this observation, Dr

Hargreaves attends to the oxygen saturation readings provided by the monitoring, highlighting the improvement and acknowledging that the critical situation is beginning to come under control. Dr Williams visually checks again with the bronchoscope and Dr Hargreaves checks the X-ray. It is, therefore, a matter of public consensus, produced through the interactions between the team and the technologies, that this intervention is legitimated and becomes accountable as the appropriate action, and the misplaced tracheostomy tube becomes one of the correct diagnoses.

Tracing the Threads of Accountability

Adamson (1997) points out that diagnosis is a process of trial and error and that there is no such thing as an incorrect diagnosis in the present: 'a diagnosis only becomes wrong with the passing of time' (1997: 149). The above scenario indicates that the reverse could also be said – that a correct diagnosis is something that can only be established in retrospect. Perhaps it is more generally that the veracity of a diagnosis – whether correct or not – can only be a post-hoc attribution. This is not to say that doctors are not concerned – prospectively – with the accuracy of their diagnoses. This scenario shows the reluctance to act without proper warrants especially when care lacks the organization and security of a routine. Legitimating actions, by explicitly identifying the warrants for interventions and the recognition of these amongst the team, not only enables the doctor to be convinced they are acting appropriately but also renders publicly available the accountability of these actions.

Neyland and Woolgar direct attention to how this distinct *ethnomethodological* sense of accountability feeds into the specific sense of *professional* accountability:

> That actions are rendered recognizable now increasingly means that they should be tested for the adequacy of their production. (Neyland and Woolgar 2002: 263)

However, some ambiguity persists as to whom accountability is owed. The particular public to which actions are rendered accountable is often unspecified and varies considerably in ethnomethodological studies of accountability. Moreover, the nature of the 'public observation' involved also varies:

> It is not always clear whether accountability involves the mere 'recognizability' of actions (for example, that it is an answer to a question) or whether it also involves sanctionable consequences. (Neyland and Woolgar 2002: 263)

And this, it seems, is the distinction between the ethnomethodological sense of accountability and the professional one. Thus far we have concentrated on how accountability is interactionally achieved amongst participants and we have only alluded to the implications beyond the immediate setting – in that participants may be aware that their actions might later be inspected by yet unspecified persons in unspecified situations. This scenario, however, illustrates the connections between different audiences and how the different senses of accountability are related. When it became clear that the patient's condition was deteriorating rapidly the consultant, Dr Williams, requested that the nurses contact the patient's relatives and ask them to come in. They were waiting in the relatives' room:

> *Dr Williams, Lucy and I leave the intensive care unit and walk a short distance down the corridor to the relative's room. It is a smallish room with a kitchen area and sitting area. The family – a young man, mid-late twenties (son) and an older woman (wife) – are seated drinking tea.*

Dr Williams sits in the far corner of the room facing them both, Lucy sits on the sofa next to the son and I stand behind Lucy. Dr Williams introduces us all, he tells them the patient is stable now but earlier on they had had some difficulties. He begins by going back to the previous day when the tracheostomy was inserted then talks them through today's events when they had difficulty ventilating. He explains that this may have been for two reasons, firstly the tracheostomy was pressed against the wall of the trachea, so they have changed from the tracheostomy back to a tube going in the mouth and down into the throat. The other reason was a pneumothorax. Dr Williams explains that a pneumothorax is a small hole in the lung that leaks out a pocket of air that then compresses the lung. He said at one point the patient's oxygen saturation, which they like to keep at around 100, went down to about 75% for a period of about 4 or 5 minutes, Dr Williams said they were really struggling during this period. He continues that they have now changed to an endotracheal tube, which goes into the mouth and down the throat, and put chest drains in each side, and explains that the patient's oxygen saturation is now back up to 98%.

The relatives express relief, exhale slowly: 'Thank you doctor'.

Dr Williams goes on: 'I have to be honest with you, at one point it was touch and go, and I thought we were going to lose him'. The wife is visibly shocked.

Dr Williams describes what the patient now looks like: 'He has 4 drains in (gestures where they are) and a tube down his throat.'

> *Dr Williams asks the family to wait a few minutes longer whilst they clear up the equipment after which the relatives could see the patient. Dr Williams, Lucy and I go back to ICU.*

When the consultant anaesthetist talks with the patient's family the account is necessarily simplified so as not to overload the family with superfluous medical details. The consultant conveys only those diagnoses and interventions that have been retrospectively verified as correct, appropriate and accountable actions – the mispositioned tracheostomy tube *and* the pneumothoraces – as causes for the patient's condition. Here, then, the search for a unifying ontology is abandoned and the patient is presented as having *two separate diagnoses that co-exist but don't cohere*. There is no longer any need to unite these problems, each diagnosis and associated interventions has been warranted and legitimated separately by a number of different sources.

The consultant's explanations are oriented to giving the family a reasonable understanding of the events – the physiological problem with the patient's body (a hole in the lungs), the difficulties with the technological device (the tracheostomy tube pressed against the wall of the trachea) and the interventions incurred (insertion of chest drains and an endotracheal tube). But notwithstanding this simplification, Dr Williams takes care to convey some very specific details: that the oxygen saturation fell to approximately 75% for a period of four or five minutes. He doesn't elaborate on the meaning of this but uses this detail to emphasize the criticality of this period. It is possible that here he is oriented to a potential future state of the patient, and potential future discussions with the family in which he may have to account for any sequelae of this period of desaturation. After confirming that the ventilation problems are now resolved and the oxygen saturation levels are now 98%, Dr Williams again emphasizes the severity of the situation: 'I thought we were going to lose him'. To those present, with experience and training in critical care, this needn't be verbalized, but accountability goes beyond those present, and the very real possibility that the patient might have died has, in Dr Williams' opinion, to be made recognizable to the relatives.

Conclusion: Incoherence and Accountability in Tension

When issues of professional accountability are questioned, it is often retrospectively, with action decontextualized and scrutinized by various actors – clinicians, managers, patients and relatives – that were not necessarily involved in the contested situation, nor will they necessarily share the 'professional vision' of those practitioners involved. 'Professional vision' is the 'socially organized ways of seeing and understanding events that are answerable to the distinctive interests of a particular social group' (Goodwin 1994: 606), it refers to the process through which practitioners learn to see the 'objects' with which they work. The particular features of an 'object' are not self-evidently present but are made visible through the embodied work of the practitioner. Therefore, what is visible to the competent practitioner, will not be obvious to the uninitiated.

In adjudicating on matters of professional accountability, codes of conduct serve as a measure against which practice may be compared. Codes of conduct are composed by a profession's governing body, they articulate a profession's agreed standards and advise the reader on the responsibilities of its practitioners. They serve a normative function in that they reify a preferred manner of professional activity. However, being premised on an individual, cognitive mode of decision making and activity, such codes of conduct downplay the complexity of real-world, situated decision making and the extent of involvement of other human, technological, environmental and material factors; they emphasize the *control* of practitioners. In these documents, therefore, professional accountabilities crystallize on certain actions and particular actors.

Our argument, following many other critiques, most notably Suchman (1987, 2007), is that this cognitive model of decision-making and action does not map onto practice very well, and we suggest that this causes a particular problem for practitioners where accountability is concerned: by focusing primarily on the actions of individual practitioners, other significant elements of practice (such as the agency of unconscious bodies) are erased. As Hutchins suggests, these texts *over*-attribute knowledge to individual actors:

> [W]hen the context of cognition is ignored, it is impossible to see the contribution of structure in the environment, in artifacts, and in other people to the organization of mental processes (Hutchins 1996: 62).

Our aim, in this chapter, has been to illustrate, in line with recent moves in science and technology studies, the incoherences that form an integral part of medical practices. The disunity of medical practices, medical knowledge, objects, devices and bodies is a theme that has come under significant analytical attention in recent years (see, for example, Mol 2002, Law 1999, Dugdale 1999, Berg and Mol 1998). However, we sought to add accountability into this analytical frame, and to highlight the elements of risk involved in working in such complex, dynamic, multifaceted situations, and how these risks are addressed by practitioners.

The first scenario shows how routine practices guide the anaesthetist into practising safely and accountably. The skill of the anaesthetist lies less in the detective work of determining the diagnosis and more in learning what constitutes the boundaries of 'normal'. A practitioner is expected to account clearly and concisely for their actions, but even in very mundane situations, patients' bodies do not always comply by presenting a clear, concise and *coherent* set of signs and symptoms. Routine checks provide a sense of security here, and as checking becomes a familiar, regular activity it becomes both ingrained in practice, and the sense of certainty it provides becomes expected of practice. Certainty in knowing and doing is highly valued in healthcare settings.

In our second scenario the problem with incoherent bodies comes into focus: bodies that offer multiple, plausible but incompatible explanations for their presentation do not provide a lead for action. The lack of an organizing script – a routine – means that a course of action must be pieced together and clinicians must work overtly to legitimate, as far as is possible, each step, action or intervention. In the final scenario rationales for action were frequently verbalized, the consultant showed great care to organize the team's actions step by step, and accountability was explicitly achieved. Events were observed and commented upon – decidedly 'witnessed'. This scenario demonstrates how the omnipresent sense of accountability in which healthcare is practised, relates to a more formal sense of professional accountability in which actions may be retrospectively inspected, judged and potentially followed by professional and legal sanctions. This second scenario showed that whereas certainty may be highly valued, it is also an *ideal*, and in some circumstances, practice, actions and interventions must go on in spite of intense uncertainty. This creates vulnerabilities for practitioners where accountability is concerned and is in part countered by the more explicit witnessing of events that goes on between participants in critical circumstances as compared to routine practice.

Neyland and Woolgar (2002) suggest that ethnomethodological studies of accountability tend to take the relevant 'public' to be the body of immediately co-present participants and are often unclear about whether and how different kinds of audiences are implicated. Our second scenario shows that health care professionals operate with a broader notion of accountability, one that extends beyond the immediate environment. Even whilst engaged in a critical period of care, the practitioners demonstrated an awareness of another 'public' – the relatives – and in fact asked for them to be called in. Furthermore, in discussions with the relatives, it seems possible that certain details were conveyed in order to foreground potential future discussions. Without elaborating on the meanings, the anaesthetist 'plants' precise details such as the level of oxygen saturation and the number of minutes. As Garfinkel points out, a situation is informed by its history and its future: 'By waiting to see what will have happened he learns what it was he previously saw' (Garfinkel 1967: 77). Accordingly, the anaesthetist does not know, at this time, the consequences of this critical period but is no doubt aware that there may be some that he will subsequently have to explain. Finally, then, this suggests that although the appropriateness of actions, for example the correctness of a diagnosis, is a post-hoc achievement, this doesn't prevent healthcare professionals from being prospectively oriented.

The development of understanding clinical practice as a process of distributed decision making, with decisions shared among humans, devices and routine practices, has been an incisive analytical resource within STS, but it fails to acknowledge that practice may not necessarily be viewed this way when questions of professional accountability are raised. In these circumstances, practice is often scrutinized retrospectively, with actions decontextualized and contrasted against ideal models of practice inscribed into guidelines and codes of conduct. We have aimed to highlight the tensions between understanding practice as something fluid, unstable and multiple and the expectations of certainty inherent in healthcare practices and the need to act sometimes in the absence of such certainty. By tracing the different manifestations of accountability and the links between them, it is possible to discern how and why disunities must, on some occasions, be addressed, not necessarily made to cohere, but in some way be comprehended so that *actions can be made accountable*.

References

Adamson, C. 1997. Existential and clinical uncertainty in the medical encounter: an idiographic account of an illness trajectory defined by Inflammatory Bowel Disease and Avascular Necrosis. *Sociology of Health and Illness*, 19(2), 133–159.

Atkinson, P. 1984. Training for certainty. *Social Science and Medicine*, 19(9), 949–956.

Atkinson, P. 1995. *Medical Talk and Medical Work*. London: Sage Publications.

Berg, M. 1992. The construction of medical disposals: medical sociology and medical problem solving in clinical practice. *Sociology of Health and Illness*, 14(2), 151–180.

Berg, M. and Mol, A. (eds). 1998. *Differences in Medicine: Unraveling practices, techniques, and bodies*. Durham: Duke University Press.

Button, G. and Sharrock, W. 1998. The organizational accountability of technological work. *Social Studies of Science*, 28(1), 73–102.

Dugdale, A. 1999. Materiality: juggling sameness and difference, in *Actor Network Theory and After*, edited by J. Law and J. Hassard. Oxford: Blackwell, 113–135.

Garfinkel, H. 1967. *Studies in Ethnomethodology*. Englewood Cliffs, NJ: Prentice-Hall.

Goodwin, C. 1994. Professional Vision. *American Anthropologist*, 96(3), 606–633.

Hutchins, E. 1996. Learning to navigate, in *Understanding Practice: Perspectives on activity and context*, edited by S. Chaiklin and J. Lave. Cambridge, UK: Cambridge University Press, 35–63.

Joyce, K. 2005. Appealing images: Magnetic resonance Imaging and the production of authoritative knowledge. *Social Studies of Science*, 35(3), 437–462.

Konner, M. 1988. *Becoming a Doctor*. New York: Penguin.

Law, J. 1999. After ANT: complexity, naming and topology, in *Actor Network Theory and After*, edited by J. Law and J. Hassard. Oxford: Blackwell Publishers, 1–14.

Mol, A. 2002. *The Body Multiple: Ontology in medical practice*. Durham: Duke University Press.

Neyland, D. and Woolgar, S. 2002. Accountability in action?: The case of a database purchasing decision. *British Journal of Sociology*, 53(2), 259–274.

Singleton, V. 1998. Stabilizing instabilities: the role of the laboratory in the United Kingdom Cervical Screening Programme, in *Differences in Medicine: Unraveling practices, techniques, and bodies*, edited by M. Berg and A. Mol. Durham: Duke University Press, 86–104.

Suchman, L. 1987. *Plans and Situated Actions: The problem of human–machine communication*. Cambridge: Cambridge University Press.

Suchman, L. 2000. Organizing alignment: A case of bridge-building. *Organization*, 7(2), 311–327.

Suchman, L. 2007. *Human–Machine Reconfigurations: Plans and situated actions.* 2nd ed. Cambridge: Cambridge University Press.

Yakel, E. 2001. The social construction of accountability: Radiologists and their record-keeping practices. *The Information Society*, 17(4), 233–245.

PART 2
Simulating Bodies

Medical technology can take many forms, some life saving, some life maintaining, some for show and some for educational purposes. Much of this technology can be very expensive. And much of it can also be very flashy. It is easy to find examples of both in the simulator industry. This is a field dominated by the dream to recreate the patient, ostensibly so medical students can learn and do medicine on a simulator instead of a person, saving patients from being the guinea pigs of the 'see one, do one, teach one' learning paradigm that is so prevalent in the medical apprenticeship. This is an honourable motive, certainly, though sometimes one can also suspect a Frankensteinian desire to create for the sake of creating.

For social scientists, the development of simulators begs questions of what is being (re)created and represented. The human anatomy? Pathologies? Patients? Body parts? The answers are as many as the simulators are diverse, and medical simulators are diverse. If one stretches the definition to include static models, then simulators have existed for centuries, and are extensions of the desire to describe, reproduce and study the human anatomy without a steady supply of cadavers. Just as anatomies in various forms and from different time periods have been analysed for the pre-existing understandings of class, race, gender and disease that they recreate (Cartwright and Penley 1998, Jordanova 1999, Laqueur 2003, Schiebinger 1993, Stolberg 2003), so too can simulators, even if they are more advanced and incorporate specific practices, be open to this type of analysis.

The chapters in this section represent three different approaches of analysis. The simulators themselves are also very different. While all three are simulating the female reproductive organs, the simulator in Rachel Prentice's study is a haptically enabled gynaecological simulator, which means it has surgical instrument handles attached to computer-controlled mechanical motors which create a force feedback sensation to accompany a computer generated visual representation of the womb and ovaries. The body is presented virtually. Users of this simulator practise performing minimally invasive surgical procedures on the reproductive organs, and through the forces attached to the handles they 'feel' what they are doing inside a female abdomen while they 'watch' their movements on the computer screen. In contrast, the birthing simulator in Jenny Sundén's chapter is a physical model of a full female body which pushes out a simulated baby. It is made of rubber and mechanical parts, can bleed, and is a very tangible machine. The simulator in Ericka Johnson's chapter physically recreates the female reproductive organs in rubber and silicon to allow students to train giving a specific type of gynaecological exam.

Each chapter looks at the specific practices involved in creating these simulators, but from different theoretical and disciplinary perspectives.

Prentice's analysis is based on ethnographic observation at an interdisciplinary medical informatics laboratory and on interviews with people from a wide variety of professions (with, for example, knowledge of anatomy, surgery, computation, education, cognition and engineering), all working on the simulator. Her material shows how different disciplinary fields come together to discuss and recreate objects and characteristics, like the elasticity of an organ, which are negotiated between computer engineers and medical doctors. Prentice does this by focusing on what happens at and around the interface of hands and instruments during the design process, watching how the body becomes mathematical, how it is described using equations. As she points out, the design of a surgical simulator articulates surgical skills for both the computer and the users. Her observations show how simulator design forces the articulation of surgical skills, some of which otherwise often remain tacit. But her analysis also shows how bodies and machines are constructed together during simulator design, a process she calls 'mutual articulation'.

Taking a slightly different approach, though also using interviews in conjunction with analysis of teaching instructions, media reports and marketing materials, Jenny Sundén presents an intersectional analysis of a birthing simulator from a decidedly posthumanist theoretical position. By closely reading the simulator and looking at historical parallels in anatomical wax models, Sundén addresses the politics of simulation, examining sexual difference and sexuality as well as race and national belonging. Her work is a feminist intervention in that it interrogates how the bodies of the simulators are materialized, how they are stabilized and, ultimately, through the unpredictability of use, also destabilized.

Sundén's work draws some of its theoretical inspiration from feminist science studies philosopher Karen Barad. Barad's theory of agential realism is also the basis of Ericka Johnson's analysis of the simulated body (and practice) in the final chapter of this section. Here it is argued that simulators are not reproducing ontologically pre-existing anatomies. They are not reproducing the body as a physical object. Rather, simulators are recreating very context specific medical practices that allow and create disciplinarily and culturally produced knowledges of the body. These phenomena of knowing the body are then materialized in the simulator as if they were a neutral reproduction of the body. As the research presented in her chapter follows a simulator from one culture to another, it becomes apparent that simulator developers and users may wish to think about what and whose practice and experience is being simulated. Likewise, this approach also opens a discursive space to consider patients' experiences of medical practice, a topic rarely discussed in simulator literature.

Together, these three chapters constitute a counter-example to the hegemonizing, truth-making tendencies of western medicine (and, like Berg and Mol (1998), problematize the very idea of one 'western' medicine). Though not specically addressed in each chapter, read together their analyses comprise an attack on the philosophical principles behind the evidence-based Medicine movement. Though the work does not necessarily support the counter argument of Evidence-Based Medicine, that medicine is an art rather than a science and does not function well within clinical guidelines (see Pope 2003, Timmermans and Berg 2003), it does undermine the assumption that results from random controlled trials can be applied across varying contexts without considering the social and structural specifics of the context in which medicine is practised. Much of the debate about Evidence-Based Medicine has focused on clinical guidelines, and technologies can also be read as guidelines. For example, the simulators that are analysed in this part are built to convey very specific ideas of correct medical practice, reifying clinical practice guidelines into machines for training and teaching. Yet, as with clinical guidelines, 'technological guidelines' can be problematic if they are posited to be universal while the practice they are meant to guide is very place and culture specific.

Thus the universal and the specific are common themes in the following section, despite the three chapters being very different in their methodology, approach and presentation. Prentice, for example, carefully articulates how understandings of the body are congealed and materialized in the technology of a simulator, while Sundén instead posits that there is no clear-cut causality between human and nonhuman bodies, no obvious referential links between simulators and patients. Johnson's chapter lands somewhere in between when focusing on how phenomena of knowing recreate medical practices in the simulator. Yet taken together, all three of these chapters show how the 'natural' body is formed and reformed in the practices of simulator culture, how actors – technologies and others – work together to create and recreate the medical bodies, understandings and experiences being simulated.

References

Berg, M. and Mol, A. (eds). 1998. *Differences in Medicine: Unraveling practices, techniques, and bodies*. Durham: Duke University Press.

Cartwright L. and C. Penley (eds). 1998. *The Visible Woman: Imaging technologies, gender, and science*. New York: New York University Press.

Jordanova, L. 1999. *Nature Displayed: Gender, science and medicine 1760–1820*. London: Longman.

Laqueur, T. 2003. Sex in the flesh. *Isis*, 94(2), 300–306.

Pope, C. 2003. Resisting evidence: the study of evidence-based medicine as a contemporary social movement. *Health: An Interdisciplinary Journal for the Social Study of Health, Illness and Medicine*, 7(3), 267–282.

Schiebinger, L. 1993. *Nature's Body: Gender in the making of modern science*. Boston: Beacon Press.

Stolberg, M. 2003. A woman down to her bones. The anatomy of sexual difference in the sixteenth and early seventeenth centuries. *Isis*, 94(2), 274–299.

Timmermans, S. and M. Berg. 2003. *The Gold Standard. The Challenge of Evidence-Based Medicine and Standardization in Health Care*. Philadelphia: Temple University Press.

Chapter 4
The Anatomy of a Surgical Simulation: The Mutual Articulation of Bodies in and Through the Machine[1]

Rachel Prentice

Surgical learning traditionally has included intensive and structured training of a resident's skills of seeing, interpreting and intervening in a patient's body. Residents now receive most of their training in the operating room, working on actual patients under the close supervision of an attending surgeon. In the last decade, however, researchers in universities and private companies have begun to develop virtual reality training systems, modelled on flight simulators, that might one day train medical students outside the operating room, potentially freeing attending surgeons' time and giving students some practice before they work on patients. Surgical simulators also could be used to train experienced surgeons' skills with emerging visualization technologies and minimally invasive surgical techniques (Rheingold 1991, Katz 1999). The ideal virtual reality simulator would provide visual and physical experiences similar to minimally invasive surgery, teaching the fine motor movements needed to clamp, cut or suture virtual tissues, giving students and surgeons opportunities to practise their skills *in silico* before trying them *in vivo*.

Traditional methods of practising skills outside the operating room include tying knots on drawer handles and suturing skin-like objects, such as banana peels. Several types of virtual and mechanical simulators have been developed to supplement or replace these methods. This Chapter deals only with virtual reality simulators. To build virtual reality simulators, researchers have broken down and reformulated knowledge about patients' bodies and surgeons' actions in ways that are technologically compatible with digital computers. The computer as a surgical teaching tool thus becomes a crucial non-human actor in this research arena (Latour 1993, Haraway 1997). In this chapter, I dissect the research that went into creation of a surgical simulator developed by an interdisciplinary medical informatics laboratory at Stanford University School of Medicine to teach minimally invasive gynaecological procedures, such as the removal of an ovary.

---

1   Abridged from and first published by SAGE/SOCIETY as: Prentice, R. 2005. The anatomy of a surgical simulation: The mutual articulation of bodies in and through the machine. *Social Studies of Science*, 35(6), 837–866.

To provide trainees with a 'muscular gestalt' (Dreyfus 1992: 248–249), that is, generalizable physical skills relevant to the work of surgery, the simulator must facilitate a visual and kinaesthetic interaction between the surgeon-user's body and the virtual patient's body. In computer device research, haptically enabled instruments provide physical feedback from a virtual object to the user, creating the sensation of interacting with a material object.[2] Adding haptics to a simulator creates a tight link between sensation and action, a significant research challenge for simulator makers that is neatly captured in singer Cassandra Wilson's question, 'Is there any way to feel a body through fibre-optic lines?' (Wilson 1999).

The construction of haptically enabled surgical simulators involves three distinct but related research areas: graphic modelling, haptic interface design and studies of haptic cognition. Each research area requires surgeons, computer experts, engineers and others to develop new understandings of the model patient's body and the user's body and to incorporate these understandings into computer software and interface devices. Surgical simulator makers must parse the physical components of surgical skill. Looking at technical practice in medicine can illuminate the construction of bodies in medical work in new ways (Casper and Berg 1995). Studying haptically enabled simulators as they emerge provides an opportunity to examine surgical practice and the construction of surgical knowledge by following how researchers construct a digitally and mechanically mediated relationship between hands and patient. This paper shows how studying the construction of a medical teaching technology can reveal facets of surgical practice that are not readily apparent when observing traditional operating room instruction. The process of simulator construction reveals the shaping of the patient's body by the surgeon and, reciprocally, of the surgeon's body by the patient. It also reveals how bodies and machines are mutually constructed during simulator design. I call these processes mutual articulation.

Mutual Articulation in Surgery and Simulation

In this section, I describe how the concept of mutual articulation provides a means of studying the acquisition of surgical skill and the development of surgical simulators. Examining the role of hands follows a recent trend in science studies toward an emphasis on the objects of medical knowledge as they are brought into being through practice, 'Instead of the observer's eyes, the practitioner's hands become the focus point of theorizing' (Mol 2002: 152). Studying the relationship between hands and object in surgery and surgical simulation moves the focus of the observation away from visual and cognitive models toward a focus on what

---

2   Stanford's simulator requires at least three pieces of hardware: a graphics computer to run the simulation, an interface device, and another computer connecting the interface device with the graphics computer. I use 'computer' and 'simulator' interchangeably throughout this chapter.

happens at the interface of hands and instruments. Although anatomy and surgery are undeniably visual, the role of physical interaction in the development of surgical knowledge remains underexplored.

'Mutual articulation' follows from Bruno Latour's concept of 'articulation', which describes how bodies come into being through sensory interactions with the world (Latour 2004). Latour argues that the body is most usefully imagined as an interface that becomes increasingly differentiated as it interacts with more elements in the world. Bodies and body parts come into being through the process of learning to articulate differences. Thus, the sensing body becomes increasingly articulate as the senses learn to register and differentiate objects. Latour cites the example of a kit the perfume industry employs to teach future perfume makers the art of smelling. Using this kit, students learn how to differentiate extremely dissimilar smells and then to make progressively finer distinctions. Skilled perfume experts become known as 'noses'. The metonym reveals how sniffing skill and body part become synonymous, how they come into being together. The play on multiple meanings of the word 'articulate' as 'jointed', in the sense of a body having joints, and 'speaking intelligibly' (OED 2004, articulate), suggests that bodies and knowledge come into being together. Viewed from this perspective, much of medical education is a process of articulating two bodies – the patient's body and the physician's body. Acquiring knowledge, whether through the senses or through the mediation of instruments, becomes a process of articulating differences in the world.

The concept of articulation works well with cases like the perfume kit, in which the teaching tool is standardized and stable. In surgery, however, knowledge of the object is embodied in the surgeon at the same time that the surgeon brings that object into being. I argue that patient and surgeon shape each other through a process of mutual articulation. The physician sculpts the anatomical body from the indistinct tissues of the patient's body (Hirschauer 1991), even as this sculptural practice defines and reinforces the surgeon's skill. Mutual articulation is particularly important when creating models from complex objects, such as human bodies. With each surgery, the surgeon creates a version of the model from a body's broad anatomical variations and fleshy opacity.

Focusing on mutual articulation of practitioner and body encourages re-examination of some classic ethnographic work on medical learning. Medical anthropologist Byron Good describes medical students' first explorations of human bodies in the anatomy laboratory as primarily visual training. Students spend their first weeks in the anatomy laboratory learning to distinguish among the reds and whites of different tissues. Many medical students describe their difficulty separating everyday bodies from biological bodies at the beginning of their medical training: 'I'll find myself in conversation … I'll all of a sudden start to think about, you know, if I took the scalpel and made a cut [on you] right here, what would that look like' (Good 1994: 73). Bringing greater attention to hands in this story brings forth another dimension to this statement: The student describes this process of looking as initiated by the scalpel. This student's knowledge of the body's insides develops while he dissects. Seeing is inextricably bound up with sculpting.

To take another example, ethnographer Stefan Hirschauer says physicians acquire two bodies. They learn an 'abstract body', which is the body as it is represented in anatomy texts and plastic models. They also acquire their own bodies as experienced practitioners. Hirschauer describes how surgeons sculpt the body, reproducing the abstract body of anatomical representation in the patient's body. Although he connects abstract anatomical knowledge as contained in atlases to the skills needed to produce those images, he says, 'the body of the anatomic atlas, with its clearcut divisions, different colors, numbered and labeled structures, is present in the surgeon's mind' (Hirschauer 1991: 310). Hirschauer creates a separation between the skilled work of hands and the visual knowledge of the atlas, which he says resides in the mind. Considering anatomical knowledge as it is practised in the act of sculpting the anatomical body – studying practice at the interface of a surgeon's hands and a patient's body – eliminates worries about the completeness or accuracy of mental models and about the surgeon's ability to translate mental knowledge into physical action. Hands, eyes and mind are no longer considered separately. Practising on patient bodies teaches young doctors how to make the fine visual and visceral distinctions among tissues that they will need as surgeons. Attending surgeons use real bodies, and the contrasts between them, to teach students to see and to feel differences among tissues. Students learn these distinctions through the process of sculpting bodies. Practitioner and body mutually articulate each other as the student learns to sculpt the surgical site from the undifferentiated, unarticulated patient's body.

In simulator design, model bodies and user bodies must be articulated for the computer. The process of construction of a surgical simulator reveals how surgical skill must be articulated for the computer and, ultimately, for its users. The objectification of the relationship of hands, instruments and anatomies breaks the process of surgery into many components, forcing surgeons and programmers to make explicit elements of the tactile experience of surgery, such as the elasticity of a uterus or the delicacy of an ovary, that often remain tacit. The construction of a surgical simulator makes explicit the two-way movement of mutual articulation. Engineers and programmers literally build the relationship between hands and machines by decomposing the action of hands into two components: action and sensation. Hands learn while they do. Eyes and other senses also learn while they do, but the connection is much less direct. Simulator researchers explore the body as an interface to understand the elements of information required to pass from hands to object and back. And studying simulator research can provide a wealth of new questions for observational studies of surgery, particularly about such areas as haptic knowledge and the social aspects of surgery that cannot be taught with a simulator (Collins, De Vries and Bijker 1997, Prentice 2004).

The Ethnographic Setting: Merging Disciplines

The Stanford University Medical Media and Information Technologies (SUMMIT) laboratory, where I did ten months of participant observation, starting in late 2001, occupies half a floor of a burnt-sienna stucco office building at the northwest corner of the Stanford University School of Medicine. The laboratory has twin roles: information technology research and service to the medical school. Much of SUMMIT's work falls within the emerging field of medical informatics, which seeks to apply computer science and technologies to medicine (Forsythe 2001: 3).

To build a virtual reality simulator, researchers must create body objects that are incorporated in the computer. This requires a crucial epistemic move: the body must become mathematical, described using equations the computer can interpret. Actions and sensations surgeons usually experience physically must be calculated. In the world of surgical simulation, a virtual body must interact with both computer and user as a mathematical and a visual-physical entity. The laboratory director describes the mathematics of modelling bodies:

> The only way the computer can understand things is, in this case, through geometry. It needs geometry. It needs to know how to compute a sequence of forces with equations, which previously, in a sense, [surgeons] did in their heads. You knew how to predict what was going to happen. You didn't solve an equation to do that, it was just part of the experience. So it's the computer that forces you to put that mathematical construct on.

Surgeons predict the consequences of their actions based on their experience as it becomes incorporated in their bodies and others' experience distilled in papers, procedural scripts and apprentice-style teaching. In contrast, computers must understand bodies and their actions mathematically. The feel of surgery, which surgeons' bodies typically experience phenomenologically – as practice – must be parsed, calculated, incorporated into the computer's programming, and ultimately, fed back to the human user, who then will experience the sensations of performing a surgical procedure phenomenologically.

Materializing the Virtual Patient

Simulator research at Stanford, and most virtual reality simulator research elsewhere, focuses on minimally invasive procedures. To perform a minimally invasive procedure, a surgeon inserts a camera and instruments through small incisions in the body and performs the procedure while looking at a monitor that shows surgical action taking place inside the body's interior. Because minimally invasive surgery already occurs 'on-screen', simulating these procedures is easier than with open surgery.

The simulator requires a user, graphic models of patient body and surgical tools, an interactive device designed to look and act like the surgeon's end of an instrument, a computer to manage the haptic device and a separate computer to run the simulation. Making the system work requires definition of how these components work together. Materializing tools and bodies in cyberspace requires what are, in effect, three feedback loops that make up the interaction between user and model. The first – or virtual – feedback loop defines the interaction between instrument tips and model body as the model responds to the instruments and, in turn, provides haptic feedback to the user. This is the domain of computer modelling. Researchers – programmers and surgeons – wrestle with the question: how can we create a graphic and physical model that accurately represents the body interacting with the instrument? The second – or mechanical – loop describes the interaction between the user's hand and the instruments as the instruments respond to user and model. This is the domain of mechanical engineering research, which aims to answer the question: how can we ensure that our device works properly – feeding correct haptic information to the virtual world and back to the user's hands? The third – or cognitive – loop connects the user's mind, his or her intent, to the user's hands, while hands and device interact. The cognitive loop represents the domain of haptics research and this question predominates: how does a body learn? Each of these loops represents a research area among simulation experts. Each requires descriptions of the virtual patient's and the material user's bodies as they interact with the simulator. Although each component of the simulator defines the relationship between model and user slightly differently, the components attempt to give the user a seamless experience of surgery.

Modelling: Constructing the Model Patient's Body

SUMMIT's laparoscopic simulator contains a model of the female pelvis made from ninety-five digitized photographs of pelvic cross-sections. The sections came from an anonymous 32-year-old woman who willed her body to Stanford before she died. Anatomists at Stanford froze the pelvis in an upright position, then ground layers off at roughly 2-millimetre intervals. After removing each layer, they took a photograph of the newly exposed cross-section. A gynaecologist then used the collection of cross-section photographs as the foundation for Stanford's virtual reality simulator. He named the collection the Stanford Visible Female, linking it to the National Library of Medicine's better-known Visible Human Male and Visible Human Female, which were created using similar techniques.[3] He scanned the ninety-five cross-section images into a computer. He then spent

---

3   Visible Human Project information and images can be viewed at www.nlm.nih.gov/research/visible/visible_human.html. (see also Cartwright 1997, Cartwright 1998, Waldby 2000, Csordas 2001). Birke (1999) briefly discusses both the Visible Human Project and the Stanford Visible Female.

more than a year tracing the structures he wanted to model into files using an early version of PhotoShop®, a commercial image-manipulation application: one file for each structure on each cross-sectional image. He describes this process, called segmentation, simply as 'drawing circles' around each structure he wanted to model and saving the contents of each 'circle' as a 'mask' with its own computer file.

The gynaecologist initially segmented only the reproductive system, leaving the six pelvic bones and many muscles as undifferentiated aggregates labelled 'bone' and 'muscle' respectively. Subsequent iterations differentiated pelvic bones and muscles and added less critical features, such as fat. The gynaecologist segmented the reproductive organs and a collaborating orthopaedist segmented the bones and muscles. They produced 2,200 masks from 95 cross-section slices encompassing the female reproductive system and the surrounding musculo-skeletal system. This division of labour occurred because each physician had a slightly different area of anatomical knowledge, which speaks to the extreme specialization of surgical-anatomical knowledges and to the difficulty of producing a comprehensive model body.[4] Segmentation includes several of the 'transformative practices' Michael Lynch identifies in relation to model-making, including 'upgrading' the images by making strong borders between tissue types and 'defining' the images by sharpening contrasts (Lynch and Woolgar 1988: 160–161). But segmentation is not done to make the cross sections readable by human eyes. Rather, anatomists segment cross-sectional images to create outlines that are integrated into computer-modelling programs; that is, to articulate cross-sections for computers.

Up to this point, medical experts – the two surgeons – did the work of delineating body parts. The next modelling steps multiplied the body in another realm of practice: the world of computer modelling, a subspecialty of medical informatics. A computer-modelling student took the segmented masks and computationally stacked them, creating models of organs, muscles, bones and other features (as stacked slices of bread create a loaf). To connect cross-sections into a surface model, the student transformed stacked outlines into a 'mesh', a digital, mathematically generated net that mapped the model's contours, much like a nylon stocking maps a leg. Modelling using this technique takes advantage of a digital photograph's resolution into pixels. Once gynaecologist and orthopaedist outlined the structures to be modelled on the two-dimensional cross-sections, the modelling student wrote computer algorithms to connect the outlined pixels across adjacent cross-sections, creating a geometry the computer could understand. These

---

4   An anatomist at the University of Washington, who works on computer applications for teaching anatomy, told me that research funding also stands in the way of creating comprehensive anatomical applications. Funding agencies will pay for new applications, usually limited to one area of the body, but claim that applying new computer technologies to an entire body is production work, not research, and ought to be done by the private sector. However, this anatomist claims, and others confirm, most companies have found the labour of creating a comprehensive computer body model not worth the cost.

connected pixels formed a mesh conforming to each structure's surface. Because this model is made of both graphic pixels and the mathematical mesh, the model body is simultaneously a graphic and a mathematical representation of a body – a representation that can be viewed and manipulated by a human user in ways the computer can calculate. These graphic models are 'silicon second natures', digital artefacts that mirror natural objects, but also offer to replace them as resources for medical learning and research (Helmreich 1998: 11–12).

Modelling transforms the photographic cross-sections into a neat, three-dimensional model of a uterus that has already had fat dissected away, in other words, a graphic model that resembles a surgical site that a surgeon has already sculpted. The surgeon physically – using a computerized drawing pen instead of a scalpel – articulated a model that represented his experience. The model body then affirms for the gynaecologist that this computational procedure worked and has produced a tool he considers adequate for teaching surgical anatomy to simulation users.

The model pelvis is a laboratory object: it is the image of the original object (in this case a human body), detached from its natural environment, and no longer beholden to the original's temporality (Knorr Cetina 2000: 27). Unlike a living or dead human body, the model body can travel through a computer network, can be pulled apart and put back together, or modified to reflect pathologies, all without causing it harm. The model body becomes an 'immutable mobile', a digital reconstruction of the original with the advantage of 'mobility, stability, and combinability' (Latour 1986: 7). But the model in this state is useful primarily for teaching anatomical structures.[5] It is visual, but it cannot yet interact with the user as a material body would. It is not yet a patient and it is not yet prepared for surgery because surgery, at its most basic, physical level, involves interactions of bodies and instruments. Before the model pelvis could become what one Stanford researcher calls a 'patient-on-demand', it had to become responsive to surgical action. In Latourian terms, it had to become articulate, or able to be 'moved, put into motion by other entities, humans or non-humans' (Latour 2004: 1). To make the pelvis deformable, a programmer added algorithms to the model that describe how tissues stretch, separate or come together – that is, how tissue deforms – when pulled, cut or sutured. The programmer began with the mesh structure of the surface model and defined the lines connecting points on the mesh as springs. Pulling on any point of the virtual mesh causes the surrounding virtual springs to stretch, 'deforming' the model according to well-defined physics equations that describe the resistance of springs. Spring-based deformations are useful for small, relatively slow movements of tissue, as are common in surgery. Stiffer springs lead to tougher-feeling tissues.

To set values for spring stiffness, the gynaecologist and the programmer developed heuristics describing the feel of pelvic tissues. These mathematical

---

5   Available at: http://summit.stanford.edu/ourwork/PROJECTS/LUCY/lucywebsite/ infofr.html [accessed: 1 March 2003].

descriptions are constructions based on the gynaecologist's physical memories – what he calls 'haptic memories' – of the feel of performing surgery on various tissues. The gynaecologist expressed his haptic memories in terms both of his sense of differences among tissues and his sense of the feel of a particular tissue.[6] To develop the haptic program, gynaecologist and programmer created algorithms that attempt to represent the surgeon's physical experience in a form the computer can use. To do this, the programmer had to learn something about surgery. He learned the physical differences between structures in a woman's reproductive system. He also learned some terminology of anatomy and surgery to create a description of 'how the world works' at a deeper level than typical surgical instructions to cut, clamp or suture. In effect, the engineer developed a physical model of the movements behind each of those verbs.

Traditionally, tissue stiffness is known only through surgeons' bodies. Constructing a quantitative model of a patient body's physical response to surgery only becomes necessary when the knowledge moves from body to computer. The redefinition of a patient's body from the body experienced by the physician to the body defined for the computer is an important new articulation of bodies. Moments where these reconstructions become evident can be both revealing and amusing. During a demonstration, the programmer runs into a technical glitch and tries to describe to the gynaecologist how the uterus feels:

> Hey, do you want me to reset your uterus there? … Do you want me to bump up the stiffness so it behaves like muscle? Now it's behaving like a thin skin. I think that's something I learned from you [the gynaecologist]: that the uterus is basically like a tough muscle. Now it's behaving like a thin skin.

The idea of 'resetting' a uterus comes from computer science and shows how the conceptual vocabulary from that discipline contributes to defining the body in the world of virtual anatomical modelling and surgical simulation. Verbally, the programmer describes what he has learned from the surgeon about tissue feel. Mathematically, he attempts to approximate the surgeon's bodily experience, translating knowledge of a body's feel into equations describing the stiffness of springs. The virtual model body is put into motion as a function of the movement of springs. This is the type of 'mathematical construct' the group director refers to when she says knowledge that once was primarily experiential must be articulated mathematically when translated into a computational idiom. In turn, the differences in tissue feel incorporated into the model will help articulate the students' bodies. Tissue feel can be described, but only using relative terms, such as 'delicate' and 'tough' (Pinch, Collins and Carbone 1996). Students can use these descriptions to guide them while relative differences in tissue feel become embodied knowledge.

---

6 The model is an ideal body: it does not take into account variations among patient bodies or in sense of feel experienced by different surgeons, though these are additions that simulator makers say they will incorporate into future iterations.

But the computer requires experiential knowledge of difference to be articulated as mathematical values. The model's deformability does not, cannot, exist apart from the thing with which it interacts, in this case, the surgeon's body as mediated by instruments. Deformability is a quality of model bodies defined exclusively at their interface with other bodies. Values of tissue feel used in deformable models are products of the mutual articulation of bodies.

Interacting: Characterizing the User's Body

By making the virtual model deformable, programmers built the possibility of movement into the model body, but it could not yet be put into motion by a user. The next step in making the surgical simulator was to create an instrument to act upon the body. Because the user activates the instrument, which then acts upon the model body, the instrument becomes, in effect, a bridge from a body in the real world to a model body in the virtual world.[7] A bridge can take the form of several types of device, but ones I have seen all exist both on and off the screen. This existence in both worlds resembles many gaming devices but medical researchers pay more attention to giving users a realistic feel for surgical interaction. The coupling of haptic action and reaction is tighter and more rigorously defined and is itself a unique research area. SUMMIT's gynaecology simulator uses a two-handed, or 'bi-manual' device, which is a heavy, metal box with two protruding handles. Each handle has a scissor-like mechanism at the end that allows the user to manipulate virtual instrument tips. When a user turns the instrument on, graphic representations of surgical instrument tips – the patient ends – appear on the computer screen in the same space as the body model. A multi-processor graphics computer uses a method known as 'collision detection', which tells the instrument tips and model body to react when they touch. Outside the computer, the surgeon's ends of the instruments resemble surgical instruments whose virtual tips move as the user moves the handles, giving the illusion that real handles and virtual tips are continuous. Closing the scissor-like handle in the real world clamps the virtual instrument tips in the virtual world. When the user pulls the handle, virtual tip and tissue move with it, allowing what the gynaecologist calls 'tool–tissue interactions'. The device also transmits the effects of those actions on instrument and model back to the user's hands.[8]

---

7   I do not use the obvious word 'interface' here, though it is technically correct, because it has visual implications that I want to avoid.

8   Some experiments have been done with haptic interaction between two users in remote locations, but technically this creates a problem separating signals that are feeding forward from users' bodies from signals that are simultaneously feeding back to users' bodies. Human nervous systems have no trouble with this kind of 'signal processing,' but it still is a challenge for machines.

Within the context of the mechanical feedback loop, the user's body emerged in relation to the haptic device as engineers designed the device and began to study how it operates in practice. Designing a device that interprets the signals it receives from the human user and feeds the haptic response back to the user gives rise to a fascinating problem: characterizing the human user's effect on the system. During an eight-hour meeting of laboratory researchers with an external reviewer, who was an expert in educational technologies, participants tackled the question of how to consider the user's body as it interacts with the device:

> Mechanical engineer: We will have to do a study that accounts for variability among subjects.
> …
> Mechanical engineer: The dynamic response slows if a human hand is holding the device.
> Laboratory director: It's like having a sloppy, wet mass holding the thing.

Human bodies, viewed here as research objects, create several problems for investigators. Not all bodies affect the device the same way. And users' bodies slow the device down, compromising its ability to faithfully transmit the sensations of interacting with the model. The research question becomes how to manage the effects of this 'sloppy, wet mass' (or many, varied sloppy, wet masses) on the device's response. In surgery, the surgeon's body and tools, when they're performing well, are the unproblematic agents of surgical action. This is the essence of embodied tacit knowledge: with years of practice, surgeons learn to use tools as extensions of their bodies. Technique becomes largely unconscious when all proceeds smoothly (Polanyi 1966). But the effect of the surgeon's – or user's – body on the bi-manual device and the virtual simulation must be characterized mechanically and compensated for by the simulator, so the interaction of cyberbody and material body feels like an interaction between two material bodies. The user's and the model body's ability to mutually articulate each other depends on programmers', surgeons' and instrument-makers' ability to create a good enough representation of the feel of surgery. This requires articulating the user's body for the instrument and for the programs that control the instrument. Researchers must account for the sloppiness and variabilities of user's bodies. The user's body must be articulated for the instrument, so it can articulate the feel of doing surgery for the user.

Embodied Cognition: Integrating and Translating Skill

The cognitive feedback loop – the work that happens between hand and mind – takes up the question of what we learn through our bodies and how what's transmitted to the body gets interpreted and learned. A former physicist does haptics research at Stanford. She wants to better understand the role of physical learning in surgery, which she argues is necessary for the development of effective devices, including surgical simulators. She sums up the research project as the characterization of 'somato-conceptual' intelligence:

> Haptic sensations are personal. I cannot tell you exactly what I feel. It's personal. It's felt by the touching person only. It's determined by the touching forces. Each person exerts different forces. There's a different coefficient of forces for muscle, so we experience different things.

In this researcher's study of haptic knowing, material bodies become bodies that exert forces on and receive forces from objects. But bodies vary, so experience also varies. This concept of haptic learning reduces physical experience to a set of forces exerted upon and received by muscle, so the interaction of muscular forces with an object determines experience and learning. The contribution of other types of experience – of memory, knowledge culled from procedural scripts and explicit instruction, gets bracketed.

Studying the path from physical force to learning presents problems for researchers, so the problem gets redefined in terms of the force transmitted to the hands and the user's interpretation of that force. During the same review, researchers tackled the problem of how to understand what's happening inside the user's body:

> Haptics researcher: How do you make it so everybody feels the same thing?
>
> Reviewer: It gets metaphysical very quickly. If we all touch the table, do we all feel the same thing?
>
> ...
>
> Surgeon: What is felt by the user? What is the force? What is the interpretation of force by the user? Is it possible to measure?
>
> Haptics researcher: Different surgeons would make the same interpretation when they feel the same lump.
>
> Reviewer: That's as far as you can go. If everybody says it's a ring, you're in good shape.
>
> Mechanical engineer: Or 85 percent of them.
>
> Reviewer: But if you want to get to their subjective experience, then it's the metaphysical problem. …You could frame it as a signal to noise problem. You can't guarantee the same experience for everybody. But if you can build enough signal into it so most people give you the same interpretation….

Laboratory director: There may be various sources of signal: how do you know what they're telling you?

Surgeon: What in the brain it is, you can't measure it.

Reviewer: You know right where they are and you know what they're interpreting.

This conversation reveals a process of defining the surgeon-user's body in a way researchers can manage. They do this by defining the user's body in relation to the device. They begin with a broad question: how can we ensure that simulator users all have the same physical experience? They recognize that, if they try to answer the question in terms of subjective experience, it becomes difficult to examine using the tools of medicine, cognitive science and engineering. What a user senses through his or her body – whether studied as forces on muscles or descriptions of experience – is inaccessible to scientific research. If haptic knowledge consists of forces exerted on users' bodies and the interpretation of those forces, then studying the connection between force and interpretation becomes very difficult. The researchers then reformulate the user's subjective experience as a question of consistency of interpretation or, in more scientific terms, reproducible results. They realize they cannot know what bodies experience directly, nor whether two people experience the same sensations when touching the same object. They cannot know whether many users' internal experiences of touching an object, such as a lump, are identical, but they know that many surgeons would give identical interpretations of that object. As the reviewer suggests, shifting the definition of haptic experience away from metaphysical questions about internal experience – away from the body's physical and subjective insides – and towards the body's interface with an object, might allow researchers to elicit consistent interpretations.

Defined as a body that palpates and interprets a lump, researchers can study what the body knows. As scientists, however, they can go one step further. They can augment the signal from the object to encourage more consistency among interpretations. By defining haptic cognition as a relation of signal to noise, they can ensure that the device sends a strong enough message to the user's body that most users give the same response. By observing where on the model the user is working, they begin to understand what signals are strong enough to provide a consistent interpretation. The pathway between the user's body and his or her understanding – the mind–body connection – becomes, in effect, black boxed. It cannot be characterized the way a device might be, or mathematized, the way a model patient's body might be. Rather, the user's body in haptics research gets defined in terms of the signal the rest of the system sends to the user's body and the fidelity with which the user interprets that signal. The question is no longer what the body is, but how the body interprets action; the ontological body becomes the interpreting body. The challenge shifts from trying to interpret what happens inside the user's mind and body toward understanding how to create a model body that surgeons can be sensitive to in identical – or mostly identical – ways.

Vision, Touch, Embodiment, Knowing

The simulator is an assemblage of hardware and software shaped by knowledges from multiple disciplines. Simulator research falls into three areas – modelling and deformation, interactive device-making and studies of haptic cognition. Research into each of these areas requires definitions of the model patient's body, the user's body, and how they interact in simulated surgeries. Within each research area, the physical connection between user and model must be delineated. Simulator makers must make mathematical models of surgical actions that usually remain tacit, such as the movements a surgeon makes when clamping, cutting or suturing, and the response of tissues to those movements. I have laid out how each of the three research areas articulates the user's body in relation to the simulated model body and vice versa. What remains to be done in this section is to consider the implications of mutual articulation for studying the teaching of manual skill.

The deformable model's utility as a teaching tool is limited without values representing haptic feel. The representation of the gynaecologist's physical experience that gets incorporated into the model shapes how the model will react to the user and how the model will shape the user's experience.[9] The model body's resistance to surgical instruments is defined in relation to the gynaecologist's embodied memories and the resulting algorithms describing the model's resistance will, in turn, shape the user's body. The haptic interface must compensate for the fleshiness of the user's body well enough that the mutual shaping of model and user will provide a meaningful learning experience for beginning surgeons. Thus, researchers will study many bodies, so they can incorporate a model of their variations into the device. The model's ability to articulate the user's body will be measured in terms of users' interpretations. At each stage of this research, the user's body is articulated in relation to the simulation system and vice versa.

Haptics – researching and designing an interface that feeds sensory information to the user's hands – makes the mutual articulation of the user's and the model's bodies apparent because the connection between the hands and the model must be carefully constructed. Technologically and physiologically, the link between the object's effects on the user and the resulting action is much tighter with touch than vision. The dual nature of hands – they are sensors and actuators – connects actor to object much more directly than vision, smell or hearing (Reiner 2004). Hands simultaneously perceive an object and act directly on it. The effects of touch can be measured as effects on the object. Simulator researchers at Stanford realize this: they know that a poorly designed model of tissue or a poorly designed

---

9   The gynaecologist plans to incorporate values for haptic feel based on the experiences of many surgeons in a future iteration of the simulator.

interface may fail to give students a feel for actual surgery. With a simulated model body, researchers can study the forces users exert when dissecting tissues directly. Researchers also know they can observe how the model reacts to the body's actions, making the study of the connection between model and cognition more direct. Because hands themselves contain the means of both sensation and action, they embody mutual articulation in a way that forces researchers to place tight constraints on the connection between sensing and acting. The reviewer cited above makes the critical point about touch and cognition, 'You know right where they are and you know what they're interpreting'. The hand, as a perceptual instrument that senses while it acts can make studying the interpretations that result from these perceptions and actions easier to study than other senses. Simulator researchers, if they can make haptically enabled simulators work properly, can enhance the student's tactile learning. With hands, how sensation, action and interpretation intertwine can be constructed at the interface with an object, as the user's ability to articulate the model body through anatomical sculpting and the model's ability to articulate the user's body in terms of surgical skill.

The concept of mutual articulation for understanding surgical simulation addresses a problem that arises when discussing simulation. Latour's concept of articulation specifically attempts to avoid a world of subjects and objects in which the subject houses an internal representation of the object whose accuracy must be verified (Latour 2004). The notion of abstract anatomical knowledge and the surgeon's ability to sculpt the body to resemble an anatomical model reproduces this concept of a representation of human anatomy housed somewhere inside the surgeon (typically imagined as inside his or her mind). Considering the creation of anatomical knowledge as the development of physical skill that comes with years of practice allows one to consider not the accuracy of an internal visual model that may or may not exist, but simply the surgeon's ability to sculpt the patient's body. Thus, surgical knowledge can be thought of at the interface between a surgeon's hands and a patient's body, as it exists in practice. The surgeon's knowledge becomes his or her ability to sculpt the anatomical model from highly variable patient bodies. Simulation reveals that the patient's body plays a role in that shaping.

With a simulated 'patient-on-demand', students may have opportunities to practise surgical procedures when they want, as often as they want, and on as many types of pathologies as can be programmed into the simulator. Haptics will change the nature of the interactions from viewing and perhaps acting upon the body with a mouse to *feeling* the cyberbody react. The incarnation of bodies in cyberspace that can provide haptic feedback will make these interactions bodily in ways unlike earlier computer technologies, undoubtedly with implications for other fields in which haptic interactions are important. Haptics research, as a field that studies how hands learn, can reveal how bodies mutually shape each other.

At each point in the creation of the surgical simulation described here, researchers pooled various disciplinary knowledges of anatomy, surgery, computation, education, cognition and engineering to develop an object (a model, a software program, a device) that has a particular relationship to the user's body. At each point, then, researchers are working to create interpretations of what human bodies are in relation to these objects; that is, to articulate the body in new ways. These technological knowledges of human bodies are multiple, but not unconstrained. The simulator must not only articulate patients' and users' bodies as they relate in surgery, it must also help incorporate knowledge of those relations – surgical skill – into the student's body.

References

Birke, L. 1999. *Feminism and the Biological Body.* New Brunswick: Rutgers University Press.

Cartwright, L. 1997. The visible man: The male criminal subject as biomedical norm, in *Processed Lives: Gender and technology in everyday life,* edited by J. Terry and M. Calvert. New York: Routledge, 123–137.

Cartwright, L. 1998. A cultural anatomy of the visible human project, in *The Visible Woman: Imaging technologies, gender, and science,* edited by P.A. Treichler, L. Cartwright and C. Penley. New York: Routledge, 21–43.

Casper, M.J. and M. Berg 1995. Constructivist perspectives on medical work: Medical practice and science and technology studies. *Science, Technology & Human Values,* 20(4), 395–407.

Collins, H.M., DeVries, G.H. and Bijker, W. 1997. Ways of going on: An analysis of skill applied to medical practice. *Science, Technology & Human Values,* 22(3), 267–285.

Csordas, T.J. 2001. Computerized cadavers: Shades of representation and being in virtual reality, in *Biotechnology and Culture: Bodies, anxieties, ethics,* edited by P. Brodwin. Bloomington: Indiana University Press, 173–192.

Dreyfus, H. 1992. *What Computers Still Can't Do: A critique of artificial reason.* Cambridge: MIT Press.

Forsythe, D.E. 2001. *Studying Those Who Study Us: An anthropologist in the world of artificial intelligence.* Stanford: Stanford University.

Good, B.J. 1994. *Medicine, Rationality, and Experience.* Cambridge: Cambridge University Press.

Haraway, D. 1997. *Modest_Witness@Second_Millenium.FemaleMan_Meets_ Onco Mouse: Feminism and Technoscience.* New York: Routledge.

Helmreich, S. 1998. *Silicon Second Nature: Culturing artificial life in a digital world.* Berkeley: University of California Press.

Hirschauer, S. 1991. The manufacture of bodies in surgery. *Social Studies of Science* 21(2), 279–319.

Katz, P. 1999. *The Scalpel's Edge: The culture of surgeons.* Boston: Allyn and Bacon.

Knorr Cetina, K.D. 2000. *Epistemic Cultures: How the sciences make knowledge.* Cambridge: Harvard University Press.

Latour, B. 1986. Visualization and Cognition: Thinking with eyes and hands. *Knowing and Society: Studies in the sociology of culture past and present,* 6, 1–40.

Latour, B. 1993. *We Have Never Been Modern.* Cambridge: Harvard University Press.

Latour, B. 2004. How to talk about the body? The normative dimension of science studies. *Body & Society,* 10(2–3), 205–229.

Lynch, M. and Woolgar, S. 1988. *Representations in Scientific Practice.* Cambridge, MA: MIT Press.

Mol, A. 2002. *The body multiple: Ontology in medical practice.* Durham: Duke University Press.

OED *Second On-line edition.* 2004. (dictionary.oed.com)

Pinch, T., Collins, H.M. and Carbone, L. 1996. Inside knowledge: Second order measures of skill. *The Sociological Review*, 44(2), 163–186.

Polanyi, M. 1966. *The Tacit Dimension.* Garden City: Doubleday & Company.

Prentice, R. 2004. *Bodies of Information: Reinventing bodies and practice in medical education.* Cambridge, MA: Massachusetts Institute of Technology.

Reiner, M. 2004. The role of haptics. *Immersive Telecommunication Environments. Circuits and Systems for Video Technology, IEEE Transactions*, 14(3), 392–401.

Rheingold, H. 1991. *Virtual Reality.* New York: Simon & Schuster.

Waldby, C. 2000. *The Visible Human Project: Informatic bodies and posthuman medicine.* New York: Routledge.

Wilson, C. 1999. Right here, right now, *Traveling Miles.* Blue Note Records.

Chapter 5

Blonde Birth Machines:
Medical Simulation, Techno-corporeality
and Posthuman Feminism

Jenny Sundén

New technologies of reproduction are rapidly transforming cultural understandings of kinship, family, body, sexuality and origin. Because of such changes, reproductive technologies have become a dynamic site of research across disciplinary boundaries. In the humanities and the social sciences, discussions of reproductive technologies interrogate the historical, political and cultural signification of technologically transformed parental definitions and practices, of new beginnings (and of endings), of the reconfiguration of the very limits of humanness and of 'life itself'. Techno-corporeality, the ways in which technologies are becoming (or perhaps, were always) entwined with our bodies, experiences and existences, comes in many shapes and guises in the domain of reproduction. Whereas considerable research has been devoted to technologies such as artificial insemination, *in vitro* fertilization (IVF) and 'artificial womb' technologies (see Clarke 1995, Davis-Floyd and Dumit 1998, Franklin 1997, Franklin and Ragoné 1998, Haraway 1999, Hartouni 1997), considerably less attention has been paid to the design and use of birth machines in the field of medical simulation.

Meet S575 Noelle™ – a wireless maternal and neonatal computer interactive simulation system from Miami-based Gaumard Scientific – one of the latest incarnations of cutting-edge birthing machinery.[1] S575 Noelle™ (pronounced as *Noël*, referring to its release near Christmas) is delivered with: one fully computer interactive and automated delivery system (the manikin body assembly); placenta with umbilical cord; episiotomy trainer (set of three); urinary bladder; a lid covering the abdomen (and a special lid for C-sections); a lifelike birth canal;

---

1   Gaumard Scientific traces its history to 1946. The founder was a World War II army physician, George Blaine, who worked on reconstructive surgery and childbirth technologies. One of the first projects he introduced in 1949 was a childbirth simulator: 'The body of the simulator was approximated by translucent thermoplastic, the abdomen by padded cotton, the vulva was approximated by two hemispherical pieces of latex, and the baby was a rag doll' (Interview with Vice President of Gaumard, John Eggert, 22 November 2006). Gaumard has developed and delivered Noelle models since 1999, the '575' being the latest incarnation from 2008.

postpartum haemorrhage; one full-term neonate; interface modules for ECG, pulse, ultrasound, defibrillation, cardioversion, and pacing of Noelle and neonate; two 17-inch touch-screen monitors; one computer for the instructor to control the monitors and communicate wirelessly with the system; one student laptop to control fetal delivery, neonate condition and the monitors; instruction manuals and teaching tips.

Bringing out the age-old Frankensteinian fear of technology-out-of-control in its merging of technology with the female body, Noelle is designed to give a number of birth scenarios.[2] It can be in labour for hours or give birth unexpectedly fast, and be programmed to display a range of different birth complications. In his article, 'Robot birth simulator gaining in popularity', Associated Press business writer Paul Elias mentions how this 'full-sized, blond, pale mannequin is in demand because medicine is rapidly abandoning centuries-old training methods that use patients as guinea pigs, turning instead to high-tech simulations' (Elias 2006). Noelle is a first-rate high-tech simulation, eventually delivering a plastic doll – a baby robot – that can change colors 'from a healthy pink glow to the deadly blue of oxygen deficiency … wired to flash vital signs when hooked up to monitors' (Elias 2006). Both 'mother' and 'baby' produce realistic pulse rates and are able to breathe. The latest edition to the Noelle series is simulated blood in a uterine assembly, attached under the lid of the abdomen. When a port is opened, this produces a blood-like fluid from the inside of the uterus, the walls of the birth canal or both. An instructor can reduce bleeding as students perform fundal massage. Noelle varies in price, ranging from $3,200 for the most basic model to a $38,000 fully interactive, wireless version. The motto for the wireless Noelle is to simulate 'care in motion'.

Departing from a posthuman feminist understanding of technobodies, this chapter critically explores simulations of birth, the lifelike, and techno-corporeality through a close encounter with a (primarily) blonde, (primarily)

2　In Mary Shelley's *Frankenstein*, the monster's tragedy is his solitude, his exclusion from human relations in general, and from an intimate connection with a female counterpart in particular. He begs Victor to create a female monster, but halfway through her construction, Victor decides to destroy her. While the monster vengefully watches him through the window, Victor violently terminates his second act of (pro)creation, since this female monster 'might become ten thousand times more malignant than her mate', she may even 'become a thinking and reasoning animal'. The monster had promised to hide from human society, but she had not. There was no guarantee that she would voluntarily adapt to the subordination of femininity. Moreover, the monster may hate her deformed body more than he hates his own, or, perhaps even worse, she 'might turn with disgust from [the monster] to the superior beauty of man' (Shelley [1818] 1994: 160). This fear is a central theme in James Whale's horror film *The Bride of Frankenstein* (1935). Mary Jacobus points out that the fantasy of the female monster who longs for men instead of monsters is a terrifying threat to male (hetero)sexuality. This threat is not only tied to the she-monster's hideous deformity that excludes his image of desire, but to the frightening autonomy of her refusal to reproduce in the image in which she was made. See Jacobus (1982).

white birthing machine. The text draws on a range of sources, notably technical manuals, instruction videos, as well as an interview with the simulator's 'founding father', but it also take into account technological imaginaries of simulator bodies in terms of how the simulator is imagined in popular science contexts. The focus of this exploration is on the design of simulators, and not on actual use in clinical settings (which would be the subject for a different investigation). Then again, thinking about design for medical practices is thinking about use in the sense that design processes and practices always inscribe and anticipate use and users in certain ways (and not others). An investigation of techno-corporeal imagery and becomings in medical simulation, their possibilities and limitations, the text critically addresses the politics of simulation. The argument is performed in three parts. It sets out with an account of the 'birth' of birth simulators themselves – the act of creation in a domain of technological procreation – investigating the status of the 'real' as well as of 'realism' in the simulation world. Second, it moves on to explore some historical parallels or predecessors to medical simulators in the shape of anatomical wax models. Finally, in response to recent feminist discussions of difference in terms of 'intersectionality' (how various power relationships co-construct one another in multiple ways), the discussion will reveal how this particular reproductive machinery is entwined with issues not merely of sexual difference and sexuality, but also of race and national belonging.[3] The chapter, starting with the birth of simulators, ends, conversely, with a brief contemplation of simulation and death.[4]

Design Beyond Realism

In the 1990s, people at Gaumard realized that they needed to take their work on motherhood and birthing experience in a different direction. While they had previously worked with models of the female body in parts, such as obstetric phantoms, they now envisioned that models of birthing needed to be divided into three elements, namely, the mother, the foetus and the neonate. On 22 November 2006, I conducted an online interview with John Eggert, the Vice President of Gaumard Scientific and an engineer with a long history in medical simulation.[5]

---

3   For a discussion of the possible affinities and affordances linking the current intersectionality discussion to the field of cyber/cyborg-feminism, see Sundén (2007).

4   I am indebted to Professor Thomas Söderqvist and his research group at Medical Museion in Copenhagen, as well as to the organizers and participants of the TAP (*Thesis Antithesis Prosthesis*) seminar at the University of Gothenburg, for productive comments on earlier versions of this text.

5   Eggert situates himself as a creative father of sorts of Noelle, even if the simulator is an ongoing, collaboratively designed configuration. It was Eggert who responded to my initial email contact with Gaumard, investigating the possibilities of interviewing people from the Noelle design team: 'I am the creator. How can I help?' Eggert also performs alone

It became fairly obvious that we needed a full-sized mum that would articulate properly. We needed a foetus that could be birthed either vertex or breech or anything else. And we needed to have a neonate that would respond appropriately … And then, it is pretty apparent that you'd need a mechanical solution, and you'd need an electrical hardware solution, and you'd need a software solution to conduct the orchestra.[6]

Such a complex cybernetic machinery of mechanical, motor-driven hardware bodies, interlinked with, displayed, monitored and operated by screen-based scenarios, is certainly a challenging design project. In medical debates about the use of simulators in medical education, there is a clear emphasis on the need for cost-effective, low-risk, educational strategies to meet all the more complex technological development, paired with a heightened awareness of patient care and safety (see Deering et al. 2006: 107, Schuwirth and van der Vleuten 2003: 37, Wright et al. 2005: 26). Traditionally, the psychomotor skills and clinical reasoning skills required to be a clinician were acquired via an apprentice-style 'see one, do one, teach one' model. Today, medical simulators are introduced as mediators and problem-solvers, taking the place of humans as experimental subjects.

Discussions of the usefulness of simulators enter in intriguing, and not always consistent, ways into the slippery terrain of 'realism', 'the lifelike' and 'the real'. Realism, for example, as a literary mode is no less constructed than say fantasy or concrete poetry, but is harder to reveal as such. Literary realism, seemingly operating as a transparent mode, 'is characterized by an inability or a refusal to know itself as writing; illusionism, a kind of willful self-blindness destined to induce in its reader a reciprocal self-blindness'(Boumelha 1988: 81). Realism, traditionally associated with literature from the Renaissance and on, is characterized by its focus on individual experience and bounded by its mission to represent the 'real' conditions of social existence:

> Realism involves a fidelity both to the physical, sensually perceived details of the external world, and to the values of the dominant ideology. … Realism's desire to 'get the details right' is an ideological practice, for the believability of its fidelity to 'the real' is transferred to the ideology it embodies. The conventions of realism have developed in order to disguise the constructedness of the 'reality' it offers, and therefore of the arbitrariness of the ideology that is mapped onto it (Fiske 1987: 36).

The desire in realism to 'get the details right' has an obvious resonance in the simulation world. On one hand, simulation is said not to be intended to replace learning in clinical settings, but rather to provide a controlled and safe environment

---

together with the simulators in the instruction videos on Gaumard's homepage: <http://www.gaumard.com/index.html> under 'Videos' [accessed: 27 March 2009].

6   Interview: John Eggert, 22 November 2006.

for practising. 'As such, simulation imitates, but does not duplicate reality – it is a controlled "real-world-like" medical setting' in which the simulator body mimics the processes of a living body: a beating heart (or, actually, several), internal movements, and rotations, and so on (Ypinazar and Margolis 2006: 3). On the other hand, there is a desire to create scenarios that masquerade as 'reality', that take the place of 'the real' in ways that make the participants forget about its constructedness. This understanding approaches Baudrillard's (1994) notion of simulation as that which does not pretend, but produces itself as that which is simulated, hence rendering unclear the difference between true and false, real and imaginary (Baudrillard 1994). Or, in Eggert's words (words that recur like a mantra in the simulation community): 'Isn't the classic phrase that you want to suspend disbelief?'[7] In this sense, simulators are thought of as mimetic devices, as stand-ins for 'the real', as critically close approximations If being critically close has bearing on discussions in medical simulation, a relevant question is then to what, more exactly, such critical closeness refers. In other words, what is positioned as and understood to be 'the real' in medical simulation?

As feminist science and technology scholar Ericka Johnson points out, there are typically double concerns in discussions in the simulation world as to what constitutes a successful, or 'valid', simulator: Does the simulator mimic a real body realistically? Does it teach medical procedures accurately (Johnson this volume)? The method commonly used to evaluate simulators is double blind clinical trials. Rather than relying on measurements of whether simulator bodies modelled in 'lifelike' ways have significant impact, these tests speak primarily of how well the simulators mediate the knowledge and experience of medical practices (see Deering et al. 2004, Halamek et al. 2000, Wright, Taekman and Endsley 2004). Johnson argues that while medical simulators do provide models of the patient body, the body being modelled in the simulator – rather than constituting an anatomically pre-existing given – is actually the experienced body. Her main point is that medical simulators, more than anything else, articulate medical practices, which begs critical questions concerning whose practice, and experience, is being simulated (Johnson 2008).

When asked about what kind of competence, knowledge and experience was constitutive in designing Noelle, apart from the most obvious ones in the mechanical engineering and programming fields, Eggert spoke about the accumulative, dynamic nature of simulator design and the importance of taking into account the company's history of having designed, developed and sold childbirth simulators for fifty years. Implicit in this history is, for example, extensive customer input from people around the world, which becomes a knowledge base for members of the company. Then again, he also delivered an interesting answer that has everything to do with family bonds and reproductive capacities:

---

7   Interview: John Eggert, 22 November 2006.

JE: We have on our staff two physicians who work with me on a regular basis. One of which is my son. He is an internist, pulmonologist and critical care specialist.

JS: Did you bring in people from the other side of the spectrum, so to speak, like women who have experience of giving birth?

JE: Those that we brought in were and are still in the company, and would include people like my wife.

It is imperative to point out that the Noelle project provides multiple models of practised bodies and bodies as practices, so to speak. The Noelle body has never been one, but is the (provisional) result of multiple bodies and body-technologies, a cyborgian assemblage of an ongoing process of modelling and remodelling, a continuous transformation. In Eggert's words, 'the Noelle project, which we started years ago, in fact will never be completed.'[8] Designing for medical practices is itself a practice, as well as a kind of use, in the sense that design practices inscribe and anticipate use. Given the open-endedness of design for medical practices, and how it must anticipate the use of the simulator, this process is certainly not without its limitations. Rather, what the simulator body can do, is regulated, restricted and controlled in multiple ways. As will become clear, such restrictions have everything to do with how simulator design practices incorporate the idea(l)s of technological progress and a kind of embodiment that is peculiarly disembodied.

As important as it is to try and trace the bodies, models and technologies that, in their way, shape the simulation, it is equally important to understand that this is never a one-way process – as seems to be the underlying assumption in the rhetoric of realism and simulations of 'the real'. Alongside Lisa Cartwright, I find it crucial to ask 'whether conventions of realism are in fact the most useful means of "learning more" about, or "better representing" the body' in medicine (Cartwright 1998). Moving beyond realism to better understand medical simulation, however, is not merely a matter of revealing how realism masquerades as the universal, and hence conceals the cultural specificity and situatedness of technologies. This is because such discussion keeps insisting on a division between the real and the simulated, between biological bodies and those of machines, even in *critiquing* the principles of realism. Even if the universalism of realism in simulation is questioned by asking whose reality, more precisely, is being simulated, the notion of a pre-existing reality possible to re-present and model (with the simulator) remains. Such an understanding obscures the fact that there is no clear-cut causality between human and nonhuman bodies, no obvious referential link.

---

8   Interview: John Eggert, 22 November 2006.

Techno-corporeality and Posthuman Feminism

If (human) bodies are thought of as pre-existing simulation, as originals of sorts against which the simulators are measured as more or less successful incorporations, every alternative understanding of the many connections between human and nonhuman bodies, between nature and culture, is effectively eliminated.

Feminist science and technology scholars have consistently decoupled nature from the natural in showing that 'nature', much like culture, is something that is formed and re-formed. This decoupling has also served to disengage the die-hard coupling of woman and nature, or woman-as-nature. Interestingly, women and nature appear to be re-coupled in much feminist work on reproductive technologies. Reproductive technologies – whether understood as artificial insemination, *in vitro* fertilization, 'artificial womb' technologies or ultrasound scanning – are often articulated independently of/as separate from women, their experiences and (supposedly) natural bodies. As Irina Aristarkhova has pointed out, 'very few feminist researchers to date have articulated other than the most negative attitudes toward "reproductive machines", mostly on the grounds that women are already being exploited as "wombs" and "machines of reproduction"' (Aristarkhova 2005: 52).[9]

It is not surprising that feminist critics of reproductive technologies are attempting to reclaim women's bodies as a strategy against what is generally referred to as the medicalization of women's bodies, as well as against tendencies to exclude the maternal from the procreational equation. In these discussions, the body of the woman/mother is violently invaded, inscribed, disciplined or controlled by (masculine) medical science and technologies. Alternately, their bodies and their reproductive capacities are sidestepped altogether and ultimately replaced by machines.

In feminist criticism of technoculture more generally, there is a similar line of thought that emphasizes how the (sexed) nature/culture split prevails even in intense fusions of human and machine. Machine bodies in Hollywood science fiction, as pictured in films such as *Robocop* and *The Terminator*, typically illustrate an exaggerated, metallic masculinity that highlights traditional couplings between male bodies and machinery (see Cockburn 1983, 1985, Oldenziel 1999, Wajcman 1994, 1995). Although a synthesis of human and machine that renders unstable the very boundaries of the human subject, the maleness of these cyborg bodies is not only left intact but hyped-up (Holland 1995, Springer 1991, Springer 1996). Even if such readings of machine bodies rightfully draw attention to how the sexed body does not necessarily vanish out of sight in corporeal linkages with technologies, they seem to sidestep, entirely, the fact that cyborg bodies are haunted by contradictions. If (reproductive) technologies are, too hastily, seen as a

---

9   For discussions that clearly complicate the techno/body division, see, for example, Haraway (1991, 1999). See also Charis Thompson's more optimistic take on technologies of reproduction as new possibilities for women, in Thompson (2005).

male domination/denial of repressed female bodies, this builds on the problematic notion that there would exist such a thing as a (feminine) sphere untouched by technology. Jill Marsden points out how such commentaries imply a 'separation or distinction between technological 'agency' and the 'matter' of its operations'; in this sense, it then becomes possible to speak of 'natural' nature, either irresponsibly wished away (as in the Frankensteinian death of the mother) or ideologically determined (as a resource for masculine exploitation and control) (Marsden 1996: 8). Consequently, these arguments effectively eliminate every productive pairing of *women* and machines. They also eliminate an understanding of the materiality of the body, not as passive or culturally determined, but as an active force of its own becoming.

Elsewhere, I have argued for how Australian 'corporeal feminism' as formulated by feminist philosopher Elizabeth Grosz can be productively put to use in cyborg-feminist projects (see Sundén 2003). In relation to Grosz, for whom the body is understood as something partial, incomplete, relational and always in the process of becoming otherwise, but nonetheless as always sexually specific, the discussion of women and/as reproductive machines could take a different direction. In *Sexy Bodies: The Strange Carnalities of Feminism*, Elizabeth Grosz and Elspeth Probyn argue for a mode of understanding (the sexing/queering of) bodies along a Deleuzian notion of becoming; of bodies conceived as activities, processes, movements, lines and motions of making (Grosz and Probyn 1995). This is not the time or place for a thorough exposition of the possible affinities and implications of corporeal feminism for feminist science and technology studies, but merely an opportunity to point out a possible direction for such an endeavour. For Grosz, the body is neither a pre-representational biological presence, nor a purely discursive inscription, but an 'open materiality' and a site for political, social and cultural struggle:

> It is an open materiality, a set of (possibly infinite) tendencies and potentialities which may be developed, yet whose development will necessarily hinder or induce other developments and other trajectories. These are not individually or consciously chosen, nor are they amenable to will or intentionality: they are more like bodily styles, habits, practices, whose logic entails that one preference, one modality excludes or makes difficult other possibilities (Grosz 1994: 191).

In thinking of bodies in terms of becoming, there is the possibility of distinguishing between different modes of becoming, between different ways in which bodies become meaningful. Design for medical practices could, in similar terms, be thought as a set of potentialities which may be developed, and yet whose development will hinder other ways in which simulations may take shape. In an attempt to challenge the boundaries of constructivism, an exploration of the technological and cultural shaping of bodies is not enough. It is important also to examine how sexually specific yet hybrid bodies come to matter, and will matter differently, partly due to their very materiality. If Grosz's early work was an effort to think the body as that which marked discourse with its own force and difference, in her later work on Bergson and Darwin, Grosz expands this site of force not only beyond the body, but beyond the human altogether (Grosz 2004). This is a relocation of the argument, from its previous investment in human bodies and/as culture, to a heightened interest in intersections of nature and culture, life science and cultural theory. This reorientation, then, also potentially expands the discussion of corporeality beyond the bodies of humans, to also include non-human bodies and matter. In a similar way, feminist physicist Karen Barad argues that feminist philosophy of the body (in her case primarily Butler's notion of performativity) can be productively de-anthropomorphized and put to use for science studies (Barad 2003).

This shift of emphasis, from an interest merely in culture, to a focus on intersections of nature and culture, could imply a willingness to let a feminist thinking of bodily becomings speak to relationships between human and nonhuman bodies and to how they are implicated in one another. What I am getting at is a *posthuman feminist* understanding of techno-corporeality. Along with Barad, in her definition of a posthumanist perspective, I argue for feminist interventions and interrogations, which '[call] into question the givenness of the differential categories of 'human' and 'nonhuman', examining the practices through which these differential boundaries are stabilized and destabilized'(Barad 2003: 808). In thinking with and through reproductive machines, it is important to recognize how these technologies, rather than being something external to and possibly invasive of the body, are actually connected in multiple ways with what we have come to think of as our bodies. In her interrogation of the temporality of the technobody, Gail Weiss speaks of the interface between bodies and machines, of the 'significance of an *intercorporeality* that defies any attempt to affirm the autonomy of the body apart from other bodies or from the disciplinary, technological practices that are continually altering and redefining them'(Weiss 1999: 163).[10] She traces the relationality between bodies and between bodies and machines in temporal terms and envisions the temporality – and, indeed, the embodiment – of technobodies as nothing other than our own:

> The durée of the technobody – whether this body be that of a newly cloned sheep; 'a test-tube' baby; a woman in labour hooked up to technological devices that record fetal movement, fetal heartbeat, maternal blood pressure, and contractions; a boy with a liver transplant; a woman with a prosthetic leg – arises out of a violent effort and requires a violent effort in order to see the interconnections that link this durée with our own. Indeed, what is most violent,

---

10   See also Catherine Waldby's use of Weiss's term *intercorporeality* to address notions of embodiment and tissue transfer. She argues: 'the idea of intercorporeality contributes to a denaturalization of the relations between the limits of the body and the limits of the "I" understood as a discrete entity. In this regard, it may help to conceptualize that most literal kind of boundary confusion involved in tissue transfer' (Waldby 2002: 241).

I think, is the recognition that technology is part and parcel of our own durée (Weiss 1999: 170).

The question is not whether or how women can be saved from (reproductive) technologies, but one of working with and through our couplings with machines responsibly. To acknowledge the relationality between human and nonhuman bodies is not to give in to a certain masculine script of technological development and progress, but to envision the only site possible for intervention, infiltration and possible redesign.

Woman as Birth Machine

Woman as enunciated by the patriarchy as a birth machine, predestined for the reproduction of the labour force in capitalist society (where men are the real source of capital), is far from a new figuration. In her writing on scientific disembodiment, pregnancy and the unborn, medical historian Barbara Duden argues that human foetuses today, as well as (pregnant) women, rather than being conceptualized as natural facts are engineered constructs of modern society (Duden 1993). To this, I would add that the notion of being engineered also entails the possibility of re-engineering, of being formed differently, an argument rarely present in the discussion of the 'technologization' of women's bodies.

Reproductive machines have circulated in Western cultures in many shapes and guises. Medical simulators and birthing machinery, such as Noelle, come out of a long tradition of, for example, obstetric phantoms and anatomical wax models. Wax models – or waxes – were introduced as didactic tools toward the end of the 17th century, and remained in use well into the 18th century. Apart from their educational purposes, they also made for thrilling public displays on the boundary of art and medical science. In Ludmilla Jordanova's account of wax models, she puts forth how these 'Venuses' (as they were called), shipped out from northern Italy 'on silk or velvet cushions, in passive, yet sexually inviting poses', were intriguing modulations of art, medical science, reproduction and eroticism (Jordanova 1989: 44).[11] Even if not all waxes were female, those that were male were most often either upright, fleshless muscle men, or merely parts of men, such as male torsos.

According to Jordanova, the differences between male and female waxes are even more striking in view of how the female bodies of wax are detailed, adorned and supplemented. With minute attention to detail, the bodies of the female wax models resemble Roman statues in how they depict the female shape. Instead of the smooth, stone-like impression of cold marble, the use of wax painted with oil

---

11   For discussions of female wax models as erotically inviting, see also Bronfen (1992) and Showalter (1991).

colours, so it can be mistaken for human skin, makes for an uncanny realness.[12] Human hair frames their faces and covers their sexes; they have body parts that can be removed, revealing the texture underneath the skin, and are sometimes supplemented with small foetuses. Many wax Venuses strike poses from famous art works (as their name suggests), which not only links art to science, but points, according to Jordanova, to realism as a guiding principle in multiple fields:

> Eyebrows, lashes, head and pubic hair were added painstakingly and serve no other function than to make the body as lifelike as possible. They add nothing to the anatomical detail of the model; they even form a bizarre and striking contrast to the exposed internal organs and muscles that look like chunks of meat. Here we have more than realism; a verisimilitude so relentless that is becomes hyper-realism (Jordanova 1989: 47).

Attention to detail is everything in simulation, which brings Noelle in line with previous displays of the reproductive female body in medicine, yet in a different way. Jordanova distinguishes between lifelikeness and anatomical detail and argues that the adorned body of the waxes had nothing to do with how these bodies model anatomy, with how they function as didactic tools. In Noelle, there is perhaps a similar contrast between, for example, the human-like hair on the head and the internal motor rotations that gradually push out the baby. But even if perfectly washable, combable simulator hair adds nothing as such to the process of delivery, it feeds into and foregrounds affective responses on the part of the human user. In performing birth and birthing 'as if' the nonhuman body of the simulator is, in fact, human, attentiveness to detail in the simulator body is not set apart from medical practices, but becomes an intrinsic part of them. Elias describes a training session in which, in a state of emergency, the Noelle was wheeled off to an operating room 'where she gave regular birth to twins after a frenzied 20-minute operation' (Elias 2006). One of the nurses expressed concern as to whether or not the simulator body was appropriately covered ('We wheeled her through the hallway with her gown open'), effectively destabilizing the distinction between simulator and simulated, nonhuman and human bodies (Elias 2006).

Then again, ways of depicting female bodies for 'medical purposes' do not always relate to concern with dignified cover-ups. On the contrary, bare naked

---

12   Departing from Sigmund Freud's 1919 essay 'The Uncanny', the anthology *The Uncanny: Experiments in Cyborg Culture* is an investigation of cyborg imagery and cyborg bodies. In the introductory chapter, the editor Bruce Grenville uses Freud's understanding of the uncanny as something not new or strange, but frighteningly familiar, to understand today's cyborgs: 'I argue that the cyborg is uncanny not because it is unfamiliar or alien, but rather because it is all too familiar. It is the body doubled – doubled by the machine that is so common, so familiar, so ubiquitous, and so essential that it threatens to consume us, to destroy our links to nature and history, and quite literally, especially in times of war, to destroy the body itself and to replace it with its uncanny double' (Grenville 2001: 21).

waxes were put on display as still lives for an audience to learn from, and to be thrilled and perhaps aroused by. Jordanova makes the case that the female wax models invited sexual thoughts in the form of 'mentally unclothing the woman. Of course, these models were already naked, but they gave an added, anatomical dimension to the erotic charge of unclothing by containing removable layers that permit even deeper looking into the chest and abdomen' (Jordanova 1989: 55). Noelle is 'layered' in a similar manner as the waxes, allowing the medical team to remove parts and, in a sense, look into the interiority of the body and its reproductive machinery. Even though there are occasional news photos of Noelle clad in a hospital gown, most of the time the Noelle simulator is on display completely naked.

The nakedness of Noelle's body is even more striking in comparison with some of its male counterparts, such as the emergency (or EMS) simulator SimMan from Norwegian Laerdal. SimMan is routinely portrayed on the company website wearing pants and a shirt, sometimes with one sleeve rolled up over the elbow to facilitate the insertion of IV needles.[13] If not fully clad, in news shots from training sessions around the world, SimMan may appear bare from the waist up, while visual evidence of the whole body laid bare is rare. Disrobing Noelle, then, becomes not a process of removing garments, but rather a matter of removing and/or replacing body parts, such as the 'lid' covering the abdomen, the cervix (which often breaks), and so on. As Eggert points out in a discussion of the design and inter-changeability of body parts, 'the cervix is an enormously difficult design exercise', since the material used needs to be enormously elastic, feel soft when touched, yet have longevity.[14] In comparison with, for example, an arm, cervixes are not long-lived: 'the cervixes are replaceable, they snap in and out … Whereas arms literally want to be in the field for years without having to be replaced or without having significant maintenance done on them'.[15]

In contrasting eyebrows and pubic hair with 'the exposed internal organs and muscles that look like chunks of meat', Jordanova traces a representational shift from 'realism' to 'hyper-realism'. Medical simulators like Noelle similarly seem to enter, not realism, but rather a (materialized) Baudrillardian hyper-realism in ways that, while challenging the distinction between human and nonhuman bodies, produces a hyper-real body that is curiously *dis*embodied (Baudrillard 1994). This techno-corporeal formation relies on a selective bodily awareness that allows the birthing body to have hair that can be washed and combed, breasts perfectly shaped, and so on, but that discriminates quite clearly against bodily fluids, odours and sounds. Even if Gaumard provided bodily fluids thirty years ago, the typical customer response would be that the less messiness, the better, to avoid having to bother with any clean-up. In terms of audio, screaming is an add-on choice

13   See, for example, the first page of the 2007 Product Catalogue from Laerdal: http://www.laerdal.no/document.asp?docID=14668676 [accessed: 16 April 2007].

14   Interview: John Eggert, 22 November 2006.

15   Interview: John Eggert, 22 November 2006.

of sorts, performed by the instructor. It is a scream wired into the body from the outside, but not something clearly linked with certain stages or incidents in the delivery phase. In line with customer requests, and in line with the idealization of female bodies in technoculture, the Noelle comes together as a rather dry, quiet, odourless configuration.[16] Human wet-ware has primarily entered the simulator indirectly, such as in the instruction manual reminder to lubricate the birth canal before each delivery. Interestingly, one of the latest editions to the Noelle simulator series is simulated blood postpartum, which points at a change of attitudes on the part of the customers. Another interesting development tendency is the change from a relatively quiet delivery (Noelle had previously no speech), to models with nearly a hundred pre-programmed phrases to be initiated by the instructor. Noelle's speech concerns everything from experiences of pain and discomfort, to comments on how the pregnant body has felt recently. But if SimMan can beg for his life ('Don't let me die'), and draw attention to the fact that he is not alone ('I have a family'), the Noelle scenarios rarely get more dramatic than 'worst pain', 'going to be sick' and 'help me'.

The Detachable Feminine and Simulations of Whiteness

A virgin birth machine, the Noelle body is not only one, but at least two. In being delivered with a foetus as well as a neonate of indeterminate sex, Noelle is many. However, this possibly frightening multiplicity in the crossing of wires and reproductive sexuality seems to be taken care of by the male engineer with god-like master commands at his fingertips: 'David Isaza, an engineer with Gaumard, sat in a corner with a laptop, sending wireless signals to Noelle. With a keystroke, he can inflict all sorts of complications, overriding any preprogrammed instructions' (Elias 2006). Noelle, with its high-wired womb and always ready to dilate cervix and vulva, is in a sense the techno-incorporation of a new, automaton Virgin Mary, giving birth to the One endlessly. Interestingly, the newborn robot is peculiarly sexless, its apparently seamless crotch avoiding every straightforward linguistic determination. Is this a pointer in the direction of a high-tech, queer future open to ambiguity and trans-sexuality? Or, is it rather a way on the part of the mannequin designers of not having to pick sides?

---

16   The dryness of this cyborg body parallels in a sense the dream of techno-disembodiment, of leaving the body and all its limitations behind in cyberspace articulated by (primarily male) cyberenthusiasts in the early 1990s. In their Cartesian separation of mind from body, cyberspace is completely freed from the messiness of the physical and miraculously becomes a space of the mind. The dream of getting rid of the all too human wet-ware in simulator birthing bodies is of course not the same, but still carries a similar tendency of not blending high-tech, computer interactive bodies with the messiness of human embodiment.

The answers to these questions are perhaps not as clear-cut as they may at first appear, at least not in relation to SimMan, which puts an interesting spin on the simulation of reproductive heterosexuality. At first sight, SimMan simulates the reliable breadwinner and family father (through uttering canned phrases such as 'I have a family'). In the next instant, however, SimMan may come across as a thought-provoking trans-sim. An article entitled 'Dolls give students a dose of reality' reports on how interchangeable body parts of simulators put a twist on bodily specificity in simulation. Nursing senior Sharon Williams at the University of Pennsylvania recalls how one time she had to insert a catheter in one simulator and was met with a surprise: 'I think I am doing it on a male because the doll had a male face', she says. 'I pulled down the sheet, and there was a female part!' (Leiman 2003) Another report clarifies that 'SimMan can become a woman, with the addition of a wig, breasts and reproductive organs' (Hartford Hospital 2003).

In a true transvestite, drag queen fashion, the 'he' becomes a 'she' with the addition of (female, one must assume) reproductive organs, breasts and, not to forget, a wig. This makes one wonder whether some sort of male reproductive organs have to come off first, before anything else can be added. Or, if this sexed transformation rather proceeds from a non-genital, non-reproductive default mode, to which 'the feminine', in the form of reproductive machinery, is a possible add-on. At moments like these, it is quite striking how the production of the simulator body is curiously queer – even in the midst of (heterosexually infused) reproduction.

Even though the Noelle model comes in 'three ethnic colours', Gaumard offering what Eggert refers to as 'a Northern European, a Southern European and an Afro', as a multicultural solution to the simulation of racial difference, the simulator is routinely portrayed and sold as white.[17] In her *White Women, Race Matters*, Ruth Frankenberg makes clear that whiteness is both a privileged location, a perspective from which to understand the self and others, and a set of cultural practices that are usually unmarked and unnamed: 'Naming whiteness displaces it from the unmarked, unnamed status that is itself an effect of its dominance' (Frankenberg 1993: 6). The naming of whiteness makes possible the viewing of practices and subject positions as racialized, as well as racist. Similarly, Richard Dyer, in *White*, stresses that 'whiteness needs to be made strange' (Dyer 1997). White is that peculiar sign that is both a colour and not a colour, both visible and invisible. It is that which visibly makes and marks white people as white, while simultaneously working as a signifier of privilege, of what it means to be white, which is invisible (unmarked, unspecific, universal). To make white strange is to uncover the specificity of whiteness, to adapt a wider notion of the white body, of whiteness as involving something that is in but not merely of the body (Dyer 1997).

Making Noelle white-skinned does not avoid the issue of race, but unwittingly marks the simulator body as unmarked, unspecific and universal. Then again, the

---

17   Interview: John Eggert, 22 November 2006.

moment Noelle leaves for a training session in Afghanistan, the meaning of its whiteness along with its national belonging and dependence on smooth technology shifts significantly. Elias tells the story of Robbie Prepas, a Laguna Beach midwife and consultant to Gaumard, who has experience using various Noelle models in Afghanistan (Elias 2006). Afghanistan has, according to the US State Department, the second-highest infant mortality in the world. Evidently, there is some serious work for Noelle to do in this country. In 2004, Prepas was working for the Centers for Disease Control and Prevention to train Afghan medical staff. Prepas and her colleagues used different versions of Noelle, 'including one that worked by hand crank to move the mechanical parts. ... But while the Noelle mannequins were helpful, power failures and other technological glitches hindered the mannequins' effectiveness. Still, Prepas said Noelle is becoming standard issue in the United States' (Elias 2006).

The site-specific performativity of Noelle should be emphasized. In the US, the simulator appears to perform flawlessly, but in Kabul its machinery does not work as well, which appears to prevent Noelle from becoming standard issue. It is not clear what technological glitches, apart from the power failures, hindered the effectiveness of Noelle and the delivery of its robot-babies in Central Asia. It appears rather self-evident that white, digitized high-tech bodies would not operate smoothly in a nation into which you must bring a mechanical version that works by hand crank. On the other hand, it is doubtlessly hard to provide a safe, clean environment for childbirths and newborn children in a country such as Afghanistan, fighting to gain some sort of stability in the aftermath of the US invasion and a drawn-out war. If the Noelle project can help save the lives of children and (becoming) mothers, not least in particularly exposed locations, there is a lot to gain by it. As Eggert puts it, 'You have to hope for the best, but you have to be prepared for the unexpected. ... Simulators can help prepare for the unexpected.'[18] Situated in the midst of paradoxical simulatory possibilities and limitations, Noelle not only repeats oppositional relationships between women and machines, East and West, but holds, simultaneously, the possibility of differentiation, of doing things differently.

Death and Simulation

> In 1776, [a] Jaquet-Droz android, a 'Musical Lady' that played the harpsichord, was exhibited in London. As she played the five tunes in her repertoire, her eyes would move coyly from side to side, and her bosom would heave lightly, as if she was breathing. The machine was advertised as 'a vestal virgin with a heart of steel,' but one member of the audience thought her heart might be otherwise (Wood 2002: xiv).

---

18   Interview: John Eggert, 22 November 2006.

Female machines are a complex species. Eighteenth century automatons were clockwork constructions, accentuating by their fundamental principles their immortality – as well as the mortality of their makers. A prominent maker of entirely mechanical automatons, predecessors of our modern-day robots, Jaquet-Droz made a range of captivating technobodies. His 'Musical Lady' played her instrument dressed in a beautiful, elegantly detailed gown worthy a woman at the French court, crowned by an intricately coiffured wig. Occasionally displayed without her skirt, not only the fine workings of the clockwork machinery were uncovered, but also a pair of shapely legs, covered with delicate silk stockings. The configuration of woman as clock – and clock as woman – is a complex yet manageable creature, mechanical yet lifelike, predictable and pleasing. Jennifer Gonzales points out that in the history of making mechanical bodies, automatons are imbedded in the mechanical innovations connected with keeping time. These are cyborgs that appear more trapped than liberated by their mechanical parts (González 2000). Immersed in time differently from humans, clockwork bodies mark time, but do not sense the force of time propelling the human body closer to death.

In her *Edison's Eve*, Gaby Wood argues that although androids do not understand death, they are themselves incorporations of mortality: 'Rather than being copies of people, androids are more like *mementi mori*, reminders that, unlike us, they are forever unliving, and yet never dead. They throw the human condition into horrible relief' (Wood 2002). As such, automatons embody the very antithesis of our mortality, the negative of human knowledge of finitude. What then is the status of death in machines of reproduction, in machines that reproduce birth, the beginning of life as it were, from which death as the ultimate ending is never far off? Is death present in the Noelle simulation of birth and beginning life? Or, is this machinery rather of the clockwork variety, performing beyond the utmost limit of lived time? If closure is an essential component in the poetics of life, intimately tied to the pleasure of being alive, perhaps the one thing that both prompts and enables us to live, how is closure configured in the simulator? In other words: does Noelle die? A comprehensive answer to these questions must be made elsewhere, as this one is by necessity fairly brief.

Noelle – as mother unit – does not die, unless its machinery breaks down beyond repair. In the manual for S565 Noelle™ (this document has not been updated with the introduction of the S575 Noelle™), there is one passage on death that identifies possible scenarios for becoming mothers, but not hard-coded in the Noelle system: 'After delivery the uterus normally contracts reducing postpartum bleeding. Under certain conditions, contraction does not occur and extensive bleeding may continue. If this condition is not recognized and treated in a timely manner the new mother may go into shock and die.'[19] However, the newborn Noelle baby, the neonate, will not always make it. In 'Teaching Tips' for S565

---

19   The S575 Noelle Manual is available at: http://www.gaumard.com/download/manuals/40_S575.pdf [accessed: 27 March 2009].

Noelle™, scenario seven is called 'Gloria cord prolapse', which involves a woman, Gloria, and a prolapsed cord emergency: 'Prolapsed cord emergencies are life or death situations. This scenario presents a disastrous intrapartum complication that results in foetal death. … Despite heroic efforts of the student team, Gloria's baby fails to recover. The student team must now learn how to comfort the living.'[20] As previously mentioned, Laerdal's SimMan can speak of death ('Don't let me die') and also has the ability to die: 'SimMan's equipment includes several injured body parts that can be changed depending on the scenario. In the most extreme circumstances, SimMan's internal organs could begin to shut down and he could die' (Newton 2003).

The fact that the death of the mother is not part of the set-up is intriguing and has several different implications. It clearly sets Noelle apart from the configuration of motherhood, death and the making of artificial bodies in *Frankenstein*. Feminists reading *Frankenstein* have often made sense of Victor's creation of the monster, not as the making of a man by another man, but through the more familiar framework of female sexuality, reproduction and ultimately abortion (Donawerth 1997, Gilbert and Gubar 1979, Moers [1977] 1978, Veeder 1986, Youngquist 1991: 339– 359). Such readings miss the point that the creation of the monster depends on the absence, or even death, of the mother (Homans 1986). Frankenstein's reanimation of a dead body in pieces introduces a way of creating life that no longer needs a mother, and actually, all mothers introduced in the narrative end up dead. The lack of a dying-mother scenario for Noelle instead brings the simulator in line with 18th century automatons as machines without end. The becoming mother not being able to die may temporarily spare students from traumatic delivery experiences, but simultaneously obliterates an essential component of life and what it means to live, which further adds to the dis-embodiment of this particular technobody.

The absence of death, moreover, makes for an interesting contrast to the conventional ending for machine heroines. From classic examples of female androids of fiction in E. T. A. Hoffman's 'The Sandman' (Olympia) and Villiers de l'Isle Adam's *L'Eve future* (Hadaly), to more recent cinematic incarnations such as Ridley Scott's *Bladerunner* (Pris) and Jonathan Mostow's *Terminator 3* (the terminatrix), machine women tend to be rather volatile incorporations of violent sexuality with disastrous implications. The fear of machines that become uncontrollable is entwined with the fear of female sexuality that gets out of hand (Huyssen 1981). As manifestations of such masculine anxiety, the female machine must usually 'die' at the end of the story. The Noelle simulator is certainly different in significant ways, in neither being a work of fiction nor made for seduction. Yet, this performative machinery is one without end, and as such the very inversion of the regulatory cultural script for female technobodies. I have argued, often and elsewhere, for the posthuman feminist necessity of alternative female machines (ones that, for one thing, do not die at the end of the tale). Noelle doubtlessly

---

20   The S565 Noelle 'Teaching Tips' are available at: http://www.gaumard.com/ download/manuals/39_S565tips.pdf [accessed: 27 March 2009].

produces birth-giving bodies in a selective fashion. Unable to move away from its position flat on its back, it is a prime simulatory performance of female passivity for trans-national trade and training. Then again, this female technobody is quite rare: it is unstoppable and will ultimately outlive, so to speak, its own maker.

References

Aristarkhova, I. 2005. Ectogenesis and mother as machine. *Body & Society* 11(3), 43–59.

Barad, K. 2003. Posthumanist performativity: Toward an understanding of how matter comes to matter. *Signs* 28(3), 801–831.

Baudrillard, J. 1994. *Simulacra and Simulation*, translation by Sheila Faria Glaser, Ann Arbor: University of Michigan Press.

Boumelha, P. 1988. Realism and the ends of feminism, in *Grafts: Feminist cultural criticism*, edited by S. Sheridan. London and New York: Verso, 323–329.

Bronfen, E. 1992. *Over Her Dead Body: Death, femininity, and the aesthetic*, New York: Routledge.

Cartwright, L. 1998. A cultural anatomy of the visible human project, in *The Visible Woman: Imaging technologies, gender, and science*, edited by P. A. Treichler, L. Cartwright and C. Penley. New York: New York University Press, 21–43.

Clarke, A. 1995. Modernity, postmodernity, and reproductive processes, ca. 1890–1990, or 'Mommy, where do cyborgs come from anyway?', in *The Cyborg Handbook*, edited by C. Hables Gray, H. Figueroa-Sarriera and S. Mentor. New York: Routledge, 139–156.

Cockburn, C. 1983. *Brothers: Male Dominance and Technological Change*. London: Pluto.

Cockburn, C. 1985. *Machinery of Dominance: Women, men, and technical know-how*. London: Pluto.

Davis-Floyd, R. and J. Dumit. 1998. *Cyborg Babies: From Techno-sex to techno-tots*. New York: Routledge.

Deering, S., Poggi, S., Macedonia, C., Gherman, R. and Satin, A.J. 2004. Improving resident competency in management of shoulder dystocia with simulation training. *The American College of Obstetrics and Gynecology* 103(6), 1224–1228.

Deering, S., Brown, J., Hodor, J. and Satin, A.J. 2006. Simulation training and resident performance of singleton vaginal breech delivery. *Obstetrics & Gynaecology* 107(1), 86–89.

Donawerth, J. 1997. *Frankenstein's Daughters: Women writing science fiction*. Syracuse, NY: Syracuse University Press.

Duden, B. 1993. *Disembodying Women: Perspectives on pregnancy and the unborn*, translation by Lee Hoinacki, Cambridge, MA: Harvard University Press.

Dyer, R. 1997. *White: Essays on race and culture*. London: Routledge.

Elias, P. 2006. Robot birth simulator gaining in popularity Associated Press. Available at, for example: http://www.usatoday.com/news/health/2006-04-15-robot_x.htm [accessed: 27 March 2009].

Fiske, J. 1987. *Television Culture*. London: Methuen.

Frankenberg, R. 1993. *White Women – Race Matters: The social construction of whiteness*. Minneapolis, MN: University of Minnesota Press.

Franklin, S. 1997. *Embodied Progress: A cultural account of assisted conception*. London: Routledge.

Franklin, S. and Ragoné, H. (eds). 1998. *Reproducing Reproduction: Kinship, power, and technological innovation*. Philadelphia: University of Pennsylvania Press.

Gilbert, S.M. and Gubar, S. 1979. *The Madwoman in the Attic: The woman writer and the nineteenth-century literary imagination*. New Haven and London: Yale University Press.

González, J. 2000. Envisioning cyborg bodies: Notes from current research, in *The Gendered Cyborg: A reader*, edited by G. Kirkup, L. Janes, K. Woodward and F. Hovenden. London and New York: Routledge, 58–73.

Grenville, B. (ed.). 2001. *The Uncanny: Experiments in cyborg culture*. Vancouver: Vancouver Art Gallery, Arsenal Pulp Press.

Grosz, E. 1994. *Volatile Bodies: Toward a corporeal feminism*. Bloomington and Indianapolis: Indiana University Press.

Grosz, E. 2004. *The Nick of Time: Politics, evolution, and the untimely*. Durham and London: Duke University Press.

Grosz, E. and Probyn, E. (eds). 1995. *Sexy Bodies: The strange carnalities of feminism*. London and New York: Routledge.

Halamek, L.P., Kaegi, D.M., Gaba, D.M., Sowb, Y.A., Smith, B.C., Smith, B.E. And Howard, S.K. 2000. Time for a new paradigm in pediatric education: Teaching neonatal resuscitation in a simulated delivery room environment. *Pediatrics*. 106(4), e45.

Haraway, D. 1999. The virtual speculum in the new world order, in *Revisioning Women, Health, and Healing: Feminist, cultural, and technoscience perspectives*, edited by A. Clarke and V. Olesen. New York and London: Routledge, 49–96.

Hartford Hospital 2003. *Rounds*. Hartford Hospital's wellness magazine. [Online, summer]. Available at: http://www.harthosp.org/rounds/PDF/2003 [accessed: 15 December 2006].

Hartouni, V. 1997. *Cultural Conceptions: On reproductive technologies and the remaking of life*. Minneapolis: University of Minnesota Press.

Holland, S. 1995. Descartes goes to Hollywood: Mind, body and gender in contemporary cyborg cinema, in *Cyberspace, Cyberbodies, Cyberpunk: Cultures of technological embodiment*, edited by M. Featherstone and R. Burrows. London: Sage, 157–174.

Homans, M. 1986. *Bearing the Word: Language and female experience in nineteenth-century women's writing*. Chicago and London: University of Chicago Press.

Huyssen, A. 1981. The vamp and the machine: Technology and sexuality in Fritz Lang's 'Metropolis'. *New German Critique* 24/25, 221–237.

Jacobus, M. 1982. Is There a Woman in this Text?. *New Literary History, A Journal of Theory and Interpretation*. XIV(1), 117–141.

Johnson, E. 2008. Simulating medical patients and practices: Bodies and the construction of valid medical simulators. *Body and Society* 14(3), 105–128.

Jordanova, L. 1989. *Sexual Visions: Images of gender in science and medicine between the eighteenth and twentieth centuries*, New York: Harvester Wheatsheaf.

Leiman, M. 2003. Dolls give students a dose of reality. *The Daily Pennsylvanian*, [Online, 20 January]. Available at: http://www.temple.edu/ispr/examples/ex03_01_20b.html [accessed, 27 March 2009].

Marsden, J. 1996. Virtual Sexes and feminist futures: the philosophy of 'cyber-feminism', *Radical Philosophy* 78, 6–16.

Moers, E. [1977] 1978. *Literary Women*. London: Women's Press.

Newton, T. 2003. *A Life or Death Simulation*. [Online]. Available at: http://www.wku.edu/echo/previous/archive/2003oct/stories/simman.htm [accessed: 27 March 2009].

Oldenziel, R. 1999. *Making Technology Masculine: Men, women and modern machines in America, 1870–1945*. Amsterdam: Amsterdam University Press.

Schuwirth, L.W.T. and van der Vleuten, C.P.M. 2003. The use of clinical simulations in assessment. *Medical Education*, 37, Suppl. 1, 65–71.

Shelley, M. [1818] 1994. *Frankenstein: Or, the modern Prometheus*. London: Penguin Books.

Showalter, E. 1991. *Sexual Anarchy: Gender and culture at the fin de siècle*. London: Bloomsbury.

Springer, C. 1991. The pleasure of the interface. *Screen*, 32(3), 303–323.

Springer, C. 1996. *Electronic Eros: Bodies and desire in the postindustrial age*, Austin, TX: University of Texas Press.

Sundén, J. 2003. *Material Virtualities: Approaching online textual embodiment*. New York: Peter Lang Publishing.

Thompson, C. 2005. *Making Parents: The ontological choreography of reproductive technologies*. Cambridge, MA: MIT Press.

Veeder, W. 1986. *Mary Shelley and Frankenstein: The fate of androgyny*. Chicago and London: The University of Chicago Press.

Wajcman, J. 1994. Technology as masculine culture, in *The Polity Reader in Gender Studies*, edited by A. Giddens, D. Held, D. Hillman. Cambridge: Polity Press, 216–225.

Wajcman, J. 1995. Feminist theories of technology, in *Handbook of Science and Technology Studies*, edited by S. Jasanoff. Thousand Oaks, CA: Sage, 189–204.

Weiss, G. 1999. The durée of the technobody, in *Becomings: Explorations in Time, Memory, and Futures*, edited by E. Grosz. Ithaca and London: Cornell University Press, 161–175.

Wood, G. 2002. *Edison's Eve: A magical history of the quest for mechanical life*. New York: Alfred A. Knopf.

Wright, M.C., Taekman, J.M. and Endsley, M.R. 2004. Objective measures of situation awareness in a simulated medical environment. *Quality and Safety in Health Care*, 13, suppl. 1, 65–71.

Wright, M.C.,Taekman, J.M., Barber, L., Hobbes, G., Neman, M.F. and Stafford-Smith, M. 2005. The use of high-fidelity human patient simulation as an evaluative tool in the development of clinical research protocols and procedures. *Contemporary Clinical Trials* 26(6), 646–659.

Youngquist, P. 1991. Frankenstein: The mother, the daughter, and the monster. *Philological Quarterly* 70(3), 339–359.

Ypinazar, V.A. and Margolis, S.A. 2006. Clinical simulators: Applications and implications for rural medical education. *Rural and Remote Health* 6(2), 527.

Chapter 6

Simulating Medical Patients and Practices: Bodies and the Construction of Valid Medical Simulators[1]

Ericka Johnson

Why and how can a gynaecological simulator that has been 'validated' in one context, that is accepted by experts as a functional and realistic model of the body on which to teach gynaecological exams, not be considered functional when it changes contexts and is used in another country?[2] To think through this problem, which grew out of reflections upon the ontological basis of the simulator's different functionality within the US and Swedish contexts, I examine the use of the terms 'reality' and 'validity' in medical simulator literature and then apply Karen Barad's concepts of agential reality and intra-action to the gynaecological simulator's development. This provides a new way of thinking about how knowledge can be created in and from a simulator.

Barad asserts that we need to think about what and how we know as phenomena instead of as knowing subjects and known objects. She proposes two terms which are of particular use for my analysis of bodies in medical simulators. The first term is intra-action, which is used to indicate that 'a phenomenon is a specific intra-action of an "object" and the "measuring device"; the object and the measuring agencies emerge from rather than precede, the intra-action that produces them' (Barad 2007: 128). Intra-action can help to articulate how the female reproductive organs are produced through gynaecological practices before they are (re)produced in the simulator. Intra-action works within the theoretical framework of agential reality, the second term I will be using, which examines how discursive practices are related to material phenomena, and addresses 'the material nature of practices and how they come to matter' (Barad 2007: 45).

---

1   First published by SAGE/SOCIETY in Johnson, E. 2008. Simulating Medical Patients and Practices: Bodies and the Construction of Valid Medical Simulators. *Body and Society* 14(3), 105–128. Reprinted with permission.

2   The research on which this chapter is based is an examination of the development and implementation of a digital mannequin that represents the female pelvic anatomy. As part of this project I have interviewed actors involved in the invention, development and marketing of the simulator.

The idea that discursive practices and materiality are interrelated is not new. Barad draws much of her inspiration from feminist work on materiality (esp. Butler) and the field of feminist science studies (esp. Haraway). That social relations and politics are embedded in the materiality of technological artefacts is a founding concept within the field of Science and Technology Studies (STS), from which Barad also pulls ideas. Here, the politics of objects are often taught through the story of Winner's (actually, Moses') bridges in intro-STS courses (and problematized by Woolgar and Cooper (1999), though this does not seem to be taught as often) (Winner 1980). STS, and in particular Actor Network Theory (ANT), provide a vocabulary for speaking about the politics of the material world, considering artefacts and humans as actants. As Latour points out, the use of the term 'inhuman' to describe technologies is a misnomer, and one that hides the translation, delegation and prescription mechanisms embedded in the construction of technologies for very human purposes and by very human engineers (Latour 1988: 303). He clarifies these concepts through his well-known exploration of the 'hole-wall' and 'door closer'. Technologies are seen as delegates of social relations, and prescribe back to the users the values and structures they were built to enforce (Latour 1988: 310).

ANT terminology puts words to the way technologies can be created and used to reproduce social relations. Later ANT-inspired analysis is helpful to talk about how 'existing' objects are not so stable and defined as we might be inclined to think. ANT-and-after ideas have offered alternative, more flexible understandings of objects and what they do as actors (see Law and Singleton 2005: 347). Playing on the ANT term immutable mobile, later work has also shown how objects do not necessarily remain the same as they move across contexts and through time; rather, objects can be very *mutable* mobiles (de Laet and Mol 2000). Likewise, the definition of an object can resist closure completely, oscillating between various understandings and definitions even within the same context and at the same time (Dugdale 2000).

Thinking about the gynaecological simulator I have been working with in terms of delegation and prescription, one could posit that it is used to prescribe a specific way of examining the patient. The simulator delegates what an instructor would say to a student. 'Press this hard, right here, to feel the cervix,' the simulator seems to communicate through its computer screen. And one could make the argument that teaching the bimanual exam on a simulator, with standardized responses to pressure, on a standardized female anatomy, on a machine that is movable across contexts, countries and practices, is a textbook example of an immutable mobile. But one could also, after watching the simulator be used in practice, make the argument that this simulator is actually quite mutable. For example, rather than just using it as a teaching tool for doctors in training, the gynaecologists I worked with in Sweden brought the simulator into their examination rooms, removed the abdominal skin and used the simulator to explain upcoming bimanual exams to their patients, even letting the patients give an exam on the simulator, both to explain what they were going to experience and as a way of educating the patient about her own anatomy. This 'misuse' of the simulator as a teaching tool for a completely different audience shows how the artefact is flexible, even within the context of one hospital. That it changes in how it is understood (from student training tool to patient educator), by whom, and when attests to the oscillations of meanings that it moves through.

These are all interesting observations. But how does one interrogate the validity of the knowledge of the body found in the simulator? How can we express (and understand) the way knowledge about the world (and social relations) is initially generated to then be replicated in technological artefacts? To address these questions, I have turned to Karen Barad's agential reality and the concept of intra-action as a useful way to think about our relationship with medical simulators and the 'valid' models of the medical body that they provide for users. Within the theoretical framework of agential reality, intra-action articulates how the circumstances of experiencing an object are what define the object. This is very relevant to understanding how the patient body is known in medical practice and how the phenomenon of knowing the patient body in specific practices is then used to create valid models of it in simulators. As I will explain below, as designers work to create models of the human body, they are thinking about how their models are experienced by the users, and – though to a less articulated degree – how the patient bodies they are simulating are experienced by medical practitioners. Barad's theoretical work, which understands reality as things-in-phenomena, as our participation within nature (Barad 1996: 176), is therefore a useful tool for examining simulator practice and debates about validity because it shifts an analysis away from discussions of things and users, subjects and objects, to the phenomenon of knowing as the basic unit of existence (Barad 2003: 815).

Thus, in this chapter, I will use the concepts of agential reality and intra-action to show that the gynaecological simulator refracts phenomena of knowing the female reproductive organs through the bimanual pelvic exam as performed in very specific ways. By expounding upon this example I hope to show the analytical usefulness of these terms for more general simulator studies, and for understanding how the body is produced as relational phenomena. Importantly, as I will discuss at the end of this article, by interrogating the bodies reified in medical simulators, the concept of agential reality directs analysis to the practices of knowing the patient body that are then materialized, reconstructed and taught in the simulators. Recognizing the primacy of practice in the discussions about simulators and their use is important, as it highlights that it is often very context specific practices that are being standardized in the physical artefacts used to teach them. It also opens up a discussion of the question of *whose* experiences of medical practice are articulated by the simulators.

Valid Patient Simulators?

Although a large variety of medical simulators exist, their introduction to medical education invariably tends to bring up a standard discussion of validity (or 'fidelity', 'realism' and 'authenticity', the terms are used loosely and slightly interchangeably in the medical literature).[3] The typical concern is whether or not simulators actually represent the 'real' body and if they are really teaching medical procedures correctly; no one wants medical students to spend their time training on a false model of the body or practising an incorrect procedure and then damaging patients when they transfer their knowledge and skills onto a living patient.

Medical debates about simulator validity have tended to focus around how well the body is modelled, with the understood subtext being how realistic the representation of the human anatomy is. In common usage, the term simulation generally refers to imitations or representations of a separate, distinct, 'real', although Baudrillard has problematized this category with his work on simulacra (Baudrillard 1994). As it is often conceived, the referent being simulated can be a system or process, or it can be an object. Or, as in medical simulators, it can be both – an operation upon a body, for example. The use of the term simulation, rather than reproduction, also carries with it the concept of distilling and representing essential characteristics rather than the entire object; creating a model of the essence rather than the whole.

Medical simulator developers tend to use visual representations and tangible examples of the anatomy to source and support their models of the body, everything from traditional, dissection generated anatomies to advanced imaging technologies like MRI and CT scans. Which technology is used to visualize the anatomy is very relevant to what is seen and then reproduced. As Thacker notes, technologies of visualization interact with institutional structures and economies of bodies to produce 'particular, performative spectacularizations of the anatomico-medical body' (Thacker 1999: 320), though I would argue that these epistemological aspects are not always sufficiently considered when such visualizations are used in the design of simulators. For example, virtual reality simulators sometimes use data from the visible human project to construct organs and internal volumes which claim to mimic an actual body, but which bodies are mimicked, how they are known and what they say about our understandings of the human subject and pathologies are questions generally left to the humanities and social sciences (see Cartwright 1998, Waldby 1999, 2000). Likewise, there seems to be little reflection within the simulator community over the way these various methods of gathering information about the patient body influence, or to use Barad's ideas, intra-act, with the body to create the phenomenon of knowing it that is then called an anatomy.

When developing medical simulators, information and communication technologies are also being integrated into models to then send signals and

---

3   See, for example, the articles in the 2003 special edition of *Medical Education* 37 (supplement 1) dealing with simulators.

responses back to the users. Likewise, many medical simulators combine both visual and tactile stimuli. Visual images are often created on a computer monitor, representing the interior of the body or giving performance feedback through graphs and numbers. The tactile elements of a medical simulator can take the form of a mannequin or artificial body part. The tactile can also, however, be created virtually through the use of haptic feedback computer programmes that allow a user to 'feel' a virtual object with a surgical tool or other medical instrument.

However, and of relevance to the theoretical discussion here, one of the primary considerations used to evaluate medical simulators, whatever form they take or technologies they use, is how well the simulation recreates the *experience* of medical practice. When calibrating and evaluating a simulator, medical experts are often asked to test how the simulator mimics the 'real thing', where the real thing is the practice of a medical procedure. Thus the simulator community relies on 'objective' representations of the physical body (i.e. information gathered about an ontologically separate body that is not bothered by epistemological considerations) as a foundation for the validity of their simulators, but their evaluation criteria often draw on knowledge about and clinical experiences of medical practice. The implications of this two pronged approach is what I will explore here.

At the heart of this dual approach is a conflict between what a simulator is and what it represents, a conflict that is really a discussion of ontology and epistemology, of what is known and how it is known, something often discussed and debated in the fields of Science, Technology, Medicine & Society and Feminist Science Studies (as elsewhere). This debate raises questions about how knowledge is created in situated practice, whether knowledge can be considered a phenomenon rather than a representation of an ontologically separate truth, and if it is best analysed through how the world is experienced, including a respect for the way technologies can shape the phenomena we know (see Barad 2007, Haraway 1998, Mol 2002, Suchman 2007). It also points to the importance of considering who does the knowing (Harding 1991) and what the objects of knowledge are, as illustrated by debates about medical testing and the gendered body (Oudshoorn 1994, 2003, Shaw et al. 2004) and the patient's experience of and participation in medical practice (Cussins 1998). Applying these critiques of knowledge production to the development of medical simulators highlights questions about how evidence of the body is created, maintained and taught to new practitioners.

Simulators as Examination Tools

When looking at articles about the use of simulators in medical education,[4] the issue of validity seems to address two related but different aspects of simulator

4   To examine how this concept and the terms around validity are used, I have chosen to analyse it in the special supplement of *Medical Education* on the use of simulators (autumn 2003) and other articles about simulators which bridge the questions of simulator use and development between engineering and medical actors.

use. The first and perhaps most common area of usage is the question of how a simulator can test or examine a user's knowledge of a medical procedure, and how 'valid' a representation test results are of the actual knowledge acquisition or demonstration. The discussion about validity in these cases tends to focus on the question of whether or not one can make a valid assessment of a student's or doctor's skill by testing it on a simulator (Dawson and Kaufman 1998: 481). This use of the term validity, and use of the simulators, as well, touches on a much older debate within medical education about how exams, certification and credentialing can guarantee that the professionals being licensed to practice medicine actually know what they are doing.[5]

To address the use of simulators as assessment tools, many medical studies try to justify simulator use against other, more traditional, methods of examination. One approach is to demonstrate through case studies that exam results produced from a simulator actually match those the same students receive when being examined by more tradition forms, like paper based tests (see Pugh and Youngblood 2002). Another method of validating simulator test results is to compare the test results of experts with those of residents, and extrapolate that better results by experts say something about what skills the simulator was actually measuring (Tsai et al. 2003: 74). Perhaps the most rhetorically convincing argument for using simulators as valid testing tools comes from the field of surgical simulators, where simulators provide a place for students to engage in the traditional method of learning, and to demonstrate their knowledge in practice, but without actually endangering real patients (Schuwirth and van der Vleuten 2003). This argument tends to connect back to the medical aphorism, particularly common within surgery, that a medical student should 'see one, do one, teach one' as they learn medicine, and points out that the last thing a patient wants to be is a medical student's 'do one' guinea pig (Dawson and Kaufman 1998).

Simulators as Patient Models

The other area in which validity becomes an issue is the question of which model of the patient is being simulated. It is in these discussions that validity is frequently interchanged with the terms realism and fidelity. Concern is expressed over how well the simulator actually mimics the patient body, with directives for future development addressing very technical aspects like, 'The color of tissues must be realistic, and the surface texture maps must accurately reflect the simulated organ' (Dawson and Kaufman 1998: 481). In this use of the term, a valid simulator recreates the body realistically. Barad's concept of agential reality, addressing 'the material nature of practices and how they come to matter' (Barad 2007: 45), is useful here to demonstrate what phenomena of knowing produce the 'realistic body' being recreated.

---

5   For a review of this in the history of American medicine, see Starr (1982).

I posit this because closer examination of this use of the term validity indicates that the issues being discussed are not how well the simulator mimics the body, but how well the simulated medical practices recreate those medical practices carried out by experts. As with some of the attempts to validate simulators in testing situations, references to the use of experts appear in this literature. For example, in the development of a haptic urological simulator, in which both tactile and visual stimuli are reproduced, engineers working on the simulator mentioned in their report of the technical development that 'Observations of actual operations on humans and animals showed that a urological operation can be divided into two phases, i.e. the insertion phase and the main operation' (Papadopoulos, Viachos and Mitropoulos 2002: 2), indicating that during their development process they used actual practice as a model for the simulator, rather than solely relying on anatomical representations of the body. Their statement also reveals elements of time and narrative in their practice. The 'realism' that they were trying to incorporate into the simulator was not merely referring to the urological anatomy, but was describing specific participation with the patient body by medical experts through time. As a result, the simulator mimics practice not anatomy, and simulates participation with the body. It simulates specific practices carried out through time, not ontologically pre-existing bodies independent of experience, because the urological body being simulated is that of the intra-action between the patient's urological system (and all of the technological, cultural and economical structures that contribute to its very situated presentation, see Barad, 1998) and the medical practices of the surgery.

The same group of technicians mention that, after initial development of the simulator, they sent the machine out to 'potential users' for testing and evaluation. Involving experts in both the design and testing stages is very common practice, as Prentice (2005, this volume) delineates, and other articles in the selected material also mentioned the use of experts to judge if the simulators were valid (Dawson and Kaufman 1998: 481, Tsai et al. 2003: 76), which means the simulators are evaluated against the knowledge of medical practice that experts have.

In many medical practices, however, knowledge about the patient body is generated through mediating technology, not in direct intra-actions only between a physician and a patient, but with the help of technological instruments – often measurement apparatuses. Simulators are, therefore, also being built to recreate technological representations of medical knowledge. In writing about the development of a natal distress simulator, for example, the developers acknowledge that they were trying to build a simulator that replicated the baseline signals (primarily read through anaesthesiology monitoring equipment) sent by a baby and the mother during birth and in response to the therapeutic interventions given to the patients. They tried to recreate these by 'comparing model responses to animal or human data presented in the literature' (van Meurs et al. 2003: 31), i.e. by replicating the way that medical knowledge is recorded, reported and read by others in the community. In this way, the simulator can send technologically mediated signals of its response to the medical interventions of users just as a patient would. The same development goal exists for other simulators, in particular the ones which are used in anaesthesiology training to teach individuals and teams how to deal with patient reactions to pharmaceutical practices in the operating room (Good 2003: 16, Johnson 2004). This type of simulator, which can take the form of a full patient mannequin that sends responses through monitoring equipment just as a human would, is sometimes called a high-fidelity simulator, in which 'fidelity is the extent to which the appearance and behaviour of the simulator/simulation match the appearance and behaviour of the simulated system' (Maran and Glavin 2003: 24). The fidelity comes from how the simulator can relay these signals to users in a way that mimics those physical and technological responses given by patients through monitoring and mediating technology during anaesthesiology. Significantly, although not articulated as such in the medical literature, the concept of simulator fidelity is based on intra-action (see Barad 1996, 2007), that is, how we read signals to know about the patient, not recreation of the patient, and can be compared to Barad's discussion of Bohr's philosophy-physics and the way in which the apparatus of measurement 'enacts a cut delineating the object from the agencies of observation' (Barad 2007: 114).

The definition of fidelity above comes from an article in which Maran and Glavin make a distinction between engineering fidelity – replication of the physical characteristics of the real task – and psychological or functional fidelity, which they define as, 'the degree to which the skill or skills in the real task are captured in the simulated task' (Maran and Glavin 2003: 24). But, while they do not specifically comment on this, it is worth noting that in both of these examples of fidelity, it is a *task* that is being simulated, not merely a body part or a medical environment. Practice, phenomena and action are simulated, not the body as an unchanging anatomy.

Thus, it would seem as if the medical and technical professionals working with simulators are realising, though not necessarily reflecting upon, the fact that they are simulating practice (Al-khalifah and Roberts 2004, McCloy and Stone 2001, Wright, Taekman and Endsley 2004, Dawson and Kaufman 1998), a realization which also appears in an article about the testing of the gynaecological simulator. In it, the simulator's inventor states:

> Some researchers have focused on recording the hand and arm movements the surgeon makes in reference to an instrument, whereas others focus on the 'operative outcome' or end result, such as the quality of an anastomosis. The research reported here suggests it is equally or more important to capture data representing how the user interacts directly with the tissues – either by direct contact (hand to tissue) or by instrument contact with the tissues (instrument to tissue). By placing sensors on the tissues being manipulated, *the data that are captured are more specific to the procedure being performed* than to the physical attributes of the user or how a user interacts with an instrument. (Pugh and Youngblood 2002: 458–459. Emphasis added)

A concern to capture the data '*specific to the procedure being performed*' indicates that the way simulators are being designed takes into account the concept of knowledge as a phenomenon involving practice, though without actually using those terms. To demonstrate this further, I will now turn to an analysis of the interview material gathered while speaking with both the gynaecological simulator's inventor in the US and the woman in the UK who modelled the physical pelvic mannequin which the simulator uses. Through examples from the design and usage practices of this gynaecological simulator, I will show how Barad's theoretical approach to knowledge and materiality can be useful in understanding the complexity of medical simulators. In doing so, I also present a theoretical discussion of why a validated simulator can work in one context, yet be problematic in another.

Simulating the Bimanual Pelvic Exam

As described above, validity is a general concern for those working with medical simulators (Maran and Glavin 2003). It became a specific concern for me when I started to study the use of an imported gynaecological simulator in Sweden. The simulator had been designed to help teach students how to conduct the bimanual pelvic exam. It simulates a female pelvis, with the uterus, ovaries and vagina sitting inside a pelvic cavity and covered by a synthetic skin. The internal organs are fitted with special pressure sensors that can display on the attached computer if the student is 'feeling' in the right place and how hard they are pushing on the internal organs.

At the beginning of this research project, I had travelled to the US to observe a training session with the simulator at a university hospital. The medical students using the simulator there had arrived at the session having previously examined a live patient in their obstetrics and gynaecology course. They were now going to conduct a pelvic examination on the simulator, with the help of an instructor. Their work on the simulator began after the instructor first went through some of the pathologies that can present during a gynaecological exam. She then described to the students how they would conduct a speculum exam and a bimanual exam on the simulator.

The speculum exam entailed gradually inserting a Pederson speculum into the simulator's vaginal cavity and slowly opening it up to observe the cervix. After this was done, the speculum was removed and the bimanual exam was conducted, which consisted of three distinct phases. First the students were to enter the simulated vagina with one hand and feel the cervix. Then, with their other hand pressing downward from on top of the simulated patient's abdomen, the students were to lift the uterus upward with their first hand and feel the presence and size of the uterus (see Figure 6.1). The students were to note when they touched the

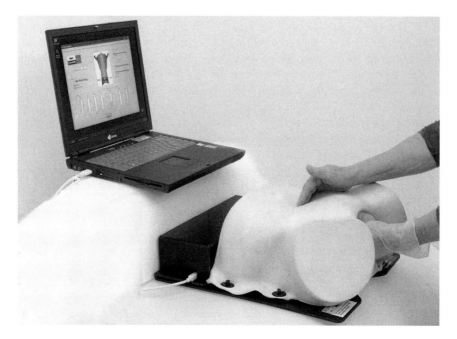

Figure 6.1   The pelvic simulator

fundus[6] of the uterus. Finally the students were to try to feel both ovaries between their internal and external hands.

As the students found and touched each of these organs, the pressure they put on them was measured by the simulator and graphically displayed on the computer screen of the laptop attached to it. At one point, towards the end of the simulation, the instructor mentioned in passing that she would not be able to really know if they were touching the organs if it were not for the pressure displays on the screen. For her work as an instructor, being presented with visual proof of what the students did was helpful. For the students, the visuals were also a way of knowing if they had really touched what they were 'looking for' with their fingers. The simulator not only gave them a model to work on, it gave them feedback about what they were doing.

After the session, the students and instructor all seemed pleased with their simulator training and talked about how the experience related to what they would encounter with patients. This satisfaction with the simulator was not shared by the gynaecologists I was working with back in Sweden. What has triggered my reflections in this article is that it became apparent that the validated simulator which worked in the US (Pugh and Youngblood 2002) was not meeting the

---

6   The fundus is the base of a hollow organ, farthest from its opening, in this case the far tip of the uterus.

demands my Swedish research partners were making of it. They were dissatisfied with the small size of the simulated pelvic bone, the cervix, which they thought was too short, and the firmness of the abdominal wall. And, perhaps most telling, they were dismayed that they could not use the simulator to conduct the pelvic exam that they teach their students; the very same bimanual pelvic exam I had observed in the US, in which a student feels the cervix, feels the fundus and tries to feel the ovaries.

I began to wonder about the source of the negative reaction from the gynaecologists in my research group, and why the simulator could be used to teach a bimanual pelvic exam in one context but not in another. And, since the simulator in question had been validated by experts, how a discussion about its performance in two different contexts could be related to validity. These thoughts lead to reflection over what the simulator is simulating. Surely the whole reason to make valid and realistic simulators is so that they simulate an objective patient body. Medical simulators are designed to simulate patient bodies,[7] and the female body is not that different in the USA, where the simulator was invented, than in Sweden. Unless, perhaps, medical simulators are not actually simulating bodies. Perhaps simulators are simulating something else. But first, a little background about the simulator's history.

When developing the gynaecological simulator, its American inventor worked with a number of different rubber and plastic models of the body already in existence before settling on the model now used. The current model had been on the market, without pressure sensors, for fifteen years before it was adapted to the simulator. When I was talking with the inventor about this process and how she conceptualized of the simulator, an interesting view on the material construction of the artefact came up. Because she had used several different models of the female anatomy in the process of designing her simulator, she had opinions about how the various anatomies they represented were modelled. She felt that some had specific mistakes in the anatomical construction that made their use problematic, and others had been designed for alternative procedures which made their use for the pelvic exam difficult. For example, one of the models she initially tried using had been designed to train students in laparoscopic surgery for tubal ligation, and therefore the plastic that the vagina was made out of was too solid to work when students were attempting a bimanual vaginal examination.. The inventor tried to convince the designer and producer of that model to make the vagina out of a softer latex by photographing the red and chaffed hands of people who examined it, i.e. reintegrating the results of (simulator) practice back into the simulator's design.

During an interview about the design process, her conceptualization of the ideal model indicated a concern with (correct) practice. She said, 'I was thinking abstractly that it didn't have to be a mannequin, it could be some glob. [...] You put your hand in a black hole and it [...] reshapes itself into either a spleen or a

---

7   For an analysis of the gendered body in simulators, see Johnson (2005).

pelvis or whatever, and the bigger element of it was the visual feedback that you got *'so you had an understanding of what you did compared to what the quote unquote experts do'* (emphasis added). For the simulator's inventor, the important aspect was not how realistically the mannequin mimicked the human body. Instead, when conceptualizing of the simulator she was focused on the way the simulator represented a practice, the expert examining the pelvis, and how information about that could be relayed to the person using the simulator. This focus on the practice of using the simulator in relation to the practice of experts giving a pelvic exam, rather than the artefact mimicking the anatomy, also appeared when talking about how the pressure sensors in the pelvic cavity were calibrated. As the sensors register the pressure a person puts on various parts of the internal anatomy, there has to be a way of determining if the touch is purposeful or accidental. To determine this, the inventor conducted a study which registered the average pressure generated when trained and practising gynaecologists examined the simulator. This was then coded into the simulator and used as a benchmark for further exams.

In addition to inserting digital sensors that register touch and pressure to parts of the anatomy, the inventor also changed a few elements of the pelvic model that she finally chose to use. She had a harder plastic inserted in the ovaries, for example, to make them easier to feel and easier to attach sensors to. She also moulded the stubs of legs, which the model originally did not have, to make the simulator look more like a female body from the outside. After making these changes, the UK based designer of the model sent the altered simulator out to a series of medical experts – practising gynaecologists – for their responses and reactions, to see if it was still a 'valid' representation of the female anatomy. The comments that came back from this prototype test, which discussed the way the uterus moved and how solid the ovaries felt during the exam, also speak of the phenomenon of knowing the female body during an exam. The model was judged based on these gynaecologists' reactions to the simulator and comparisons of it with their experiences of live patient's bodies during the pelvic exam, not, as could have been done, on dissections of female cadavers or images or scans of the female body.

One of the more interesting things the inventor had changed about the model was that she demanded the manufacturer package the simulator with an insertable 'fat pad' that could be placed underneath the skin of the abdomen to allow students to practise examining obese women. The fat pad, which is now shipped with each pelvic simulator, is a thin, silicon insert much like a slightly oversized mouse pad. The skin of the abdomen is removed from the pelvic simulator, the fat pad is inserted above the uterus and ovaries in the simulator, and then the skin is put back in place. The reason for having the fat pad is because a significant amount of the bimanual pelvic exam involves pressing upward with the hand that has been inserted into the woman's vagina while simultaneously pressing downwards with the other hand from on top of the abdomen, and then trying to feel parts of the anatomy between the hands, locating and feeling, for example, both of the ovaries. Finding the ovaries during the pelvic exam is difficult to master; the ovaries are relatively small and soft, and it can be difficult to feel them between the hands. In addition, as they are located off to the sides of the uterus, the examiner has to manoeuvre their hand inside the vagina into a position where the ovary can be caught between the internal and external hand. It is even more difficult to feel the ovaries between one's hands if the patient being examined is significantly overweight, and obese patients are becoming more and more common, both in the US and in many other western nations.

Thus, inclusion of the fat pad is a relevant consideration for teaching exams with the pelvic simulator. However, I was surprised by the fact that the simulator's pad was made of a relatively thin layer of silicon. I brought this up with the model's designer, who explained to me that fat in the body is, of course, at body temperature, and when it is that warm it is not very solid. It is bound in small capsules of sorts, but these have a tendency to move around almost (but not quite) like a liquid in parts of the body. Thus, when a patient is lying down on her back during the pelvic exam, the fat in her abdomen tends to slide downwards, off the peak of the stomach. When examining an obese patient's pelvic region, as the hands press up from inside and down from on top of the abdomen, the fat in that area is gently pushed out of the way. Not all of it, of course, but quite a bit of it. Therefore, the 'thin' fat pad gives the feeling that a doctor would have when examining a much larger patient. As the designer told me, 'When you're going in, and someone's got that much fat, it will displace quite a lot [...]. Whereas even though that silicon is very soft, it doesn't displace the same way. [...] It's a matter of judging what is simulated, or how the simulation will equate with the real life.'[8] Significantly, what she is saying is that the fat pad is simulating not the actual body of the patient, since it is not made of a gelatinous, almost liquid substance that moves out of the way and changes its behaviour depending on temperature and position. In the most literal sense of the word, the fat pad is not a valid representation of the body because it does not recreate the physical characteristics of fat. What the fat pad is simulating is the phenomenon of examining an obese patient lying on her back. The simulator then becomes a valid representation of a specific practice, of a specific phenomenon of knowing patient obesity experienced by a doctor during a pelvic exam.

The designer's description of how she thinks of patient fat and simulator fat resonates with Barad's conception of knowledge as constructed in practice. The designer did not use the terms intra-action or *phenomena*, but her design took into consideration how the simulator would be able to reflect the phenomenon of examining an obese patient, rather than simply creating an obese simulator. Just as Barad, when writing about how ways of knowing and reality are mutually constituting during scientific experiments, states that '*observations do not refer to objects of an independent reality*' (Barad 1996: 170, emphasis in the original), the designer seems to recognize that it is the way a doctor observes the obese patient's body, the practice of observing and creating knowledge, which should

---

8   Interview with model designer of the simulator, January 2005.

be simulated, not the body as an object independent of epistemology. When knowledge about the body that has been gleaned through practice is reified into a simulator, that specific phenomenon of knowing the body is simulated, not the ontologically independent body as such.

Barad uses the term agential reality to explain the practices of phenomena that create our knowledge about the world. She draws her original inspiration for this theory from the work on quantum physics by Nils Bohr. Using his explanation of light, a point of contention within the physics community at the beginning of the 20th century, Barad explains how Bohr asserted that light can be both a particle and a wave, depending on the apparatus of measurement used to examine light. What light is becomes dependent on the way it is measured or observed. From this example, Barad posits that *concepts are defined by the circumstances required for their measurements* (Barad 1996: 169–170). Light, and everything else, can not be separated from the way it is experienced. The phenomenon of knowing something is what determines what is known. As she states, '*Phenomena are constitutive of reality*'. Reality is not composed of things-in-themselves or things-behind-phenomena, but things-in-phenomena. ... What is being described is our participation *within* nature' (Barad 1996: 176). She calls this participation within nature agential reality. Fundamental to an agential realist analysis is that phenomena become the basic unit of existence, not subjects and objects. 'That is, phenomena are ontologically primitive relations – relations without pre-existing relata' (Barad 2003: 815).

The concept of intra-action is used in the theory of agential reality to explain the details and actors in the practice of knowledge phenomena. By using the neologism intra-action, Barad makes the point that within the theoretical framework of agential reality, the distinction between subjects and objects as separate entities, a dichotomy of knower and known, is erased. The term dissolves the boundary between objects and 'agencies of observation'. Intra-action signifies that the object of knowledge can not be separated from the way, the practice or phenomenon that makes it known. It is in contrast to the more common term interaction, which reinscribes the separateness of the object and the method of observation (Barad 1998: 96). Intra-action reflects Barad's dismissal of representationalism, of the 'belief in the ontological distinction between representations and that which they purport to represent' (Barad 2003: 804). The referent and the object of observation (and by extension the person doing the observing) become intra-acting subunits of a phenomenon, all of which are necessary components for the phenomenon to be observed. And what is described by the observations is not nature, but the intra-active participation of all the subunits (Barad 1998: 105). Analytically, the term intra-action becomes useful because it articulates the local, specific practices involved in making what Barad calls agential cuts. It provides a way of analysing the details in knowledge practices. It can show, for example, how a fat pad and an examiner's hand can intra-act in a way that simulates examining an obese patient even though the fat pad does not change consistency with temperature changes or move loosely throughout a cavity like human fatty tissue.

As mentioned earlier, Barad's work draws inspiration from Judith Butler's theories about gender and performativity (Butler 1990) when she asserts that technoscientific practices are also performed, and it is in the performance that knowledge is created (Barad 1998: 105). She also acknowledges the inspiration of Haraway's (1998) examination of situated knowledge for the development of her theory (Barad 1996: 166). But agential reality expands on situated knowledge by creating a way to activate the concept of situated knowledges in analysis of scientific practice through observations of practice and phenomena of knowing. In addition, and of particular interest, agential reality and intra-action expand the work of Butler and Haraway to include artefacts. By making phenomena the base unit of analysis, the concept of intra-action becomes a particularly useful tool for thinking about how we relate to the world and to technology, and, as Suchman (1998, see also 2007) notes, for considering what happens in the relations between humans and non-humans. Relying heavily on Barad's concept of intra-action in an article that considers agency for persons and artefacts, Suchman points out that 'it matters when things travel across the human–artifact boundary, when objects are subjectified (e.g. machines made not actants but actors) and subjects objectified (e.g. practices made methods, knowledges made commodities)' (Suchman 1998:11). Using the concept of agential reality, one can begin to pay attention to 'travel across the human–artefact boundary'.

Agential reality differs from (some) Actor Network Theory (ANT) (see Law 1987, Latour 1999) in that it does not merely include artefacts through the concept of symmetry and actant; it lifts the unit of analysis from actants and networks to the phenomena that create both artefacts and actors. It also places agency in the relationships between people and material artefacts, rather than with people and/ or material artefacts. 'According to agential realism, agency is a matter of intra-acting; it is an enactment, not something someone or something has. Agency cannot be designated as an attribute of 'subjects' or 'objects' (as they do not pre-exist as such)' (Barad 2001: 236, see also Suchman 1998). One of the criticisms of ANT has been that it is possible to interpret the term actant in such a way that agency is attributed to things and thereby can appear to make humans and non-humans equal, through the concept of symmetry, which hides issues of power in our relationships with the world (see Star 1991). And while ANT actually has only proposed that things and people be treated symmetrically in analysis, which is slightly different, and later ANT analyses have tended to look at enacted relationships as well, the concept of symmetry disguises the fact that 'humans and artifacts do not appear to constitute each other in the same way' (Suchman 1998: 11). Barad's concept of intra-action is able, through the emphasis on phenomena as the unit of analysis, to explain how non-human objects can be implicated in the question of agency, since agency must be seen as relational in the intra-active practices of knowledge phenomena.[9] Analysing the pelvic simulator with the concept of intra-action can explain not only that it works in one context and not in another, but why. It is

---

9   See also Mol and Law (2004) for a discussion of the body as subject and object.

easy to look at a medical simulator and assume it is a representation of the body. However, a simulator is really a representation of specific phenomena of knowing the body, which makes simulators representations of practices, practices that can vary from one context to the next.

Looking again at the bimanual pelvic exam, small, contextual differences appear between the US and Sweden.[10] Some of the differences involve interactions with the patient, and are a result of issues specific to the public/private display of the body.[11] For example, the Swedish and US exams can vary in the way eye contact is made or avoided with the patient, and how/if the patient's body is covered during an exam. But some of the differences are found in the actual medical practices of the exam. These have become reflected in the way the simulator is built and refracted by the change in context. So, for example, the simulator allows for the fundus of the uterus to be pressed up against the top of the abdominal wall and felt from above, from outside of the patient's abdomen. Feeling the fundus in this way, according to interviews with the inventor and the pelvic exam guidebook that is shipped with the simulator, is typical procedure for a (US) pelvic exam. However, the Swedish gynaecologists I work with have a different method of examining the uterus. Their exam, which they currently teach using professional patients rather than a simulator, involves pressing the uterus up against the abdominal wall and then tilting it forward, so that the examiner's hand outside of the abdomen is able to feel firmly down through the abdomen and examine the back side of the uterus, checking for possible growths on this otherwise un-observed area of the body.

A human body is flexible enough to allow for the uterus to be tilted forward during an examination. The simulator, however, is not. In the simulator the uterus is firmly connected to the plastic encasing that represents the pelvic bone and cavity, and it is not possible to flip the uterus up and backwards to examine the back side of the organ. Thus the simulator facilitates the less invasive US examination of the uterus, but not the Swedish method.[12]

The difference between examination practices and the way the anatomical representation works in one context but not in another, beg the question of how

---

10   The US and Sweden are very large categories. I use them here for the purpose of argument, but I am aware that local practices can also vary between examination rooms within the US and within Sweden.

11   See Heath (1986) and Pilnick and Hindmarsh (1999) for a discussion of this in other fields of medicine.

12   This difference is something to consider when teaching with the simulator, but it is not necessarily a fatal flaw, even for teaching the Swedish exam. At one level, this physical construction of the simulator can dictate what methods of examination it is used to teach. At another, however, it can not. The fact that the uterus does not move like a 'human' uterus and can not be examined in the same way as a woman is usually examined by the gynaecologists I work with offers a discussion point for the contrasts between a simulator and a human, and between the different methods of examination during a teaching session. It allows for Swedish medical practices to be reconstituted verbally despite the physical difficulties involved in feeling the back side of the uterus.

we can understand and determine validity in the case of simulated human bodies. I suggest that Barad's concept of intra-action is a useful way of approaching this issue. To understand it, one must shy away from simple representationalism and think of phenomena as the basic units of knowing. The first step towards doing so, when working with medical simulators, is to acknowledge that practice is the ontological basis upon which they are constructed, not an objective, epistemologically independent human anatomy.

Discussion

When it comes to thinking about how simulators are conceived of and constructed, how the valid medical body is replicated, agential reality demands that we include practice in our understanding of the object (Barad 1996: 182).[13] In Barad's theory of agential reality, it is phenomena that create reality, so it is the phenomenon of knowing the body which is built into simulators. I conclude this chapter by suggesting that it is important to recognize phenomenon as the basis of attempts to mimic the human patient in medical simulators for both theoretical and practical reasons.

During the course of my research, I saw that the pelvic simulator actually simulated the pelvic anatomy as known in a US pelvic exam. It did not really simulate a Swedish pelvic exam anatomy. There are differences in how a bimanual pelvic exam is conducted between the two countries, and these differences in practice become apparent when a material object is constructed to facilitate that practice. More interestingly, these differences highlight the fact that the gynaecological simulator is only an anatomy for a pelvic exam, which is not the same thing as a reproduction of the female pelvic anatomy.

Simulators do provide models of the patient body, but the body being modelled in the simulator is actually the *experienced* body. The importance of the *experienced* body is why, for example, during the development and testing phases, simulators are built in conjunction with experts who can demonstrate and evaluate the way medical knowledge is experienced as a phenomenon.

Concern with model validity appeared in my fieldwork with the gynaecological simulator. The inventor and the designer of the pelvic simulator both expressed concern that the simulator provide feedback on a phenomenon – a medical practice – and that the represented body be a realistic recreation of the experienced body. The inventor's concept of an 'amorphous glob' whose primary task is to provide feedback on practice in comparison to the experts showed a concern for practice and methods of evaluating practice, rather than ways to simulate the body. The modeller's design of the fat pad also demonstrated an appreciation for the intra-action between the doctor and the patient body in creating medical knowledge of

---

13 'Agential realism includes practice within theory – theory is epistemologically and ontologically reflexive of context' (Barad 1996: 182).

the obese body. The fat pad represents the practice of knowing the obese body rather than the reproduction of fatty tissue. This specific phenomenon of knowing obesity, primarily through the tactile, was then integrated into a simulator which also relies on the tactile, using a physically constructed model. Aside from the obvious implications for simulator design, the observation of how the obese body is known during a gynaecological exam also contributes to a sociological understanding of how knowledge about the body is created through social phenomena.

One implication this has is on our theoretical understandings of simulators. For medical practitioners and simulator developers, acknowledging the fundamental place that phenomena have in their work can emphasize the value of considering which experts are appropriate to use and what those specific expertises say about the standardizing of medical practice, in much the same way that analysis of anatomies has shown how these images standardized and legitimated certain culturally and historically specific ways to see and conceptualize of the body (see Laqueur 1990, Jordanova 1999, Schiebinger 1993). The body built into the simulator has a history, as models and understandings of a body do. But my analysis of the simulator shows that the history of the simulated body is a history of knowing the body in practice, and in very context specific medical practices. Because these practices are context specific, there is a political implication to constructing simulators that recreate and represent certain practices as medical norms. Feminist critiques have shown how medical practices (re)produce the female body (Cussins 1998, Diedrich 2007, Fausto-Sterling 2000, Jordanova 1999, Maines 1999, Martin 1992, Oudshoorn 1994) and these critiques are just as salient in an analysis of the simulators that reify those practices. Understanding that simulators are representing practice means that we must start to think about which practices are being recreated and taught to new medical practitioners, and start to ask how and why these practices are being standardized, rather than assuming that the simulator apolitically and objectively mimics an ontologically 'true' patient body.

Realizing that it is phenomena of knowledge that are being simulated, and not the body, also holds specific, practical, implications for those tasked with evaluating the simulators. Focusing on the measurements of the body and the standards it reproduces may not actually say that much about the validity of the simulator. Instead, considering the simulator as a representation of practice will demand the development of tools that can analyse and evaluate practice, both in the clinic and the classroom. Using experts to do this is a step in the right direction, but it should be reflective practice.

Another result of viewing simulators as reifications of practice is that their design process then demands methods to gather information about practice, rather than only relying on measurements or images of the body. Acknowledging that practice is simulated by the simulator explains why the 'anatomically correct' uterus works in one context but not in another. But there is more political capital to this argument than that. Acknowledging the fundamental aspects of practice in simulator development creates the discursive space to ask *whose* practice is being simulated; Experts'? Which experts? Which medical professionals are being made invisible? And what about patients? I ask this last question because in the work constellations of developers, designers and medical experts who cooperate in the tasks of simulator design and testing, the *patient's* experience of a medical practice is not merely silenced or made invisible, it is never even considered. But it could be otherwise. One could imagine a simulator which integrates how patients understand certain medical procedures, which integrates patient-specific phenomena of knowing medical practices.

Returning to the pelvic simulator and the practices of gynaecology, it is worth reflecting on the specific ways the body parts of the simulator are laden with meaning and how these meanings are manifested or silenced in the simulator. Again, here, one can examine the practices of the gynaecological examination for answers. Interviews with professional patients (women who allow students to train the pelvic exam on their bodies while also instructing the students in bedside manners) suggest that professional patients experience the gynaecological exam in ways that are not measured by the pressure sensitive sensors of the pelvic simulator. These women are concerned with how students approach them before the exam, the eye contact that is made during the examination, and the discretion with which certain topics are broached and discussed. Other, physical, aspects of the exam are experienced by the patients, too, besides just the pressure used to find internal organs. For example, the temperature of the examination equipment can be a significant aspect of the patient's experience, but is not recorded at all during the simulation. One could ask how incorporating these issues would change the simulator. Emphasizing that medical knowledge of the body is created through phenomena opens the discursive space in simulator design necessary to think about how, and by whom, medical procedures are experienced. This space can also let us think about the value of including patient experiences of medical practice in simulator design.

References

Al-khalifah, A. and Roberts, D.J. 2004. Survey of modelling approaches for medical simulators. *Proceedings of the 5th International Conference on Disability, Virtual Reality and Associate Technologies*, edited by ICDVRAT. Oxford: University of Reading Press, 321–329.

Barad, K. 1996. Meeting the universe halfway: Realism and social constructivism without contradiction, in *Feminism, Science, and the Philosophy of Science*, edited by L.H. Nelson and J. Nelson. London: Kluwer Academic Publishers, 161–194.

Barad, K. 1998. Getting real: Technoscientific practices and the materialization of reality. *Differences – A Journal of Feminist Cultural Studies* 10(2), 87–128.

Barad, K. 2001. Scientific literacy → agential literacy = (learning ? doing) science responsibly, in *Feminist Science Studies*, edited by M. Mayberry, B. Subramaniam and L. Weasel. Routledge: London, 226–246.

Barad, K. 2003. Posthumanist performativity: Toward an understanding of how matter comes to matter. *Signs: Journal of Women in Culture and Society*, 28(3), 801–831.

Barad, K. 2007. *Meeting the Universe Half-Way*. Durham: Duke University Press.

Baudrillard, J. 1994. *Simulacra and Simulation*. Translated by S. F. Glaser. Ann Arbor: University of Michigan. Originally published in French by Editions Galilee, 1981.

Butler, J. 1990. *Gender Trouble: Feminism and the subversion of identity*. London: Routledge.

Cartwright, L. 1998. A cultural anatomy of the visible human project, in *The Visible Woman: Imaging technologies, gender, and science*, edited by P. Treichler, L. Cartwright and C. Penley. New York: New York University Press, 21–43.

Cussins, C. 1998. Ontological choreography: Agency for women patients in an infertility clinic, in *Differences in Medicine*, edited by M. Berg and A. Mol, Duke University Press, 166–201.

Dawson, S. and Kaufman, J. 1998. The imperative for medical simulation. *Proceedings of the IEEE*, 86(3), 479–483.

de Laet, M. and Mol., A. 2000. The Zimbabwe bush pump. Mechanics of a fluid technology. *Social Studies of Science*, 30(2), 225–263.

Diedrich, L. 2007. *Treatments. Language, politics and the culture of illness*. University of Minnesota Press: Minneapolis.

Dugdale, A. 2000. Materiality: Juggling sameness and difference, in *Actor Network Theory and After*, edited by J. Law and J. Hassard. Oxford: Blackwell, 2000, 113–135.

Fausto-Sterling, A. 2000. *Sexing the Body: Gender politics and the construction of sexuality*. New York: Basic Books.

Good, M. L. 2003. Patient simulation for training basic and advanced clinical skills. *Medical Education*, 37(suppl. 1), 14–21.

Haraway, D. 1998. Situated knowledges: The science question in feminism as a site of discourse on the privilege of partial perspective. *Feminist Studies*, 14(3), 575–599.

Harding, S. 1991. *Whose Science? Whose Knowledge?* Ithaca: Cornell University Press.

Heath, C. 1986. *Body Movement and Speech in Medical Interaction*. Cambridge: Cambridge University Press.

Johnson, E. 2004. *Situating Simulators: The integration of simulations in medical practice*. Lund: Arkiv.

Johnson, E. 2005. The ghost of anatomies past: Simulating the one-sex body in modern medical training. *Feminist Theory*, 6(2), 141–159.

Jordanova, L. 1999. *Nature Displayed: Gender, science and medicine 1760–1820*. London: Longman.

Laqueur, T. 1990. *Making Sex: Body and gender from the Greeks to Freud*. London: Harvard University Press.

Latour, B. 1988. Mixing humans and nonhumans together: The sociology of a door-closer. *Social Problems*, 35(3), 298–310.

Latour, B. 1999. *Pandora's Hope: Essays on the reality of science studies*. London: Harvard University Press.

Law, J. 1987. Technology and heterogeneous engineering: The case of Portuguese expansion, in *The Social Construction of Technological Systems*, edited by W.E. Bijker, T.P. Hughes and T. Pinch. Boston: MIT Press, 111–134.

Law, J. and Singleton, V. 2005. Object lessons. *Organization*, 12(3), 331–255.

Maines, R. 1999. *The Technology of Orgasm*. John Hopkins University Press.

Maran, N.J. and Glavin, R.J. 2003. Low- to high-fidelity simulation – a continuum of medical education? *Medical Education*, 37(suppl. 1), 22–28.

Martin, E. 1992. *The Woman in the Body: A cultural analysis of reproduction*. Boston: Beacon Press.

McCloy, R. and Stone, R. 2001. Virtual reality in surgery. *British Medical Journal*, 323(7318), 912–915.

Mol, A. 2002. *The Body Multiple: Ontology in medical practice*. Durham: Duke University Press.

Mol, A. and Law, J. 2004. Embodied action, enacted bodies: The example of hypoglycaemia. *Body & Society*, 10(2–3), 43–62.

Oudshoorn, N. 1994. *Beyond the Natural Body: An archaeology of sex hormones*. London: Routledge.

Oudshoorn, N. 2003. *The Male Pill: A biography of a technology in the making*. Durham: Duke University Press.

Papadopoulos, E., Viachos, K. and Mitropoulos, D. 2002. *On the Design of a Low-Force 5 DOF Force – Feedback Haptic Mechanism*, Proceedings of the DETC – Design Engineering Technical Conferences and Computers and Information in Engineering Conference. Montreal, Canada, 29 September–2 October 2002.

Pilnick, A. and Hindmarsh, J. 1999. 'When you wake up it'll all be over': Communication in the anaesthetic room. *Symbolic Interaction*, 22(4), 345–360.

Prentice, R. 2005. The anatomy of surgical simulation: The mutual articulation of bodies in and through the machine. *Social Studies of Science*, 35(6), 837–866.

Pugh C. and Youngblood, P. 2002. Development and validation of assessment measures for a newly developed physical examination simulator. *Journal of the American Medical Informatics Association*, 9(5), 448–460.

Schiebinger, L. 1993. *Nature's Body: Gender in the making of modern science*. Boston: Beacon Press.

Schuwirth, L.W.T. and van der Vleuten, C.P.M. 2003. The use of clinical simulations in assessment. *Medical Education*, 37(suppl. 1), 65–71.

Shaw, M., Maxwell, R., Rees, K., Ho, D., Oliver, S., Ben-Shlomo, Y. and Ebrahim, S. 2004. Gender and age inequity in the provision of coronary revascularisation in England in the 1990s: is it getting better? *Social Science and Medicine*, 59(12), 2499–2507.

Star, S.L. 1991. Power, technology, and the phenomenology of conventions: on being allergic to onions, in *A Sociology of Monsters: Essays on power, technology and domination*, edited by J. Law. London: Routledge, 22–56.

Starr, P. 1982. *The Social Transformation of American Medicine*. New York: Basic Books.

Suchman, L. 1998. *Human/Machine Reconsidered. Cognitive Studies*, 5(1), 5–13.

Suchman, L. 2007. *Human–Machine Reconfigurations. Plans and Situated Actions*, 2nd edition. Cambridge: Cambridge University Press.

Thacker, E. 1999. Performing the Technoscientific Body: RealVideo Surgery and the Anatomy Theater. *Body & Society*, 5(2–3), 317–336.

Tsai, T-C., Harasym, P.H., Nijssen-Jordan, C., Jennett, P. and Powell, G. 2003. The quality of a simulation examination using a high-fidelity child manikin. *Medical Education*, 37(suppl. 1), 72–78.

Van Meurs, W.L., Couto, P.M. Sá, Couto, C.D. Sá, Bernardes, J.F. and Ayres-de-Campos, D. 2003. Development of foetal and neonatal simulators at the University of Porto. *Medical Education*, 37(suppl. 1), 29–33.

Waldby, C. 1999. IatroGenesis: The visible human project and the reproduction of life. *Australian Feminist Studies*, 14(29), 77–90.

Waldby, C. 2000. *The Visible Human Project: Informatic bodies and posthuman medicine*. London: Routledge.

Winner, L. 1980. Do artifacts have politics? *Daedalus*, 109(1), 121–136.

Woolgar, S. and Cooper, G. 1999. Do artefacts have ambivalence? Moses' bridges, winner's bridges and other urban legends in S&TS. *Social Studies of Science*, 29(3), 433–449.

Wright, M.C., Taekman, J.M. and Endsley, M.R. 2004. Objective measures of situation awareness in a simulated medical environment. *Quality & Safety in Health Care* 13(suppl. 1), 65–71.

PART 3
Linking Bodies and Machines

In the last part of this book, we address what machines do, what kind of medical practices and health care they help accomplish and how this is done. In focus are the everyday activities to 'localize' artefacts within local networks of tools, practices, professionals and patients, in order to make treatment, or any other action, possible in health care (cf Berg 1997, Timmermans and Berg 2003). Such activities, the chapters discuss, involve complex interpretations and enactments to establish linkages between humans and machines, between the 'material' and the 'social'. They involve practical tinkering, reasoning and emotion work to assess meanings and establish trust.

Socio-technologies, as shown in Part 2 of this book, reflect local practices and established orderings but also interpretations and negotiations between heterogeneous actors. These ambiguities are carried into the practices to make technologies work. As demonstrated in the following chapters, local contingencies demand efforts of sense-making, of tinkering and articulation of loose ends. Such messy, real-time work is a prerequisite for any technology to persist (Berg and Timmermans 2000, Berner 2008, Thelander 2003). Machines gain significance and sense – or not – as part of ongoing interactions, locally shared meanings, experiences and practicalities (Heath, Luff and Sanchez Svensson 2003).

Thus, there is an uncertain and ultimately undecided character to technologies-in-use. There is precariousness, both in relation to the making of 'links' (associations between humans and machines) and the institution of 'cuts' (differences between humans and machines) (Moreira 2000: 442). There are ambiguities and contradictions, as humans try to understand what devices can do and what they are, in order to negotiate the linkages and ontological differences between their actions and those of machines.

Such boundaries, or cuts, between machine and human appear in the analysis of a birthing monitor by Petra Jonvallen, the first chapter in Part 3. Considering birth as a transformation from a state of no distinction to distinction and the role of birthing monitors in this process, Jonvallen explores the feelings she experienced in a maternity ward in this painfully honest chapter. Rather than creating a narrative of detached observation by ignoring how she as an outsider reacted to the emotional and physical environment, she explores her response through the concept of the abject. Jonvallen presents foetal monitoring technology as a figure at the border of the subject and the other. In her analysis, emotions are a material effect of technological practice, considered a communicative performance located in power relations. She reflects on the boundary between the human body and medical technology, and the emotion work necessary to repress and control feelings awoken by the indistinct boundary.

Scientific medicine has been shown to be an amalgam of practices and beliefs, compromises, redefinitions, contested interpretations and temporary solutions (Waldby 2000: 466, Berg and Mol 1998, Singleton 1998). In Chapter 8, Corinna Kruse addresses ambiguity in such scientific work – in this case, work to establish the 'truth' of biomedical 'facts', and the practical and ontological links and cuts between humans and machines that such work entails. Her ethnographic study of genetic research laboratories explores how staff transforms samples into valid data. Through observations and interviews, she demonstrates that the boundary between humans and machines in the laboratory, which she explores as an arbitrary 'cut' using the ideas of Karen Barad (e.g. Barad 1998), is an essential part of producing valid data. Humans, in her material, were presented as prone to unreliable decisions, which threatened to make the data subjective. Machines, on the other hand, were objective. Yet this cut between what was considered 'human' and what was 'machine' was not a given of the technological constellations found in the labs. Rather, this was produced and reproduced through cultural practices related to agency. Classifications of machinelike and humanlike were fluid and crossed conceptual boundaries, which served to maintain the cut between humans and machines used to support the production of 'objective' data, even when 'machines' malfunctioned or required coaxing to produce data that was 'free' from human intentions.

Technological interventions and innovations which erase otherwise physical boundaries between bodies also appear in the final chapter of this section. Boel Berner traces the historical development of a complex sociotechnical system around blood donation. Her work explores the messy origins and gradual evolution of standardized practices in Sweden between 1915 and 1950, and shows how the micro-situation of blood donation changed over time. Tracing local assemblages of artefacts, practices, people and notions of blood, Berner's chapter demonstrates how the relationship between donors and recipients changed over time, altering what it meant to donate blood and who was implicated in the practice. Devices and humans were being calibrated and mutually constituted in first local, then national networks (cf. Prout 1996). From being a concern of individual surgeons, hospitals or donors, blood donation during this period became a topic for official public attention and national coordination; technologies thus partook as mediators in the construction and reproduction of novel professions, bodies and identities. Also in these developments there was no uniformity, but divergences and differences between national settings. Blood donation practices did travel across borders but not unchanged; techniques and devices were adopted, adapted or rejected depending on historical circumstances, culture or national health care organization (cf. Copeman 2009).

Together, the three chapters show how meanings of machines and humans are fluid and locally negotiated, and how the uses of tools and devices depend upon but also alter established patterns of power and experience. They also, along with the other chapters in this book, illustrate the fruitfulness of different methodological and theoretical approaches to the local and contingent. Jonvallen's chapter is based on observations and interviews among doctors and midwives; her presentation of the research integrates and interrogates her own responses to the boundary between human and machine. Kruse takes a more anthropological approach. Relying on Geertz's concept of culture as a web of significance, she studies laboratory practices as cultural practices, as a collective way of creating and communicating meaning. Her chapter also applies the theoretical lens of agential reality to illustrate the implications of differences being delineated between people and machines. Finally, and like Robert's work in the first part of this book, Berner relies on textual material, primarily physicians' accounts in medical journals and archival material. But her material is historical rather than contemporary, which engenders a different sort of narrative, tracing the multiple contexts within which humans and devices were separated or aligned. Thus, all three authors bring forward a respect for the importance of local linkages and practices, and medical work as something contingent, uncertain and changing in their studies of blood, guts and machines.

References

Barad, K. 1998. Getting real: Technoscientific practices and the materialization of reality. *Differences – A Journal of Feminist Cultural Studies*, 10(2), 87–128.

Berg, M. 1997. *Rationalizing Medical Work: Decision-support techniques and medical practices*. Cambridge: The MIT Press.

Berg, M. and Mol, A. (eds). 1998. *Differences in Medicine: Unraveling practices, techniques, and bodies*. Durham: Duke University Press.

Berg, M. and Timmermans, S. 2000. Orders and their others: On the constitution of universalities in medical work. *Configurations*, 8(1), 31–61.

Berner, B. 2008. Working knowledge as performance. On the practical understanding of machines. *Work, Employment and Society*, 22(2), 319–336.

Copeman, J. 2009. Introduction: Blood donation, bioeconomy, culture. *Body & Society*, 15(1), 1–28.

Heath, C., Luff, P. and Sanchez Svensson, M. 2003. Technology and medical practice. *Sociology of Health & Illness*, 25 (Silver Anniversary Issue), 75–96.

Moreira, T. 2000. Translation, difference and ontological fluidity: Cerebral angiography and neurosurgical practice (1926–45). *Social Studies of Science*, 30(3), 421–446.

Prout, A. 1996. Actor-network theory, technology and medical sociology: an illustrative analysis of the metered dose inhaler. *Sociology of Health and Illness*, 18(2), 198–219.

Singleton, V. 1998. Stabilizing instabilities: The role of the laboratory in the United Kingdom cervical screening programme, in *Differences in Medicine*.

Unraveling Practices, Techniques, and Bodies, edited by M. Berg and A. Mol. Durham NC and London: Duke University Press, 86–104.

Thelander, S. 2003. The social construction of safety in the face of fear and distrust: the case of cardiac intensive care, in *Constructing Risk and Safety in Technological Practice*, edited by J. Summerton and B. Berner. London: Routledge, 157–174.

Timmermans, S. and Berg, M. 2003. The practice of medical technology. *Sociology of Health and Illness*, 25 (Silver Anniversary Issue), 97–114.

Waldby, C. 2000. Fragmented bodies, incoherent medicine. *Social Studies of Medicine*, 30(3), 465–475.

Chapter 7
Emotion Work, Abjection and Electronic Foetal Monitoring

Petra Jonvallen

This chapter's focus on emotions in medical practice came out of my own difficulty in remaining emotionally detached during the birthings I witnessed during my fieldwork at a Swedish university hospital birthing centre. My research there examined how a new, evidence-based technique was being introduced into birthing practices, to build an understanding of why introduction was difficult despite the scientific evidence of its merits. In a recent article in the *British Journal of Midwifery*, midwife Gould (2006) maintains that emotion and 'instinct drive' govern British maternity services, and argues that future developments should instead be grounded in 'evidence'. At play here is a clear and traditional juxtaposing of (subjective) emotion and (objective) scientific evidence familiar in discussions of many medical practices. Such dichotomization of emotion versus scientific knowledge is historically a longstanding one, in which emotional experience is symbolically construed as female and rational science as male (Lloyd 1993). Ultimately, this dichotomization has to do with power relations since it is those with low status who are accused of being emotional and often blamed as behaving irrationally. Feminists and others have criticized this simplistic dichotomy and tried to promote experiences such as emotion as a basis for knowledge production (for example Jaggar 1989, Harding and Pribram 2004). In so doing, they have demonstrated how science can indeed be emotional and emotions rational; how thought can be sensitive and emotion 'sharp' (see Nussbaum 2001). Sociologist Ian Burkitt explains that emotions 'have a pattern to them that follows a relational "logic"'. This relational logic, furthermore, is related to power, and he argues that we cannot 'separate people's emotional responses and judgements of value from the power relations in which they are located' (Burkitt 2005: 5).

Studying emotions has been and is still largely a domain for the 'psy' disciplines, such as psychology, psychiatry and psychoanalysis, fields in which emotions traditionally have been seen as internal and private states (Lupton 1998). There are many other instances, however, where emotions are an object of study, such as in sociology (Hochschild [1983] 2003, Thoits 1989), anthropology (Lutz and Abu-Lughod 1990) and cultural studies (Ahmed 2004, Harding and Pribram 2004). Taken together, such research can be seen to represent a view of emotions that analyses them as 'in and about social life' (Lutz and Abu-Lughod 1990: 11) rather than simply in and about an inner self. Consequently, expressing and dealing with emotions should be understood 'as pragmatic acts and communicative performances' (Lutz and Abu-Lughod 1990: 11). This implies a non-essentialist notion of feelings as being co-constructed with specific circumstances in specific locations. In the words of anthropologist Rosaldo, 'the life of feeling is an aspect of the social world in which its terms are found' (Rosaldo 1984: 145). Emotions, in other words, say something about the social world in which they observably emanate; they are, however, also idiomatic expressions not always conscious or easily observable.

Recent studies analysing various technologies used in medical practice have focused on the relationship between technology and practice, claiming that one should be seen as affecting the other (Berg 1997, Mol 2002). These studies also highlight the roles of nonhuman subjects in medical practices and hence that there is a materiality that affects technology/practice. Emotions, I argue, are one such material effect that must be included in the analysis. I will use my own failure to act in a detached manner as a starting point for analysing the terms in which technology is introduced in medical practice. If emotions are a kind of communicative performance located in power relations, they need to be included in any analysis of today's often hierarchical and increasingly rationalized health care system.

Foetal Monitoring in a Swedish Clinic

My discussion is based on fieldwork performed at a Swedish birthing centre where, in late 2005, a new method of intrapartum foetal monitoring, STAN, was being introduced. The fieldwork was done over four months in early 2006. During these four months, I spent seven workdays, from seven in the morning to three in the afternoon, shadowing four different midwives and one assistant nurse. I also took part in the courses given by the medical technology company selling the intrapartum monitoring device, and spent many hours in the coffee/lunch room of the clinic talking to people there who had the time. When the coffee room was empty, as it often was on busy days, I sat in the control room to observe. In addition, I conducted fifteen interviews, mainly with midwives.

The new monitoring technology, STAN, is designed to replace foetal monitoring through cardiotocography (CTG), a method in use since the seventies in births defined as risky. STAN combines the widely used CTG with foetal electrocardiography. The main benefit of STAN is that it can help diagnose foetal oxygen deficiency during labour. Previous methods to identify foetuses suffering from oxygen deficiency rely on analysis of blood samples taken from the foetus' scalp. Such tests only indicate the state of the foetus at the time the test is taken, however, and taking scalp blood tests can be technically difficult. STAN, in contrast, monitors the ST segment of the electrocardiogram more or less in real time. It is the first foetal monitoring technique that provides good scientific results (Amer-Wåhlin 2003, Impey et al. 2003). It has been shown to decrease the number of babies suffering from oxygen deficiency by 54 per cent, and the number of invasive procedures (i.e., caesarean, forceps and vacuum extraction) by 18 per cent (Amer-Wåhlin et al. 2001). All in all, STAN offers more detailed surveillance and measurement of the foetal heart during birthing.

By the time of my fieldwork, STAN had already been introduced in most larger Swedish hospitals, although it was actually being used to varying degrees. Local guidelines had projected that STAN would be used in approximately 20 per cent of births. Buying the monitoring device, as with most other advanced equipment, involves a significant educational commitment that is apparently difficult to carry through at many clinics. At the site of my fieldwork, there were approximately ninety people working in the clinic who needed proper instruction in how to use the technology, something the head doctor referred to as a 'gigantic commitment'. Since the clinic had only fairly recently undergone a large-scale and somewhat unpopular reorganization, she expressed reluctance to make any further changes related to introducing a new method. The head doctor was thus very motivated to learn from the experiences of other clinics that had introduced the monitor, to avoid making already known mistakes. As she was somewhat sceptical toward learning only from the medical technology company ('They're salespeople … it's from my colleagues I will get the truth'), she had managed to get some funding to make a field trip to a hospital that had already undergone the 'teething problems' connected with introducing the method. Her greatest concern was how to introduce something new into a group of assumedly resistant midwives who had already expressed reservations about having 'yet another machine in the room'. From previous experience of using STAN in different clinics, it is generally understood that it is difficult to 'get staff to use it', meaning both doctors and midwives. The head doctor explained what it was she wanted from her field trip:

> … it was the introduction itself that I was interested in. How did it work in practice? What did people think about it? Were they afraid of the machine? Was it natural? Did it compete [i.e., with the birthing woman for attention]? Did it interfere with contact with the patient? Those were the questions I asked. It was a lot about personal meetings, not so much about factual knowledge.

Several assumptions underlie these questions: that it is difficult to introduce this new technology, that people tend to be afraid to use it, and that there is a risk staff will see it as conflicting with 'natural' birthing. Moreover, these questions imply that personnel do tend to see technology as interfering with the patient–clinician relationship.

In his book, *Rationalizing Medical Work*, Marc Berg (1997) analyses a set of rationalizing tools used in medical practice to avoid mistakes in everyday clinical decision-making. Built into these tools is expert or scientific knowledge of specific scenarios, knowledge designed to help individual doctors make scientifically informed decisions. Berg notes that both critics and advocates of these tools 'debate the nature of the tool and practice' (Berg 1997: 161). In so doing, both sides reify either the tool or the practice in a 'foundationalist' manner, overlooking that the qualities of both are not pre-determined, but rather constructed in relation to each other. Thus, there is no unidirectional process whereby a tool only has 'effects' on practice: medical practice and the tool are mutually shaped in specific situations. This means that predictions as to how the introduction of new tools will work out, or how they will potentially shift the control of decision-making and deskill the users in a specific practice, are not self-evident.

A site of practice consists of several different kinds of actors with specific histories, routines and interests, and there are local variations in particular sites as to how a tool is used. Berg has studied different types of rationalizing tools in the medical situations in which they were used, and argues that no tool is used exactly in the same way in every single location. He demonstrates how different staff members 'localize' the tools to make them work in particular situations (1997: 152). The tool may be said to discipline practice, but practice can never be fully disciplined. In getting a tool to work, the two processes of localization and disciplining occur simultaneously. Simply following instructions will not make the tool work. Clinical personnel will need to make adjustments and find ways to deal with the ad hoc characteristics of the specificities of local everyday work.

In dialogue with this, Annemarie Mol (2002) goes one step further and asks what happens to the body when it is analysed as part of such heterogeneous medical practice. Where does the local and mutual shaping of tools and practices render the body or the disease? She suggests that the ontology of the body is not one but several, and that tools can effect a shift in ontological status. Berg's and Mol's work has been very influential in recent theorizations of medical technology in practice (technology cannot be analysed as distinct from practice). Also, the ontology of the body has become multiple: bodies have different ontologies in different practices. This has opened up questions relating to how we know the body, indicating that there are different modes of knowing it (Mol and Law 2004).

Returning to my fieldwork, what interested the head doctor was not so much the technological nature of the technology or even the new method per se, but how it worked in the everyday life of the clinic, including more subtle issues concerning what staff groups felt and thought about it. Feelings and notions such as fear (of using the device), values (whether use of the device was seen as warranted) and feeling threatened were her concerns. Her assumptions as to what personnel would think turned out to be justified, judging from what some of the midwives told me. Notable reactions included resistance to the increased surveillance implied by the new technique: 'Everything becomes so instrumental with STAN', as one midwife put it. Learning to analyse the information displayed on the screen also takes some time: 'Well, that's hard to see when you're *there* in the [delivery] room', another midwife said during the educational session, implying that another mode of knowing the body or mode of practice was required than that implied by the new technique. It was against the backdrop of this understanding of the device that I set out to do my first round of shadowing to find out what such a mode of practice revealed about the use of a new device. To explore this, I will take into account one aspect of the (gendered) power dimensions of the organization of heterogeneous medical work, namely emotions, departing from a feminist conception of emotion work (Hochschild [1983] 2003) and including the notion of abjection (Kristeva 1982).

Power and Modes of Knowing

In one interview, a midwife got upset when I asked what she thought of the device. So far, she said, she had managed fine without it, and the midwives had never discussed it. Something in the way it was introduced signalled that it was a change of practice that had come from above; for example, midwives are put on lists to attend the obligatory STAN educational session. Not having been asked her opinion bothered her, an omission that suggested disrespect of her knowledge of birthing based on long experience. She saw no evidence from midwifery research or state of the art in midwifery that STAN technology was needed. This scepticism continued as a main theme in the interview, as well as expressions of feelings of having been ignored.

Midwifery research has shown how such lack of influence over the practice environment can lead to low use of prescribed methods (Walker et al. 2001). More generally, the observed midwives felt that many methods proposed by doctors are at odds with the methods developed in midwifery and that midwives' opinions are not given much weight. Discussions of new or complementary/alternative methodologies for pain relief, and so on, often arise during coffee breaks, but there seems to be little a midwife can do to introduce such methods at the clinic:

> I think we should be able to conduct the kind of development work that concerns our profession.[…] We should be *part* of the developments in health care and have more time to develop what we do (midwife).

This remark reflects a situation in which organizational changes often result in midwives doing tasks previously done by assistant nurses, something that makes keeping up to date with research even more difficult than before. This indeed is often seen as one of the main problems: that birthing is dominated by obstetrics and the technologies introduced by obstetrics.

The perspectives of the midwives and doctors often differ and likely follow from the division of labour between them, where the midwives deal with the normal and the doctors with the pathological births. The subject came up in an interview with a doctor, who described the situation as follows:

> It's quite natural, really. We do short visits with the patients when there is something wrong. We do not deal with the normal when nothing goes wrong. The approach to the patient is important, but not as important as it is for the midwives. What is important is that they [i.e., the patients] are adequately

taken care of in medical terms … in a humane and polite way, of course. But the encounter with the patient is not what's important, but the result: a healthy mother. That's why it is always easier to introduce [new technology] when it comes to the doctor.

The differences between the approaches of doctors and midwives are seen as a natural consequence of their division of labour. The doctors do not deal with the normal birthings; when midwives do, it is their approach to the patient that is important. Being 'humane and polite' is important, of course, according to the doctor, but secondary to the patient being properly taken care of 'in medical terms'. The doctor is annoyed by how some midwives emphasize the 'birthing experience'; she referred dismissively to actions taken to foster a good experience, such as providing a bed for the father, as 'touchy-feely stuff'. Such remarks illustrate how doctors may view being professional as being emotionally detached, and how taking care of someone 'in medical terms' becomes discursively opposed to being 'humane and polite'. In other words, the medical is constructed as rational and emotionally detached, and care work as the opposite, and doctors maintain their professional authority through devaluing that which is not 'medically' interesting (see also Cancian and Oliker 2000).

The boundaries around the medical are leaky, however, despite efforts to keep the medical 'pure'. The medical evidence that STAN is a good method needs to be situated in a messy practice. Efforts to move discussions of STAN further and to include more than biomedical issues are proposed; for example, in one of the interviews, a midwife wanted to point out that it is not she who delivers a baby, but rather the mother (and/or couple). The midwife's job is to assist. This point of view implies that there should be discussion of who does the work, and a fear that more and more women who come to the clinic do not perceive their own responsibility in birthing. This indicates a difference in where midwives and doctors draw their lines of responsibility: from a midwife's point of view it is the woman who should be in charge of her own body, whereas a doctor would be more prone to take control, often with the use of technology.

Following Mol, 'the body', as referred to in such discourses, is not constructed in the same terms by midwives and by doctors. The mode of knowledge employed in midwifery discourse implies a healthy and 'natural' body giving birth. The mode of knowledge represented by obstetrics discourse, on the other hand, implies a biomedical body possibly in a state of risk. The birthing bodies and technologies are discursively constructed in line with this natural/biomedical divide. Such discursive divides are indicated by, for example, when one of the midwives jokingly referred to the machine as 'a stupid robot' and one doctor referred to the bed for the father as 'touchy-feely-stuff'.

How such discursive dichotomization is correlated with actual practices is a different story. In practice, discursive demarcations of midwifery and obstetrics as 'humane' or 'medical' are less visible. Unlike it would seem from the local discourse, doctors were not more likely than midwives to use the new device. If anything, the extent to which a midwife or doctor used the device had to do with the number of years she had worked without it; in fact, one older doctor refused to use it at all. Mol formulates this relationship between discourses of natural and social as 'clashes between the knowledge *articulated* in technoscience societies and the knowledges *embedded* in their practices', and that it is people's 'theories [that] make modern divides. Our practices do not' (2002: 31). Thus, it is practice that merits study, because it is in practice that such common dichotomies cease to be important. Following such a line of reasoning leads us back to the statement at the beginning of the paper concerning the likewise modern divide made between rational and emotional to which the paper now turns.

Intense Emotions and Routine Emotion Work

Learning to become a professional in assisting at births involves partaking in a number of births. Midwifery students are required to attend 60 births before qualifying as midwives. Medical students spend two full weeks of training at the birthing centre at the end of their five years of training. Other hospital staff groups, such as ambulance personnel, are also trained in birthing, although only for one day; consequently, medical and midwifery students are frequently encountered in everyday birthing practice at university hospitals. During the academic term, the schedule is intensive, with one medical student and one midwife student each following a doctor and midwife, respectively. The students are scheduled so that there is only one student in a delivery room at a time. Normally, three midwives work at a time in a clinic with a capacity of eight delivery rooms. Roughly speaking, then, the probability of having a student helping out is one in three. Hence, staff groups are used to having students of different kinds involved in the work practices and have developed routines for introducing them to the patients, including giving the patients the opportunity to say they do not wish to have a student present. As a social scientist at this teaching hospital, I was placed into an existing 'student' category of people attending births, and was sometimes scheduled and treated like one of these students by the nurses and midwives. After my first day as a student observing a birthing for the first time, I wrote the following:

> 'Have you ever been to a birthing?' assistant nurse X asks me as soon as I step out of the changing room, partly, I guess, to see if I can handle it. I say no. 'Well you're lucky, because you will now. Come!' she says excitedly. I follow her as we hurry along the corridor to one of the eight delivery rooms where a woman is about to give birth. It is still dark outside as we enter. The woman giving birth is lying in bed on her side with her back turned toward the door. She is moaning and I notice a particular scent. It doesn't smell repulsive, only distinctive. She is lying on her left side and does not seem to notice or care that two additional people have entered the room (and how could she?). A woman who turns out to be her sister is with her and is massaging her back. Midwife Y is sitting on a

stool at the foot end of the delivery bed, gently coaching the woman: 'Just once more, you can almost see the head now.' She nods to me. I immediately feel I am about to cry, this being such a big event in someone's life, and I put quite some effort into holding back tears. While X and Y are busy coaching the woman, I feel out of place and start talking to the sister who has a warm smile. She is calmness itself … We are interrupted by Y who asks me if I want to see how open she is. I decline, since I do not know if I can take it at the moment, while at the same time I am really curious to see what it really looks like. From where I am standing, I see the scalp electrode cord that connects the foetus to the foetal monitor through the woman's vagina. I react to this observation (of an electrical cord in proximity to flesh, amniotic fluids, blood and faeces?) amidst all else that is new and strange. I had heard of scalp electrodes during the foetal monitoring educational session I had taken part in earlier, but somehow not realized that it indeed was a *foetal scalp* electrode. I am struck by the strong feeling that it does not appear very comfortable to have a chord coming out of your vagina (or in your scalp). I stand on the side of the bed and start to cold sweat. Severely. I get a tingling and familiar sensation. Am I going to faint? Get sick? This is definitely not good. And what am I doing here anyway? I somehow get my act together and sneak into the bathroom, which is located just behind me. I don't want to be a burden in a situation like this. I sit down on a stool and gradually start to feel that I am probably ok. I hear the woman's moaning on the other side of the door. I fill a plastic cup with water and drink it. X knocks on the door. 'How are you doing in there?' 'Oh, I'm fine', I say with quite some effort. *Sharpen up!*, I say to myself. I take a couple of deep breaths and go out into the room again. The sister has gone to the other side of the bed and is standing by the window. The woman has now turned on her other side and is pleadingly looking at me instead, and motions toward the anaesthetic hose, which is out of her reach. 'Can you give me that?' she pleads and motions toward the mask. I take the mask and help her hold it over her nose and mouth. She screams loudly straight into the mask as she is overcome by the next contraction. She's in so much pain, I have to help her. 'You are so strong', I hear myself saying, really meaning it and being surprised at how well I think I am handling the situation. For the next few minutes (five? twenty?) I help her with the mask and give her water to drink between pains. I no longer feel nauseous or faint and am wholly immersed in the process (adapted from field notes, January 2005).

This passage was written at the end of an intense day that started with the birthing described above. I was overwhelmed by the experience of fieldwork in a birthing centre, so much so that I often forgot or was unable to focus my observations on what I was there for, namely, to discern how staff groups dealt with the introduction of a new foetal monitoring device. This sense of being overwhelmed made it impossible for me to be detached enough to observe how those present worked with the technology in use. What do these displays and the controlling of emotions communicate in the birthing centre?

Being in a delivery room is an emotional experience, not only for students, fathers or sisters, but also for those who work with deliveries every day. In the lunch room, midwives often talk about how they handle and use emotions in their everyday work. They speak of how they get angry and frustrated with patients who do not do what the midwives think is best for them, or how fathers get angry at them for not being there all the time. They frequently refer to instances when they were happy when a birthing was successful. Midwives use these coffee and meal breaks to release emotional pressure, in what has been termed 'communities of coping' (Korczynski 2003), which help to reduce the negative effects of emotion management work. One midwife says she can talk for hours on the telephone about 'incidents big and small' with one of her colleagues. Lewis (2005) suggests that such 'communities of coping' are related to tension in hospitals between what she refers to as the 'feminized personal' and the 'masculinized professional'.

To my own relief, no one seemed to think my reactions were peculiar in any way. On the contrary, several times when I talked to midwives about them, my story was countered by 'You should see some of the fathers'. I did, and the emotions they displayed were very similar to mine. The midwives, however, reacted very differently to the birthing situations. Their work involved both expressing a certain 'detached concern' so common in the medical professions, and enhancing the positive feelings of the neophyte assistants: the birthing woman's partner or the midwifery/medical student. The joy and strain of this emotion management can be seen in how one midwife spoke about her work:

> It is *wonderful*, but at the same time extremely bothersome. Sometimes you almost feel that you don't want to go to work. It is physically trying and psychologically trying … you get to be part of the joy of a child being born, and you get to be part of it over and over again … and in that I get so close to those I'm working with. It is not many times in life that you are allowed to get so close to someone, as you do during that time (midwife).

Being 'close' to someone and sharing in the joy are two aspects highlighted here, as is birthing practice as being both physically and psychologically trying. Such emotional pressure is dealt with informally with the colleagues to whom the midwife feels closest.

To return to the above narration from the field, and my own lack of emotional detachment, I was excited that I was about to be part of a birthing situation, which I had not experienced previously. Taking part in a birthing is somewhat of a rite of passage at the hospital, judging from the question 'Did you get to see a birthing yet?' that X and other people asked me over the first few weeks I spent at the clinic. When answering this question, I referred to the experience described above, something that often led to discussions about the drama found in their work, and tales of the reactions of medical students and fathers when first confronted with birthing. Birthing involves a multitude of emotions on the parts of all people present in the delivery room, not just the mothers.

What I found most striking about the medical practice of birthing, as a non-medically trained social scientist visiting a birthing clinic for the first time, was how nurses, midwives and doctors engaged the woman who was birthing, painful and dramatic as it often is, while seemingly keeping their cool. The perceived detachment of midwives or doctors is a strategic one, 'a rational and pragmatic process of role and self-management' that makes the work sustainable (Hampson and Junor 2005). The concept of *emotional labour* (Hochschild [1983] 2003) refers to the efforts workers must make to align their feelings with organizational and managerial requirements. It is performed by workers who must routinely control their feelings while enhancing the positive feelings of others. In doing such *emotion management work*, according to Hochschild, workers seem to be estranged from their own feelings in a way similar to how production workers are estranged from their own labour.

Hochschild's concept has been very influential and indicates the importance of recognizing a kind of work that was often seen as inherently female, and thus accompanied by low status and pay. One criticism is that Hochschild's view of emotions sees them as conscious, observably managed and rationally understood, thereby reducing them to 'ideas that "have no autonomy from the rational world with which they coexist"' (Craib 1995 in Theodosius 2006: 894). In Hochschild's analysis, then, analysing emotions as 'in and about social life' obscures the unconscious processes involved in emotion work and emotion management. Moreover, not all emotions can be theorized (Rosaldo 1984).

Containing the Abject

As I entered the room, I also felt that I was about to cry. This feeling, as I recall it, came over me as soon as I stepped into the dimly lit room, and is perhaps connected to the importance and awe ascribed to birthing and to witnessing the seemingly consecrated practice of birthing. Perhaps my reaction was also related to the perceived contrast between the clinical corridors and clothes, and the fleshy, emotional experience in the delivery room. I put much effort into controlling and regulating my reactions. Following this sense of awe and overwhelming emotion came a strong sense of my not belonging there, that I was an uninvited observer of an unknown woman's very private birthing. Just being in the room was an intrusion on her privacy. My strong physical reaction to seeing the foetal scalp electrode, however, is more difficult to explain. Was it the individual contradictory elements of the whole situation that became too much? I am not the kind of person who faints when she sees blood, so I have difficulty believing that it was simply seeing bodily excretions and a woman in pain that was causing such strong emotional reactions.

The notion of abjection in feminist psychoanalytic theory (Kristeva 1982, Grosz 1989), that I here very tentatively use, might shed some light on how this experience can be analysed: as a figuration useful in helping to think beyond the traditional binary (scientific) rationality and (subjective) emotions. In Grosz's words:

> Abjection is what the symbolic must reject, cover over or contain. The abject is what beckons the subject ever closer to its edge. It insists on the subject's necessary relation to death, corporeality, animality, materiality – those relations which consciousness and reason find intolerable. The abject attests to the impossibility of clear borders, lines of demarcation or divisions between the proper and the improper, the clean and the unclean, order and disorder, as required by the symbolic. Symbolic relations separate the subject from the abyss that haunts and terrifies it. (Grosz 1989: 73)

The abject, delineated as a frontier that is neither subject nor object, makes us feel 'beside ourselves' and serves as a reminder that fixing permanent boundaries between self and other is impossible (Kristeva 1982). The abject can be seen as a borderline figure of that which is between subject and object. The foetal monitor symbolizes the proper, clean and orderly and as such negates the abject, that is, of death, the corporeality of excrement and the animality of the birthing process. It seems as though the discourses in which foetal monitoring is embedded imply a wishing away of such a terrifying abyss. Symbolically speaking, then, the biomedical discourse rejects and covers the abject.

Dealing with abjection is distributed unequally across professional groups, however. The work is delegated downward in the hospital hierarchy, as evident from the following words of a midwife, when we spoke about the general division of labour between midwives and assistant nurses:

> Say that I have a patient who starts to bleed intensely ... the assistant nurse doesn't ... [pauses] ... What she does is see to it that ... partly to see that more personnel come in, but fixes new pads.... she wipes ... and helps to measure what comes out (midwife).

Dealing with blood, faeces or amniotic fluids is the task of those at the bottom of the hospital hierarchy. No one mentions this explicitly, but it is easily observable. Midwives do this work only when an assistant nurse is not there. Only once did a discussion of how to deal with faeces during birthing come up during my fieldwork. It was during rounds in the conference room that one doctor spontaneously mentioned that she thought patients should take laxatives. She also expressed that she did not think 'we' should have to deal with this. Interestingly, she did not argue that the wiping should be delegated to nurses or midwives, but indicated that the job should be taken care of by the birthing woman, before the active phase of birthing. According to Grosz:

> The feminine, the semiotic, the abject, although inexpressible as such, are articulated within symbolic representations by those (who happen to be men)

who risk their symbolic positions in order to plunder the riches of the unspoken maternal debt. These men, if they are to avoid complete psychical/signifying disintegration, remain anchored by some threads of identity to the symbolic .... They are able to maintain their imperilled hold on the symbolic only by naming the abject, naming the space of the undivided mother–child. By naming it they establish a distance, a space to keep at bay the dangers of absorption it poses. To speak (of) the abject is to ensure one's distance and difference from it (Grosz 1989: 78).

Translating this into the context of a university hospital, the 'feminine, the semiotic, the abject' can instead, tentatively, be seen as articulated in the symbolic representations of biomedicine (in line with the symbolic dichotomy rationality/experience and male/female), here represented by the doctor naming and establishing distance from the abject. The symbolic dichotomization of emotional experience and biomedical rationality thus would seem to keep the latter free of the abject 'horrors' of animality, indistinct borders and corporeality. However, the abject does not confine itself to the seemingly clear dichotomies of emotion and rationality:

... abjection itself is a composite of judgment and affect, of condemnation and yearning, of signs and drives (Kristeva 1982: 10).

Repressing and controlling the feelings that such an indistinct boundary produces is part of becoming a responsible helper at a birthing. In fact, caring can be seen as partly about 'containing' abjection (Hughes et al. 2005) in its material form of blood, mucus, faeces and amniotic fluid. Learning to care and learning to become a nurse, doctor or midwife involves controlling such emotions while being sensitive to particularities in a way that makes the birthing safe.

Kristeva's conception of abjection mainly concerns its meanings at a subconscious level, but she also says that it has consequences for social life. The notion of abjection involved in birthing consequently reflects anxiety over indistinct boundaries, the foetus and the scalp electrode as marking this boundary. In this sense, the birthing situation is a transformation from a state of no distinction (foetus in the woman's body) to a state of distinction (baby outside the woman's body). The monitor's cord signals this liminal state of the foetus/baby-to-be. The foetus is connected to its mother through the umbilical cord, but also to the foetal monitoring machine through the cord. This scenario gives a sense of a machine on the outside that reaches in, to contact the foetus in the uterus, thereby making the transition from foetus to baby evident at an earlier stage. The visible monitor cord makes the foetus distinct before it has actually been born. So perhaps it was the confusion of the bodily boundaries between outside and inside, of seeing the cord coming out of the vagina, that helped create my physical reaction.

Toward Including Emotions in the Analysis of Heterogeneous Medical Practice

The practices of the midwives are based on observation and on the use of diverse technical devices as well as on sense and experience. New foetal monitoring devices, for them, provide merely one more piece of information needed to judge a specific situation. While some, at one level, are expressly negative toward introducing yet another technology, at another level they would not want to do without it. Integrating new technologies does not necessarily mean losing reliance on the experiential. Both doctors and midwives at the birth clinic articulate both modes of knowledge. Indeed, part of their work is to coordinate between the measurable evidence and the sensory and experiential, a coordination that usually proceeds smoothly and results in healthy mothers and babies.

So, how does an analysis of emotions and emotion work contribute to the study of technology in medical practice? The technology-in-practice approach (here represented by Berg (1997) and Mol (2002)) has given us analytical tools with which to understand how a medical technology is localized in a practice while at the same time disciplining it. Various elements at a particular site have effects on practice, be they monitors, doctors, documents or coffee rooms. My aim here has been to make visible the emotion work performed by doctors, midwives and mothers with their partners, including the more or less conscious containing of the abject, in order to make the best of a birthing situation. I have shown that the abject as such can be seen as yet another element that affects practice. By seeing the foetal monitoring device as localized in the emotion work that partly constitutes practice, a slightly different picture emerges. Focusing on emotion work in a broad sense and including notions of the abject highlights power relations in medical practice. Covering over and rejecting the abject and emotions is a sign of professionalism, and thus of status. Dealing with and containing the abject is also delegated to those in low-status positions. Framing the localization of new technology as an emotional practice thus gives a slightly different view of medical work that may help create room for the further analysis of power relationships in studies of contingent heterogeneous medical practice.

References

Ahmed, S. 2004. *The Cultural Politics of Emotion*. Edinburgh: Edinburgh University Press.

Amer-Wåhlin, I. 2003. *Fetal ECG Waveform Analysis for Intrapartum Monitoring*. Lund: Lund University.

Amer-Wåhlin, I., Hellsten, C., Norén, H., Hagberg, H., Herbst, A., Kjellmer, I., Lilja, H., Lindoff, C., Månsson, M., Mårtensson, L., Olofsson, P., Sundström A. and Marsal, K. 2001. Cardiotocography only versus cardiotocography plus

ST analysis of fetal electrocardiogram for intrapartum fetal monitoring: A Swedish randomised controlled trial. *Lancet*, 358(18), 534–538.

Berg, M. 1997. *Rationalizing Medical Work. Decision Support Techniques and Medical Practices*. Cambridge, MA: MIT Press.

Burkitt, I. 2005. Powerful emotions: Power, government and opposition in the 'War on Terror'. *Sociology*, 39(4), 679–695.

Cancian, F.M. and Oliker, S.J. 2000. *Caring and Gender*. Thousand Oaks: Pine Forge Press.

Craib, I. 1995. Some comments on the sociology of emotions. *Sociology*, 29(1), 151–158.

Gould, D. 2006. Developments in maternity services should be driven by evidence. *British Journal of Midwifery*, 14(8), 496–497.

Grosz, E. 1989. *Sexual Subversions: Three French feminists*. Sydney: Allen & Unwin.

Hampson, I. and Junor, A. 2005. Invisible work, invisible skills: interactive customer service as articulation work. *New Technology, Work and Employment*, 20(2), 166–181.

Harding, J. and Pribram, D. 2004. Losing our cool? Following Williams and Grossberg on emotions. *Cultural Studies*, 18(6), 863–883.

Hochschild, R. [1983] 2003. *The Managed Heart: Commercialization of human feeling*. Berkeley: University of California Press.

Hughes, B., McKie, L., Hopkins, D. and Watson, N. 2005. Love's Labours Lost? Feminism, the disabled people's movement and an ethic of care. *Sociology*, 39(2), 259–275.

Impey, L., Reynolds, M., MacQuillan, K., Gates, S., Murphy, J. and Sheil, O. 2003. Admission cardiotocography: A randomised controlled trial. *Lancet*, 361(9356), 465–470.

Jaggar, A.M. 1989. Love and knowledge: Emotion and feminist epistemology, in *Gender/Body/Knowledge: Feminist reconstructions of being and knowing*, edited by A.M. Jaggar and S.R. Bordo. New Brunswick: Rutgers University Press, 145–171.

Korczynski, M. 2003. Communities of coping: Collective emotional labour in service work. *Organization*, 10(1), 55–79.

Kristeva, J. 1982. *The Power of Horrors: An essay on abjection*. New York: Columbia University Press.

Lewis, P. 2005. Suppression or expression: an exploration of emotion management in a special care baby unit. *Work Employment Society*, 19(3), 565–581.

Lloyd, G. 1993. *The Man of Reason: 'Male' and 'female' in Western Philosophy*. London: Routledge.

Lupton, D. 1998. *The Emotional Self. A Sociocultural Exploration*. London: Sage.

Lutz, C.A. and Abu-Lughod, L. 1990. *Language and the Politics of Emotion*. Cambridge: Cambridge University Press.

Mol, A. 2002. *The Body Multiple: Ontology in medical practice*. Durham and London: Duke University Press.

Mol, A. and Law, J. 2004. Embodied action, enacted bodies: The example of hypoglycaemia. *Body & Society*, 10(2–3), 43–62.

Nussbaum, M.C. 2001. *Upheavals of Thought: The intelligence of emotions*. Cambridge: Cambridge University Press.

Rosaldo, M. 1984. Toward an anthropology of self and feeling, in *Culture Theory: Essays on mind, self and emotion*, edited by R.A. Schweder and R.A. LeVine. Cambridge: Cambridge University Press, 137–157.

Theodosius, C. 2006. Recovering emotion from emotion management. *Sociology*, 40(5), 893–910.

Thoits, P.A. 1989. The sociology of emotions. *Annual Review of Sociology*, 15, 317–342.

Walker, D., Shunkwiler, S., Supanich, J., Williamsen, J. and Yensch, A. 2001. Labor delivery nurses' attitudes toward intermittent fetal monitoring. *Journal of Midwifery & Women's Health*, 46(6), 352–353.

Chapter 8

Incorporating Machines into Laboratory Work: Concepts of Humanness and Machineness

Corinna Kruse

This chapter explores how machines are incorporated into laboratory practices of generating data from samples in genetic research. A research laboratory may seem far away from the medical settings discussed in the other chapters, but the clinic is not the only possible site for medical practices. Medical understandings, and with them practices, are continuously being developed. Only part of this development is carried out in the clinic; before new understandings can be incorporated into clinical medical practice, they are developed and tested in research laboratories that are seemingly far removed from doctors and their patients. These research laboratories, however, produce the knowledge that will come to be used in more obviously medical practices.

There is of course more to producing knowledge than turning samples into data; first, experiments must be designed and carried out and samples taken, afterwards, data must be assembled and interpreted, and conclusions must be drawn. However, generating data from samples is a crucial step in producing knowledge, as it makes the transition from the material to the symbolic realm (see Barley and Bechky 1994) and all subsequent steps are based on this data.

As machines come to play a greater and more essential role in producing scientific knowledge, it is important to understand the particular roles they are assigned in this production and why. This chapter will discuss these roles, showing how laboratory staff talked about machines in general and worked with individual machines, two distinctly different sets of practices that nevertheless were connected through referring to the same underlying concepts of humanness and machineness. It will argue that these concepts were intimately linked to the laboratory's central concern of producing valid data, and that machines were important tools for attaining this validity.

The Laboratories

This chapter is based on material collected through fieldwork – ethnographic observations and interviews – in five different laboratories of various sizes in the southern half of Sweden. The laboratories were associated with either of two large organizations, Swegene and Wallenberg Consortium North, and with local universities. All were involved in what might be loosely termed genetic research, working with DNA, RNA or proteins. Proteins may sound quite far removed from genetic research, but as genes encode proteins, that is, DNA can be translated to RNA, which in turn can be translated to amino acids and thus proteins, so all three of them are part of the same processes. The research was done on such diverse materials as yeast, blood and bodily tissues, ranging from basic research on how cell membranes work to searching for genetic factors in diseases to, rather tangibly, trying to develop a blood test for cancer.

Two of the laboratories studied were research laboratories, whereas the other three were so-called technology platforms: laboratories equipped with large-scale, state-of-the-art technology and the staff to handle this technology. The technology platforms were meant to give a large number of research groups access to otherwise unaffordable technology for highly specialized and high-throughput sample analysis. Their main purpose was to provide analysis services, either through the analysis of samples sent by research groups or through teaching members of these groups and subsequently helping them to analyse their samples using the platform's equipment. Work at the technology platforms thereby revolved around the transition from sample to data, a transition that was important in the research groups as well.

In all of the laboratories, machines were central to everyday work. They ranged from small, rather uncomplicated devices such as electrical scales, centrifuges and vortexes,[1] to computers and large, complex instruments such as pipetting robots[2] or mass spectrometers[3] interfaced with computers. The machines were used to relieve laboratory staff of strenuous routine work and to increase throughput. They gave access to what is impossible to see with the naked eye, and were used to increase precision and reduce error rates. Sample analyses were performed using highly specialized instruments. In the analysis process, the staff first had to put the samples into a form accepted by the particular instrument, which then created inscriptions (Latour and Woolgar [1979] 1986: 51–53), the 'raw data', as it was called by the laboratory staff. These inscriptions were usually graphs or images, which then, again with the help of machines, was turned into data by means of interpretation.

It is, however, not enough to simply produce data, data that must be understandable and presentable as a reliable and direct visualization of the sample, that is, it must be *valid* data. As one laboratory leader put it, 'if you can attack the

---

1   A small machine with a rapidly vibrating plate onto which test tubes are pressed in order to mix the contents.

2   As its name suggests, a pipetting robot is used for pipetting; these robots have multiple pipettes and can thus pipette large numbers of samples in much less time than it would take a staff member to do this by hand.

3   An instrument for measuring molecular weights.

data, then you're in trouble', going on to explain that while one should certainly be allowed to draw erratic conclusions, which later can be corrected, publishing questionable data was a serious problem.

Methods and Analytic Framework

I spent altogether about two months in the five laboratories, observing the staff at work – mostly research engineers, laboratory technicians, PhD students and postdoctoral students – and conducting informal interviews with them as well as formal interviews with laboratory leaders. Relying on Geertz's concept of culture as a web of significance (Geertz 1973: 5), I studied laboratory practices as cultural practices, as a collective way of creating and communicating meaning.

Meaning can be created and conveyed in many ways, by speech and by acts or symbols. In this way, communicating and thus creating meaning is not limited to literally telling stories, but includes conveying meanings encoded in objects or embodied in action. Geertz likens interpreting a culture to reading a text and describes culture as an 'acted document' (Geertz 1973: 10), the sentences and paragraphs and chapters of which are formed not only by words but also by things and actions. One might say that it is possible to create or act this document and thus share, create, communicate and develop meaning by *doing* things, that is, by cultural practice. Culture is not something that simply exists, but something that people *do* continually. The meanings that are shared, communicated, created and developed are done so by 'doing' or performing culture, by cultural practice.

The cultural practices I will discuss in this chapter are the laboratory practices that interwove humans, machines and valid data. In order to analyse the cultural meanings being performed, I will draw mainly on debates on humans and machines within Science and Technology Studies (STS), more specifically work that deals with agency and intentionality.

Talking About Humans and Machines

Machines were an important part of cultural practices in the laboratories. The staff spoke about and sometimes even to the machines; they tinkered with them and the environments around them, formed relationships with individual machines, and placed human beings in relation to machines in general, developing and acting upon underlying concepts of humanness and machineness. The laboratory staff's concepts of humanness and machineness emerged most clearly when they spoke about people and machines in general terms. They then usually contrasted humans with machines, as in this quote from a laboratory leader:

... why do we have a robot to do that? Well, one answer is, well, because we're lazy. The other answer is, well, nobody in this lab can, day in, day out, cut gels in this precision, without any errors ...

His words suggest a differentiation between humans and machines in terms of precision and error rates: Machines can work with consistent precision, whereas humans inevitably make occasional mistakes. Other staff members contrasted humans and machines in a similar way, usually speaking about what they called 'the human factor', a term that denoted what they apparently perceived as the perpetual risk of a person inadvertently making a mistake or breaking something. They pointed out how a machine would be more suited to a task than they were, or how a human being was prone to mistakes and accidents that could be avoided by using a machine.

For example, a laboratory technician rinsing excess fluid off glass slides remarked with a sigh: 'Oh, I wish I had a machine for this!' She was handling a lot of slides with extreme care and caution. I assumed she was not enthusiastic about performing the task because it was lengthy and terribly boring, and commented accordingly (I had not yet learned that repetitive work was not seen as a bad thing at all in the laboratory, and that staff seemed to have limitless patience for it). 'Oh, no', she answered, 'it's not that. That's okay. It's just that I'm afraid of breaking something.' A machine would remove 'the human factor' and thus the risks of mistakes and mishaps, and would in this way be safer, she said.

The laboratory leader quoted above went on to explain why he considered robots useful. He then contrasted a human being to a spot cutter, a robot that cuts tiny pieces that are to be analysed out of a gel dotted with spots of separated proteins:

Because if that spot cutter goes wrong, it would be such a dramatic and visible event, you know, oops, you've lost one gel. It's not like having a constant error rate of saying, if you pick spots out manually, you make one error in about fifty.

So that means, for one gel, when you've cut three hundred [spots], okay, you made six errors. You don't know where those errors are.

In this case, when this thing [the robot] blows up, you know, there's the gel, oops. So, big error, you may have cut all spots wrong, but you know it, so the total error rate is zero.

Central to his comparison are error rates. However, it is not so much the risk of making mistakes that is at issue; more important is the risk of mistakes that go undetected. Undetected mistakes affect the results, that is, the reliability of the data, whereas discovered mistakes can often be repaired in some way. If they cannot, they will lead to a loss of data, which, while not desirable, is still better than questionable data.

There was more to the difference between humans and machines, however. In the words of the same laboratory leader,

> if I ask [the robots] to pipette ten microlitres, they will do it, a hundred times out of a hundred ..., and [in case of a malfunction] then you see, then the computer will report ...

> [H]owever, it may well be if someone pipetted ninety-nine times, then ... makes a mistake, ... [and] doesn't notice it, or ... 'oh shit, I can't redo the whole thing, let's just hope this one disappears somehow.'

In other words, not only do humans differ from machines in being afflicted with a constant error rate, making unnoticed mistakes all the time, but they also may decide to pretend not to have noticed these mistakes.

While neither this laboratory leader nor the other laboratory staff explicitly described the difference they saw between humans and machines in these terms, the difference can be understood as one of agency and, above all, of intentionality. Humans were described as possessing the ability to act on their own, including making inadvertent mistakes and wrong decisions; machines were described as devoid of these abilities. Humans and machines were thus seen in contrast to each other, a contrast that revolved around the so-called human factor, a constant risk rooted in human intentionality.

Agency and Intentionality

Agency and intentionality are concepts that are subject to ongoing debate in STS, in which an important theme is the question of non-human agency.

Actor network theory (ANT), an approach that focuses on the interaction and entanglement of human and material agencies, argues that, since non-humans can both act and influence people's behaviour, taking material agency into account is not only possible but unavoidable (see, e.g., Johnson/Latour 1988). Using a door-closer as an example, Bruno Latour discusses how non-human actors both substitute for and shape human action; in the example, the closing of a door after people have walked through the opening has been delegated from a human porter to a mechanical door-closer. The door-closer shapes and restricts these people's actions, for example by requiring a certain amount of strength to open the door or by making it impossible to leave the door open so one can carry larger objects through it (Johnson/Latour 1988: 302) Therefore, he argues, non-human actors cannot be left out of sociological considerations (Johnson/Latour 1988: 308); indeed, the social and material are so interwoven as to be inseparable (see also Latour 1994).

Nevertheless, while claiming not to 'discriminate between the human and the nonhuman' (Johnson/Latour 1988: 303), his argument includes an implicit difference between human and non-human actors, a difference described in terms of discipline. As Latour tells the story, a non-human door-closer is needed, because the people passing through the door do not have the discipline to close it themselves, not even when they are reminded to do so by a note. Nor can a human porter be trusted to have the discipline to return to work every day and to stay alert and at his post throughout working hours. In Latour's story of the door-closer, human beings are portrayed as inherently undisciplined and difficult to coerce to perform a desired behaviour, whereas it is apparently much easier to elicit this behaviour from a mechanical device; moreover, this device can then be used to shape people's actions (Johnson/Latour 1988: 303). Thus, while ANT advocates against distinguishing between human and non-human action, at least one of its founding fathers seems to conceive of a difference in how humans and non-humans act. Humans are inherently difficult to discipline, his description implies, because they can decide to leave the door open or, in the case of the porter, decide to wander off. In other words, the humans in the example are perceived as capable of making decisions, whereas the mechanical door-closer, the non-human, is not.

Like ANT scholars, Andrew Pickering ascribes agency to both humans and the material world in his analysis of scientific activity, but, unlike ANT, he strongly and explicitly differentiates between human and material agency. Indeed, he makes the distinction into an analytical point. According to Pickering, there is one crucial difference between human and material agency, namely intentionality. Human beings have intentions and goals that guide their actions; thus understanding, for example, the intentions of scientists is crucial to understanding scientific practice. Pickering does not assume that nonhumans – he names DNA and televisions as examples – pursue goals of their own; nor does he deem it necessary to understand the intentions things might have in order to understand scientific practice (Pickering 1993: 565–566). Machines not only mediate between human and material agency, capturing, taming and materializing material agency for the benefit of their users (Pickering 1995: 7); they are also hybrids belonging to both worlds (Pickering 1995: 54). Their hybridity does not include intentionality, not even a kind of secondary, indirect intentionality, carried over from their human creators and users.

In a similar vein, Harry Collins and Martin Kusch differentiate between human and machine agency by distinguishing between 'action', which, to them, requires intentionality and meaning, and 'behaviour', which does not (Collins and Kusch 1998: 7). Like machines, human beings can simply behave, as when unintentionally blinking their eyes, but unlike machines, they can also act, that is, perform intentional and meaningful actions. The meanings of acts derive from a human agent's being a part of and understanding society; for example, winking at someone is to act, because it presupposes that the person winking knows that this is an action that makes sense in the particular society of which she is part.

According to Collins and Kusch, intentionality and understanding of one's society are strictly human attributes (Collins and Kusch 1998: 1–3).

Thus, while material and machine *agency* appear to be acceptable ideas, *intentionality*, in the form not only of intentions but also of goals, decisions and meaning, is regarded as uniquely human. Interestingly, therefore, how STS scholars reason about human and material or machine agency seems not to be so very different from how the laboratory staff in my study described the difference between humans and machines.

Their focus, however, is different. While STS scholars tend to accentuate what human beings can and machines cannot do, laboratory staff often compared machines – with their perceived lack of agency and intentionality – rather favourably to human beings; this lack made them much more precise and predictable which were much-appreciated qualities. On the flip side, it was noted that this very lack of agency made it necessary to supervise them. In this respect, machines were described as follows by a laboratory leader:

> [They have] no sense of achievement or where to go or what direction, or, somebody has got to be doing the program, you know, somebody's got to be controlling.

Not only were humans and machines perceived as opposites of each other with regard to agency and intentionality, this contrast also meant that they were regarded as suited for different kinds of tasks. Human intentionality made people suitable for being in control and for creative tasks, such as asking research questions and designing experiments. Machines' very lack of intentionality suited them for routine work and for removing as much of the human factor as possible from this work.

Machines were also preferred for making interpretations, which became clear in the cases when the staff could not use them and wholly human decisions were called for. One example was choosing spots on a gel for cutting and entering them into the spot cutter's computer. Several of the staff members doing this expressed their discomfort about making such decisions by themselves. They said they would have preferred to have the computer do this; they felt 'insecure' making these decisions. 'This is so arbitrary', they said, and felt that their decisions threatened the whole process to become 'subjective'. If the computer made these decisions, they explained, at least they could be sure that every gel would be treated in exactly the same way, with none of the arbitrariness and subjectivity they brought to it. A computer, they said, would ensure that the decisions were made objectively.

In other words, machines were perceived as performing in exactly the same way every time, as exhibiting perfectly reproducible behaviour; since reproducible laboratory work was regarded as a key to reproducible data, machines were in turn regarded as a way to attain such valid data. It was precisely this lack of intentionality that made it possible to connect machines to attaining valid data in the form of reproducible data: their predictability and inability to deviate from what they were supposed to do (malfunctions barred) meant they did not introduce errors or variation.

Mechanical Objectivity

The laboratory staff's way of contrasting humans and machines can be described by the term 'mechanical objectivity', coined by historian of science Lorraine Daston. It denotes objectivity achieved with the help of machines or technology involving machines.

Mechanical objectivity is one of several aspects of the concept of scientific objectivity traced historically by Daston (1992). In a study with Peter Galison on images and mechanical objectivity, the authors describe mechanical objectivity as being opposite to the subjectivity brought into scientific research by the individual researcher and her personal, individual idiosyncrasies, choices and judgements (Daston and Galison 1992: 82–84). That this subjectivity is perceived as dangerous is, the authors argue, a historical occurrence and not self-evident.

Photography and thus mechanically created images was incorporated into scientific practice, Daston and Galison contend, during a shift of focus from ideals or types (e.g. portrayals of ideal skeletons produced by combining features gleaned from several individual skeletons) towards depicting individuals (which nonetheless were stand-ins for types) (Daston and Galison 1992: 85–98). Machines were already associated with work-related virtues such as patience and tirelessness; accordingly, they were welcomed into this process as imaging devices, because

> Instead of freedom of will, machines offered freedom from will – from the willful interventions that had come to be seen as the most dangerous aspects of subjectivity. If the machine was ignorant of theory and incapable of judgment, so much the better, for theory and judgment were the first steps down the primrose path to intervention. In its very failings, the machine seemed to embody the negative ideal of noninterventionist objectivity, with its morality of restraint and prohibition (Daston and Galison 1992: 83–84).

Machines were regarded as producing images free of subjectivity because, unlike scientists and artists, they did not and could not choose what to include in and exclude from images. Mechanically produced images have come to be regarded as authentic, because the machine's depiction has come to be regarded as untainted by interpretation, much more than could be achieved by human self-restraint (Daston and Galison 1992: 120).

While Daston and Galison demonstrate how machines were assigned an important role in producing images understood as objective and true in changing scientific practices, they do not explain why machines were associated with non-intervention. The way of regarding machines that they trace ties in with how both STS and the staff describe machine agency: while machines certainly can do things, they lack intentionality and thus they are incapable of making decisions, creating meaning and understanding situations, which renders them incapable of subjectivity and associates them with non-intervening mechanical objectivity.

To understand how mechanical objectivity was produced and reproduced in laboratory practices and how machines were assigned the role of tools for attaining valid data, I will use Karen Barad's framework of agential realism (Barad 1996, 1998, 2003, 2007). I will argue that machines could be used as tools for making valid data because cultural practices in the laboratories made what she calls a 'cut', that is, drew a line between people and machines, ascribing each of them certain qualities and assigning each of them certain tasks.

Making Cuts

Karen Barad advocates departing from the traditional dichotomy of observer versus observed or subject versus object in science, arguing that this dichotomy is not a pre-existing given, but rather the result of artificially drawing boundaries, which is what she calls making 'cuts' (Barad 1996: 183, 1998: 95).

Instead of being a separate agent giving access to the otherwise invisible, the instrument is part of a whole, which she calls an apparatus, that produces a phenomenon (Barad 1998: 98–103). Using ultrasound imaging of foetuses as an example, she argues that the instrument:

> [D]oes not allow us to peer innocently at the fetus, nor does it simply offer constraints on what we can see; rather, it helps produce and is 'part of' the body it images (Barad 1998: 101).

The apparatus producing the foetus has a number of parts: the ultrasound instrument, the people operating it and looking at the image, the body that is to be imaged, the ability and habit to look at pictures, and cultural concepts of parenthood and of what a foetus is. 'Their child' in an ultrasound photograph that parents-to-be can show their friends and relatives is thus not simply something that was there all along and that ultrasound technology simply made visible; it is something that this technology plays a part in producing. Consequently, 'phenomena are the place where matter and meaning meet' (Barad 1996: 185).

Barad suggests using the term intra-action 'to signify the inseparability of "objects" and "agencies of observation" (in contrast to "interaction," which reinscribes the contested dichotomy)' (Barad 1998: 96). It is in intra-action, through practice, that the observer, the observed and the instrument are shaped and meaning is created. '"Subjects" or "objects" ... do not pre-exist as such' (Barad 1998: 112), Barad argues, instead, what are regarded as objects and subjects are established through intra-action, through specific practices that involve both human and material agency, as are the attributes and qualities ascribed to them (Barad 2003: 815). It is exactly this drawing of boundaries that Barad calls making 'cuts', pointing out that making these cuts always entails exclusions one should be aware of and acknowledge (Barad 1996: 183, 1998: 95). As the subjects and objects of these intra-actions do not pre-exist, they cannot be attributed or misattributed with agency (which Barad explicitly sees in association with subjectivity and intentionality); instead of a property, her concept of agency is one of enactment, 'distributed over nonhuman as well as human forms' (Barad 2007: 214). Consequently, I understand the attribution or misattribution of agency or intentionality – according to Barad, closely aligned with subjectivity, that is, being a subject or person (Barad 2007: 217) – as part of making cuts.

Barad holds a very political view of science, and, accordingly, she argues that these separations are to be seen in connection with politics. While I do not deny that science and politics are closely connected, I will use Barad's framework not to explore this connection but to understand the role of machines in making certain and objective data.

Barad's concept of intra-action and the notion of making cuts makes it possible to understand the dichotomy of humanness and machineness in the laboratories as produced and reproduced by particular cultural practices, i.e., by doing humanness and machineness. That means that contrasting humans and machines in terms of agency and the human factor and acting on these concepts *shaped* concepts of humanness and machineness. It also created – among other things, such as raw data and valid data – humans and machines in a way that had not existed before, defining them through specific kinds of agency and intentionality.

The concept of machines as infallible and predictable and thus more dependable than human beings does not seem to be specific to the laboratories I studied or even research in the natural sciences; there seems to be a widespread trust in machines in society (see Daston and Galison 1992: 83 for the virtues ascribed to machines in the 19th century), especially computers.[4] What I understand to be specific to the laboratories is how concepts of people and machines were elaborated on and fitted into cultural practice in the laboratories. These cultural practices differed between discussing machines in general and working with individual machines, although the underlying categories were the same.

Working with Machines: Maintaining Cuts

Working with machines was much less orderly than speaking about humans and machines in general. When working with individual machines, the staff encountered machines that exhibited behaviour that did not fit into the category of machineness. There were machines that seemed to act on their own and with a mind of their own, in short, machines that appeared to possess not only agency but also intentionality.

These machines' behaviour might have affected the categories of humanness and machineness, as they clearly were machines but were perceived as exhibiting

---

4   This is not to say that individual machines or computers cannot be distrusted or that people do not think it necessary to supervise machines.

qualities associated with humans. Consequently, they also might have threatened the cut between human and machines and thus the mechanical objectivity achieved through this cut.

Instead, however, machines that did not behave in a machinelike way were reclassified as almost people, and the quirks and malfunctions that made them unmachinelike were spoken of in terms of personalities and the human factor. Other studies (Gusterson 1996, Knorr Cetina 1999) describe how scientists relate to their machines as well as how these scientists speak of machines in terms of organisms or bodies. Crossing the conceptual boundaries like this, I will argue, did not blur the categories of humanness and machineness, but rather maintained them. In addition, the laboratory staff coaxed unmachinelike machines to display machinelike behaviour, a further step in keeping categories pure and maintaining the cut between humans and machines.

Crossing Boundaries

It seems that the conceptual borders were crossed mainly when machines malfunctioned, and more often with complex machines (usually computer controlled) than with fairly simple ones. A centrifuge whose lid had jammed, trapping a batch of samples inside, evoked compassion for the unfortunate colleague and several suggestions regarding how to pry 'the damn lid' open; this centrifuge, however, was spoken of simply as an object that had happened to break at an awkward moment. On the other hand, a pipetting robot that sometimes refused to start performing a task was spoken of as being not 'nice', using a Swedish adjective, *snäll*, that connotes friendliness, kindness and good-nature, an adjective that in other contexts would be used for people or pets and their actions.

The reason it did not start was also described in a way not usually appropriate for a machine. For example, the computer with which the robot was interfaced 'said' that there were disposable tips on the ends of the robot's pipettes that had to be removed first; there were in fact no tips, so the robot was described as wrongly 'thinking' that there were, and as 'waiting' for them to be manually removed. This vocabulary suggests an ascription of understanding of its situation to the robot (although, in this case, a frustratingly wrong understanding), a property usually associated with intentionality and thus human beings (see Collins and Kusch 1998).

Machine quirks were often described in terms of individual personalities; some machines, for example, were more 'sensitive' and needed more 'coaxing', whereas others had to be watched while they worked, because they were not deemed so trustworthy that one could turn one's back to them. One example was a pipetting robot that sometimes veered a little when pipetting, spilling a small amount of the fluid being transferred. It was unfavourably compared with a similar robot (neither of these looked even remotely human; in fact, all robots in the studied laboratories looked more or less like boxes or cupboards) that did not exhibit such problems and that, consequently, was said to behave much more 'nicely' (again with the connotation of being good-natured), requiring less attention. When they talked about working with these 'sensitive' machines, people frequently spoke in terms of 'knowing' the machine, of 'personal' relationships and of 'friendship', expressions that typically apply to people and relationships between them.

Machines were sometimes even assigned a gender. When talked about as entities with personalities – most often when they did not work to satisfaction, but occasionally in contrast to malfunctioning ones, like the first pipetting robot – they were referred to as 'he' instead of 'it'. In Swedish, like English, but unlike French or German, there are gender-neutral pronouns for things, whereas the gendered pronouns 'he' and 'she' are used to refer to people and sometimes animals. Accordingly, a machine should be 'it'; nevertheless, 'the machine is always a he' I was told by one research engineer, though she did not have an explanation for this, nor did she seem to need one. There seemed to be a loose pattern to the gendering of machines as machines were only assigned a gender by those who used them, while those who tinkered with a machine tended to refer to it as 'it'.

Machines might also be seen as needing protection from the supernatural. A research engineer mentioned that in the laboratory where she had worked before starting her current job, all laboratory machines had what she called 'sort of little house gods', for example small, amulet-like objects, attached to them and which were meant somehow to keep them from malfunctioning. The house gods were very useful, she said; they provided people with something at which to direct their grumbles when the machines eventually did malfunction. These house gods were rather tongue-in-cheek, and apparently uncommon in other laboratories, but still the staff at this particular laboratory had associated malfunctioning machines with the need for supernatural protection, although perhaps jokingly.

Machines with personalities were referred to as 'almost colleagues'. A laboratory technician described a quirky pipetting robot as 'a little bit human', even though it was just a machine and thus 'not supposed to' be human. Accordingly, they were said to reintroduce the very human factor they were supposed to remove from laboratory work.

Lucy Suchman argues that two factors contribute to the use of, as she puts it, 'an intentional vocabulary' when speaking about machines. On the one hand, 'the attribution of purpose to computer-based artefacts derives from the simple fact that each action by the user effects an immediate machine *reaction*' (Suchman 1987: 10. Emphasis in original). More importantly, she continues, is that human–machine interaction is increasingly based on language, making it more and more similar to communicating with people. Terms used to describe how one interacts with people thus become applicable to interactions with machines. In addition, when dealing with complex machines, their complexity makes it impossible to tie their behaviour to parts rather than the whole. A computer becomes an entity rather than a conglomerate of parts, which makes it even easier to describe in human terms (Suchman 1987: 10–16).

The last remark fits in rather well with my observations. The machines described in terms of personalities were typically complex instruments interfaced with computers. These machines consisted of quite a number of interacting hardware and software components, which in many cases made it impossible to attribute the machine's behaviour to any particular part. Thus, instead of explaining the pipetting robot's occasional malfunctions in terms of failing parts or a bug in the program, they were described in terms of a less 'nice' personality. The laboratory staff very rarely spoke about the computers with which most instruments interfaced in terms of software, instead, the instrument and computer were usually referred to as a single entity possessing particular qualities and individual quirks.

On the other hand, if a reason for a malfunction was found, it was no longer ascribed to a machine's personality. For example, a laboratory leader described how an instrument intermittently 'went berserk' as soon as the staff left the laboratory in the evening, and 'people started personalising these occasions, questioned why the bastard machine doesn't work'. However, it had clearly only been described in these terms until the staff had figured out that its misbehaviour was caused by fluctuations in the city's power supply that 'upset our machine'. These fluctuations were in turn caused by a large machine in another part of the university switching itself off once every three weeks for maintenance. It seems that as long as a reason for a machine's apparently willful behaviour could not be determined, such machines were spoken of in terms that conventionally are appropriate for people but not for objects, by attributing them a gender, or by describing them as acting with a mind of their own.

The gendering of machines appears to follow a similar pattern: machines were gendered by users, who dealt with them as wholes, and not staff members who, through tinkering with them, encountered and dealt with their parts. Finally, some machines were not spoken of at all. Those that performed without error were more or less forgotten; they were practically invisible.

Nevertheless, even though people colloquially speak about and treat machines as if they were alive and conscious, they are usually quite emphatic that machines are not actually alive and do not actually perform conscious, intentional actions. Essentially human qualities attributed to machines, as in Karin Knorr Cetina's study of physicists (Knorr Cetina 1999: chapter 5) or as seen in my fieldwork, are treated as abnormalities. In both cases, people added cautionary notes to their descriptions of machines as people. One of the physicists whom Knorr Cetina reports as saying 'we love our calorimeter', immediately modified his statement with, 'if you may say so, psychologically'. Another of her interviewees hedged, saying, 'in a way we shouldn't care at all about the detector', before saying, 'but in reality, okay, we live so long with that object, it's like a human being' (Knorr Cetina 1999: 122). Similarly, even though the staff ascribed personal qualities or even personalities to some machines and described them as 'almost colleagues', they were only *almost* colleagues, not real ones, and they were 'not supposed to' be human, not even 'a little bit'. The laboratory technician who explained to me how some machines were almost like colleagues immediately added, 'even though it shouldn't really be like this', and a laboratory leader who told me that 'most people will talk to those machines' preceded this with 'I'm not sure how willingly they admit it', indicating that talking to machines might seem a bit strange.

Apparently, all of them felt that it was inappropriate to speak about machines as people and about relationships with them in terms of friendship and even love. It seems that personhood and humanness are too closely connected to be able to speak about machines in terms usually associated with people without having to indicate that one is well aware that machines cannot actually be people. Speaking about machines as almost people was thus a way of reconciling conflicting cultural categories and meanings.

It could be argued that the boundary crossing involved in categorizing machines and people in one way and then treating them in another blurs these boundaries, mixing up the categories instead of maintaining them. At first sight, this seems curious, as in most societies great efforts are made to keep categories pure and boundaries distinct (Douglas [1966] 1994); however, it was precisely the crossing of these borders that kept the categories intact and pure and thus maintained the cut between humans and machines. By describing a machine that was 'acting up' in terms of having a personality, categories and boundaries remained largely unchallenged. Machines that were perceived as behaving like people, that is, unpredictably, individually and with apparent intentionality, were reassigned to another, more fitting, category, namely that of 'almost people', aligning their quirks and malfunctions with the human factor. The phenomenon of people ascribing individual machines or other artefacts with agency and near-personalities is of course not unique to laboratory environments; people and machines intra-act in many other contexts, continuously forming concepts of humanness and machineness. What is specific to the laboratory environments is how humanness and machineness were intertwined with producing valid data.

Coaxing

Reclassifying malfunctioning machines as almost people in certain situations was not the only way to maintain a cut between humans and machines. Another way was practices to make malfunctioning machines run reliably, that is, make them behave in a machinelike way that conformed with the idea of machineness. One laboratory leader summed up working with machines like this:

> They are very sensitive, very – it takes a lot of coaxing … to work properly, and when they work properly, they work beautifully … you just … have to spend so much time with them, [that] is all …

It was precisely this coaxing that kept machines working in a machinelike way. Machines worked reliably and predictably because the staff made sure they did.

A rather routine way to make sure that an instrument worked properly was to calibrate it. It was the person responsible for the machine (at the technology platforms it was usually a research engineer) who ran a few samples of known contents on the machine, checking whether the instrument's output was as expected and, if it was not, calibrating the machine until it was. A further routine practice to keep machines working smoothly was regular maintenance and cleaning. Machines that worked with fluids had cleaning programs that were run at the end of the week or month, rinsing any potential residue out of tubes and valves. Routine maintenance also entailed habits such as keeping track of how many times buffer fluids, for example, had been used and replacing them after a set number of times.

Coaxing could take various forms. One way to coax a malfunctioning or quirky machine back to working properly, for example, was to clean or calibrate it ahead of schedule. While coaxing could consist of rather simple acts, such as calibrating or restarting a machine that was acting in a 'weird' way, often there was a clear invocation of a personal relationship with a machine. In part, this was because determining whether a machine was working properly or acting weirdly could require considerable familiarity with it. The pipetting robot, for example, that was described as refusing to start because it wanted the non-existent disposable tips on its pipettes to be removed first, could be coaxed to work by pulling on the pipettes in a certain way. The laboratory technician – rather new at her job – who tried to start the quirky robot, explained that this was not the first time the device had acted up. She had initially assumed, she continued, that the pipettes had to be exactly aligned but were not, although she had difficulty seeing the suspected misalignment. In the end, she had to ask someone who was described as knowing the machine better and having developed a closer relationship with it, to help. This other person realigned the pipettes with a few deft pulls and pushes, making the robot ready to work.

Another way to make sure that machines worked reliably was to monitor machines while they were performing tasks, checking on them to see whether they were working smoothly and whether everything seemed in order. This was especially true for those machines assigned the status of almost people: such machines that were ascribed with willful personalities and with not being 'nice' were monitored rather closely. The pipetting robot that was often unfavourably compared with another, much 'nicer' robot, was very rarely left alone when working. A research engineer who used it explained that, although it should not be like this, it was much better to sit beside it, watch it work and, if necessary, fiddle a bit with it to prevent it from spilling. It was simply not worth going away to do a few minutes' work somewhere else, only to come back to a spoiled plate and not even know what exactly had happened, she said.[5]

The robot's classification as almost-person led to closer monitoring, which in turn meant that the human factor that it was said to reintroduce into laboratory work was eliminated as much as possible by the staff. Paraphrasing Daston and

---

5   Apart from this, she was very clear that she preferred having the robot do this task, as pipetting such large numbers of samples by hand was rather hard on the shoulder, arm and hand.

Galison (1992: 120), as these machines were themselves seen as afflicted with the human factor, they could not replace human self-restraint and perform work that was free from intervention: instead, the staff had to restrain the machines from adding uncertainty, in other words, from intervening.

Other forms of coaxing included trying to find a way of working that suited a machine. This ranged from rather general approaches, such as controlling a room's temperature and humidity to give machines regarded as sensitive the best possible working environment, to more specific approaches, such as trying to find a machine's preferred operating speed. The latter was done in one of the laboratories with a robot that placed tiny drops of liquids on glass slides. These drops had to be placed into a perfect grid pattern and had to dry into perfectly regular spots so as not to cause data loss later in the process. The robot, however, placed quite irregular drops in slightly crooked lines, causing a member of the staff to spend considerable time trying to determine whether different speeds would yield better results. There were also less marked ways of coaxing a machine to work properly, for example, by inserting samples in an especially careful way, attaching 'house gods' to it or talking to the machine while working with it.

Staff practices of coaxing machines into machinelike behaviour not only kept the notion of machineness pure, but also helped maintain the cut between humans and machines in the laboratory. On a more practical level, these practices meant that laboratory machines were as safe and predictable as the laboratory staff conceptualized them, because the staff made them so. Making machines behave predictably also meant they were coaxed into reproducible behaviour, a key factor in making reproducible data.

Conclusions

To sum up, laboratory staff incorporation of machines into laboratory work had two dimensions. By talking about humans and machines, they made a cut between the two, establishing humans and machines as opposites hinging on 'the human factor' and accordingly associated with different qualities. When working with machines, particularly with ones that did not appear to behave in accordance with the concept of machineness, they maintained the cut, on the one hand, by attributing this behaviour to machines' individual personalities, in such instances re-classifying these machines as almost people instead of machines, and, on the other hand, by coaxing machines into exhibiting machinelike behaviour. Incorporating machines into laboratory work was performative in a Butlerian sense (Butler 1999: 33) establishing and maintaining machines through specific cultural practices as safe and as producing reproducible results.

The cut these practices made between humans and machines in the laboratory made it possible to produce data perceived as reproducible and free from human intentions. Essentially, machines were used to keep the intervention of human agency out of the making of data as much as possible in striving to produce *valid* data: Inscriptions and interpretations made by machines could be regarded as authentic visualizations of samples, because machines were thought of as lacking intentionality and thus as unable to intervene by making choices or errors.

The cut between humans and machines also made mechanical objectivity possible. Machines can be regarded as non-intervening precisely because they have been and are continuously disassociated with intentionality; thus, they can become tools for capturing new discoveries, as opposed to tools for creating new knowledge. In this, concepts of machineness and humanness were central to how machines were made to fit into the laboratory practices of making valid data, entangling humanness and machineness inextricably with concepts of subjectivity, objectivity and, ultimately, valid data as free from human agency and intentionality. As Steven Shapin and Simon Schaffer point out,

> To identify the role of human agency in the making of an item of knowledge is to identify the possibility of its being otherwise. To shift the agency onto natural reality is to stipulate the grounds for universal and irrevocable assent. (Shapin and Schaffer [1985] 1989: 23).

Paraphrasing their words, machines were incorporated into laboratory practices as tools for making the data produced in the laboratories matters of fact instead of (human) interpretations.

References

Barad, K. 1996. Meeting the universe halfway – realism and social constructivism without contradiction, in *Feminism, Science and the Philosophy of Science*, edited by L.H. Nelson and J. Nelson. London: Kluwer Academic Publishers, 161–194.

Barad, K. 1998. Getting real: Technoscientific practices and the materialization of reality. *Differences – A Journal of Feminist Cultural Studies,* 10(2), 87–128.

Barad, K. 2003. Posthumanist performativity – toward an understanding of how matter comes to matter. *Signs: Journal of Women in Culture and Society,* 28(3), 801–831.

Barad, K. 2007. *Meeting the Universe Halfway – Quantum physics and the entanglement of matter and meaning.* Durham and London: Duke University Press.

Barley, S.R. and Bechky, B.A. 1994. In the backrooms of science – The work of technicians in science laboratories. *Work and Occupations,* 21(1), 85–126.

Butler, J. 1999. *Gender Trouble. Tenth Anniversary Edition.* London: Routledge.

Collins, H.M. and Kusch, M. 1998. *The Shape of Actions – What humans and machines can do.* Cambridge and London: MIT Press.

Daston, L. 1992. Objectivity and the escape from perspective. *Social Studies of Science,* 22(4), 597–618.

Daston, L. and Galison, P. 1992. The image of objectivity. *Representations,* 40, 81–128.

Douglas, M. [1966] 1994. *Purity and Danger – An analysis of the concepts of pollution and taboo.* London and New York: Routledge.

Geertz, C. 1973. Thick Description: Toward an interpretive theory of culture, in *The Interpretation of Cultures – Selected essays*, edited by Clifford Geertz. New York: Basic Books, 3–30.

Gusterson, H. 1996. *Nuclear Rites – A weapons laboratory at the end of the Cold War.* Berkeley, Los Angeles and London: University of California Press.

Johnson, J. a.k.a. Latour, B. 1988. Mixing humans and nonhumans together: The sociology of a door-closer. *Social Problems,* 35(3), 298–310.

Knorr Cetina, K.D. 1999. *Epistemic Cultures – How the sciences make knowledge.* Cambridge, Massachusetts and London, England: Harvard University Press.

Latour, B. 1994. Pragmatogonies – A mythical account of how humans and nonhumans swap properties. *American Behavioral Scientist,* 37(6), 791–808.

Latour, B. and Woolgar, S. [1979] 1986. *Laboratory Life – The construction of scientific facts.* Princeton, New Jersey: Princeton University Press.

Pickering, A. 1993. The mangle of practice – Agency and emergence in the sociology of science. *The American Journal of Sociology* 99(3): 559–589.

Pickering, A. 1995. *The Mangle of Practice – Time, Agency, and Science.* Chicago and London: University of Chicago Press.

Shapin, S. and Schaffer, S. [1985] 1989. *Leviathan and the Air-Pump – Hobbes, Boyle, and the experimental life.* Princeton: Princeton University Press.

Suchman, L.A. 1987. *Plans and Situated Actions – The problem of human-machine communication.* Cambridge: Cambridge University Press. For a rethought and expanded edition, see Suchman 2007.

Suchman, L.A. 2007. *Human-Machine Reconfigurations – Plans and situated actions.* Cambridge: Cambridge University Press.

Chapter 9

(Dis)connecting Bodies: Blood Donation and Technical Change, Sweden 1915–1950[1]

Boel Berner

Blood donation is generally depicted as an individual and altruistic act: the donor gives selflessly of his or her body to alleviate the suffering of others and prevent death. Substantial social and psychological research has gone into understanding what drives donors to give blood, and gender, age, education and other factors have been singled out in the hope of finding ways to increase the number of blood donors (cf. Healy 2000). Other studies have looked at the meaning of the donated (or received) blood for the individuals involved; for example, is the blood perceived as part of the donor's body even after donation, or as a separate, autonomous and anonymous substance? (Waldby et al. 2004).

The focus on individual attributes or attitudes about donation, however, ignores the fact that the act of donation is a social and technological one. A single individual cannot alone donate his or her blood. Moving blood between bodies today involves a complex socio-technical system of doctors, artefacts, hospitals, blood banks – in addition to medical, ethical and legal requirements. This chapter will discuss the haphazard origins and gradual evolution of this system in Sweden between 1915 and 1950. In her history of blood transfusion, Susan Lederer notes that 'In the early 20th century, blood transfusion was an invasive, dangerous, dramatic and at times successful undertaking' (Lederer 2008: 33). It was a rare practice with an uncertain outcome, and the exclusive, experimental domain of surgeons. This changed, however, during the interwar years and the Second World War. By 1950, it became a rather routine medical procedure, performed on a large scale and in a number of different clinical settings. In this chapter I will discuss what this change meant for the act of donation itself. I will focus not on individual donors' motivations or their views on blood, but on how the sociotechnical linkages of donors and users of blood changed over time.

In line with recent theorizing within science and technology studies, I will discuss how the meaning and practice of blood transfusions were constituted

---

1 Every effort was made to contact the copyright holders of Figures 9.2 and 9.3, which originally appeared in Kubanyi, E. 1928. *Die Bluttransfusion,* Berlin and Wien: Urban & Schwarzenberg.

within local assemblages of artefacts, practices and people, as well as notions of blood and disease. Such a focus on local activities and arrangements is useful for capturing the contingent, uncertain and trial-and-error evolution of medical practices, which is also noted in other research (Berg and Mol 1998, Heath, Luff and Sanchez Svensson 2003, Timmermans and Berg 2003). As John Law has phrased it in relation to modernization processes in general:

> Perhaps there is order*ing*, but there is certainly no order. This is because ... orders are never complete. Instead they are more or less precarious and partial accomplishments that may be overturned. They are, in short, better seen as verbs rather than nouns (Law 1994: 1–2).

This article will discuss the ordering and re-ordering of bodies, syringes, glass bottles, rubber tubes, chemical solutions, doctors and assistants during the period 1915 to 1950. How to best connect donors with patients was not yet a standardized practice, but rather the object of negotiation and controversy, local experimentation and professional debate. Sources used in this article are physicians' accounts in medical journals and archival material.[2] It is therefore largely their attempts at putting order to haphazard practices that will be featured here – their cutting of veins and arteries, their positioning of needles, their choices of techniques and donors, and their organizing of local blood services and 'blood banks'.

I will, however, also endeavour to give due regard to the largely silent providers of blood. Who were these donors, and how were their bodies brought into the act of donation? We shall see how initially quite intimate encounters between donors and recipients gradually changed to a more indirect and anonymous relationship. As such, the meaning of donation, as both a medical and technical act and an emerging social phenomenon, is the focus of the forthcoming analysis.

Technology Matters

Performing Direct or Indirect Transfusion?

In the middle of the First World War, scientists in several different countries announced that sodium citrate added to collected blood would prevent the blood from coagulating and becoming both useless and dangerous to the recipient. By the end of the war this insight had been put into practice in the American, British and French armies. It enabled a procedure called 'indirect transfusion', whereby blood would be collected in one location, stored for a few days in bottles with

---

2   The discussion is based on more than 100 published articles and proceedings in contemporary Swedish and Scandinavian medical journals, as well as international sources, and secondary analyses. For reasons of space, only the major sources will be referenced here, but see Berner (forthcoming).

the citrate solution, and transported to the wounded in field hospitals. This was the beginning of a renaissance for blood transfusion in Europe, after several false starts in the 19th century (Maluf 1954, Pelis 2001, Schneider 1997, Starr 1998).

In Sweden, a non-combatant country, the citrate method was largely untried until after the war. Following some disastrous early experiences in the 1870s, no further blood transfusions had been attempted until June 1916, when in a small northern town, a 14-year-old boy was admitted to the hospital with extensive injuries to his arms and legs after having been caught in a machine for several minutes. The attending surgeon, Torsten Rietz, realized that blood loss would soon lead to severe anaemia, threatening the boy's life. In desperation, Rietz attempted to save the boy with the help of a blood transfusion. The father, 'a healthy 40-year-old engine-driver', immediately volunteered as a donor. Here is Rietz' own account:

> The father was put on a table. After having had his right forearm shaved and disinfected with iodine, he was wheeled in and placed parallel to the operating table, with his head in the same direction as that of his son. The right arm of the father was laid perpendicular to his trunk with the arm's radial side facing the ulnar side of the boy's left arm.
>
> The arms were connected with a bandage. Using local anaesthetics the father's right a. radialis was uncovered to a length of ten cm. and after the positioning of a Höpfner vessel clamp, the artery was cut at the level of the wrist. Ligature of the peripheral stump. The boy's vena basilica was incised for a stretch of eight to ten cm and was also equipped with a clamp. [Rietz then describes how he used a particular 'trick of the trade' among surgeons, which involved cutting the stumps diagonally to get a larger opening of the vessels.] With the help of straight needles and black silk thread, three supporting stitches were first made, then a continuous suture. When the vessel clamps were removed, the [father's] blood flowed into the vein (Rietz 1916: 1457).

The transfusion lasted 45 minutes, after which the father felt weak and experienced a rapid fall in his heart rate. At this point the transfusion was interrupted and the father received an injection of camphor. The father's artery and the son's vein were ligatured, and the wounds closed. As for the son, '[t]he transfusion had a wonderful effect on the lad', Rietz reports. From having been pale and weak, the boy 'recovered quickly, his colouring returned, his pulse was improved'. The blood circulation in his legs seemed almost restored. Some weeks later, and after some further treatment of the wounds, the patient was discharged.

The preconditions for this somewhat intricate operation were developments in blood vessel surgery. In the United States, the French surgeon Alexis Carrel had developed a method for suturing the fine and slippery blood vessels together (the three stitches and the continuous suture referred to above), a feat that helped him win a Nobel Prize for medicine in 1912. His method was refined by George

W. Crile, who is credited with having established blood transfusion as a viable technology in the US before the First World War (Diamond 1980, Lederer 2008, Starr 1998). The Swedish surgeon did not like Crile's simplified method, but like Carrel, used fine thread and straight needles – 'the smallest number of English sewing needles (nr 16), to be obtained in a well-stocked haberdasher's shop' – to suture the artery and vein. The needle and thread were boiled in Vaseline before the operation, and Rietz also administered plenty of Vaseline or paraffin during the operation, as well as a sodium chloride solution to prevent desiccation (Rietz 1916: 1461).

This method – direct transfusion with vessel surgery – was a technically difficult procedure, demanding surgical precision and a clinical gaze to assess when the donor and recipient had had enough. Rietz later admitted, after having done several more transfusions in this way, that one problem with this method was that there was no way of ascertaining how much blood was actually transfused: 'You have to keep on doing it until the patient has recovered, and you have to stop before the person delivering the blood shows signs of exhaustion' (Reitz 1921: 154). The Carrel-Crile procedure was therefore a somewhat experimental operation that had a number of disadvantages. It demanded a highly dextrous surgeon's skills and several assistants, and could hardly be used on a large scale or in emergencies. Apart from the difficulty of ascertaining the volume of blood transfused, there was the considerable disadvantage of injuring the donor, as the radial artery had to be uncovered through a lengthy incision and then ligatured at the conclusion of the process. The donor would therefore be permanently scarred, and could not likely donate blood more than twice (Keynes 1922: 111).

For these and other reasons, Rietz and other doctors soon came to prefer *indirect* transfusion with citrated blood (i.e., the method used during the First World War), which was seen as simpler and less dangerous. Several more or less elaborate combinations of syringes, glass ampoules, tubes and bottles were now being proposed for this purpose. Some Swedish doctors favoured what was called 'Jeanbrau's ampoule', a glass flask developed by a French surgeon, with marked gradations and a narrow spout at an angle at its lower end. Using it involved exposing a suitable vein on the donor, slitting the vein wall and introducing the spout into the vein. With the help of a double balloon connected to the ampoule, the desired amount of blood could be drawn into the ampoule and mixed with the appropriate amount of citrate solution. When enough blood was collected, the vein was closed with a clamp, the spout removed, and the wound left open (see Figure 9.1). Then the recipient's vein was slit, the spout of the ampoule introduced, and the blood slowly injected into the vein. The procedure was repeated, as necessary, until the veins of both the donor and recipient were ligatured and the wounds closed (Odelberg 1920, Rietz 1921, von Stapelmohr 1930: 7).

The citrate method seemed so convenient that in a 1920 review article a Swedish doctor argued that 'the problem of blood transfusion had been solved' (Odelberg 1920: 387). By this he was claiming that the problem of coagulation that had plagued transfusion since its cautious re-establishment in the early 19th

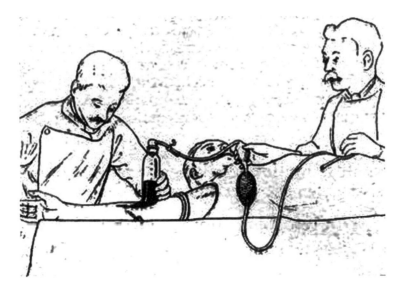

Figure 9.1   Jeanbrau's method: blood-letting in 1928
Source: Loodts 2009.

century (cf. Pelis 1997) had been resolved. While the citrate solution prevented coagulation when blood was exposed to air (which clogs tubes and prevents transfusion, and endangers the patient), not everyone felt it was a solution to the problem of transfusion.

Using Pure or Diluted Blood?

Controversy soon developed around the various side effects of mixing blood with citrate solution. Patients were suffering reactions such as fever, shivering fits, vomiting, back pain and vertigo, and many doctors, both internationally and in Sweden, became highly suspicious of these effects. One prominent surgeon, Söderlund, maintained that as a result of these side effects, the citrate method 'was doomed to disappear and also *ought* to disappear because of the dangers it posed to the patient' (Söderlund 1930: 521). He and others proposed alternate methods using what was called 'pure' or 'natural' blood, without additives. Pure blood, however, posed the classic problem: how to prevent the blood from coagulating during transmission from donor to recipient?

Once again, some doctors argued for *direct* transfusion to avoid exposing the blood to air. Using vessel sutures, as proposed by Carrel or Rietz, to transfuse 'pure' blood, was, however, not considered viable any more. Injection needles were used instead, and various complicated contraptions were inserted into and between donors and recipients to further the blood flow. One example was a German instrument called Oehlecker's apparatus, which became standard at several hospitals in Sweden. It consisted of three 50-gram glass syringes and a T-valve with two injection needles that were to be inserted into the veins of the donor and the recipient, respectively (see Figure 9.2). The two people were placed close to another, incisions were made in the arms of the donor and recipient, and the needles were inserted into the veins. Then a relatively complicated procedure of alternatively attaching syringes and opening and closing the valve took place. About 50 cubic centimetres of blood would be collected at a time from the donor

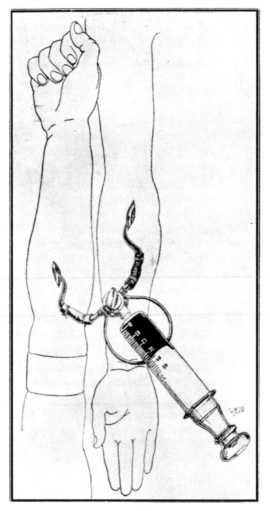

Der Apparat von Oehlecker.

Figure 9.2   Oehlecker's method

Source: Kubanyi 1928: 39.

and, after appropriately reorganizing the T-valve, injected into the recipient. From time to time, the system was flushed through with a saline solution. While one of the proponents of the method acknowledged that it was somewhat cumbersome and required several assistants to clean the syringes and administer the technique, it was effective and avoided coagulation (von Stapelmohr 1930: 47–48).

Other doctors were less convinced. The above-mentioned surgeon, Söderlund, argued strongly against using Oehlecker's method as a standard procedure due to its complexity. He argued that for blood transfusion to be a truly effective therapy, it needed to be so simple that it could be handled by the youngest assistant in a surgical ward, or even outside the hospital setting. Söderlund and others therefore preferred the *indirect* method of transfusing 'pure' blood, using flasks and needles coated internally with paraffin wax to prevent the blood from sticking to the surfaces and coagulating. Söderlund had completed more than 150 transfusions using this method (the Brown-Percy method) with paraffin-lined Jeanbrau flasks, in sick wards as well as in private homes. Some preparatory work was needed to line the interior of the flask and syringes with paraffin, and the technique also involved exposing the veins of donors and recipients (albeit with, he argued, a very small one to three centimetre incision). Overall, however, it was a much easier method to learn than the direct method, as well as faster, more efficient and very reliable (Söderlund 1930: 524–525).

Partial Accomplishments

By 1930, blood transfusion was practised in several Swedish hospitals, but the procedure was far from standardized. Rather, it reflected local doctors' preferences and skills. One author summarized the situation in 1930 as one where 'indications for a blood transfusion were still … considerably varied and contested … Opinions also diverge as to the methodology to use, and none of the existing methods has won the general approval that a perfect normal method should have' (Dahlgren 1930: 1646). Uncertainty around the practice prevailed throughout the 1930s: sometimes an indirect method with citrated blood was used with Jeanbrau's flask and a so-called Rotanda syringe, sometimes pure blood was transfused using a paraffin-lined flask; and sometimes doctors made a direct transfusion using, for example, Jüngling's, Beck's or Oehlecker's apparatuses (Gärdstam and Lilliestierna 1932, Liedholm 1936, Sköld 1936).

There was also disagreement as to where and by whom the procedure should be performed. Blood transfusion, surgeons argued, was a serious and even dangerous operation that posed mortal risks, and should only be performed by surgeons and in surgical wards (Nilsson 1936, Söderlund 1930, von Stapelmohr 1930). Several methods involved exposing and cutting donor and recipient veins, and necessitated having assistants rinse and re-organize syringes and needles or coat them in paraffin, and often under time pressure and with a risk of contamination. As one physician later recalled, a transfusion during the 1930s and even into the

1940s was normally logged as an operation, and identified with the surgeon's name (Thorén 1993: 126).

This, however, was not the whole picture. Transfusions in the 1930s were also performed in private homes and in places far away from the hospitals (Sundell 1935), and were no longer the exclusive domain of surgeons during an operation. By the mid-1930s, transfusions were also used as treatment for ulcers, anaemia, shock, infections, burns and haemophilia (Sköld 1936: 1660). This was, as one internist noted in 1936, sometimes done

> ... in competition with the surgical wards who sometimes wanted to monopolize the method for themselves, observing strict sterility, etc. But experience has shown that ... simple medical methods give as good results as the complicated surgical ones, and in addition, save the veins (Tillgren 1936: 2014).

As a result, local variations, disagreement and experimentation abounded. This existed internationally, too, where a host of different techniques were used based on local doctors' preferences and innovations, such as Unger's method, Jüngling's method, Beck's method, Merke's method, Tzanck's method, Riddell's modification of Jouvelet's method and so on. As we have seen, some of these methods were also practised in Swedish hospitals. In short, there was no established order of transfusion, but partial and local accomplishments, orderings and reorderings.

Contacting Bodies

The Donor Experience

I have found no accounts of what patients in the interwar years thought about receiving the blood of others. This may not be surprising, however, as they were often in a weakened state at the time of receiving the transfusion. Blood donors are similarly silent in the available material. One blood donor, however – Arne Tallberg, an author of popular medical literature – provided a retrospective account of his experience as a donor in the interwar years in the trade union journal *Byggnadsarbetaren* in 1962:

> At that time, 30–35 years ago, blood donation was somewhat like an unselfish sacrifice. It always took place directly from the blood donor to the patient, you were placed side by side on your respective operating table. Thus, there was a personal contact between donor and recipient and it was not least this situation that gave you a stimulating feeling of having donated a part of yourself to a fellow human being in distress (Tallberg 1962: 10).

In his account, Tallberg most likely refers to the use of Oehlecker's method of direct transfusion of 'pure' blood; as noted above this was used at several hospitals and a fairly large number of these transfusions were performed in the years around 1930 (see Figure 9.3).

What Tallberg experienced as 'personal' and 'stimulating' direct contact between donor and patient was, however, considered problematic by many physicians given the very real risk of infection. Most notably, however, this physically intimate situation was seen as *psychologically* undesirable. Some Swedish transfusionists refused to use Oehlecker's or Beck's apparatus 'for the reason that they presuppose that donor and recipient should be placed very close to each other, something which in many cases is not appropriate for psychological reasons' (Johansson 1929: 213). Schuberth and Söderlund always kept donors and recipients in different rooms, to keep the risk of infection down and diminish the 'psychic effects' (1935: 601). And Gärdstam and Lilliestierna used direct transfusion only in very special cases, since the operation, according to them, had 'the disadvantage of making too grandiose an impression ... through the placement of the two parties side by side' (1932: 7). This situation, they argued,

Abb. 18.

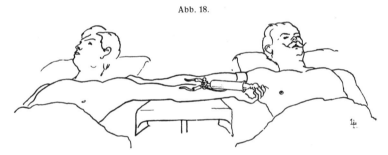

Lagerung von Spender und Empfänger bei der Transfusion nach Oehlecker.
(Erste Möglichkeit.)

Abb. 19.

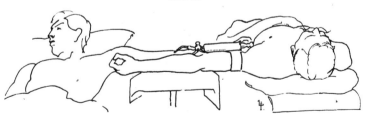

Lagerung von Spender und Empfänger bei der Transfusion nach Oehlecker.
(Zweite Möglichkeit.)

Figure 9.3   Oehlecker's method, two versions

Source: Kubanyi 1928: 40.

risked negatively influencing the recruitment of donors, who might not want to donate again after having experienced the emotional stress of lying beside – and being directly linked to – a very sick, severely wounded or even dying patient.

However, even when *indirect* methods were used the donor had to be present (albeit in a different room than the patient), since blood-letting and transfusion still had to take place within a small window of time. Blood kept in paraffin-coated containers lasted only five to ten minutes before it coagulated and became useless. Citrated blood kept longer, but it was ideally used soon after donation so that no complications would arise. As a result, this meant that the donor had to be close by or available on short notice if the need arose. Indirect transfusions also often involved a surgical incision and local anaesthesia, which necessitated some rest or diminished activity afterwards. Not surprisingly, therefore, blood donation in the early interwar period had to appeal to what Tallberg called a sense of 'unselfish sacrifice', and the pool of donors was rather small.

Finding Donors

'Of all the developments in blood donation between the wars, the greatest change was in the selection and organization of donors', one historian of blood transfusion has remarked (Schneider 2003: 193). Although the social base for the mobilization of donors varied from country to country, there seem to be some similarities among who were called upon to donate.

The most common initial source of blood in Sweden, as elsewhere, was the patient's kin and friends. In many cases, these individuals were considered morally obligated to donate.

> In most cases, I first turn to the patient's closest relatives [von Stapelmohr wrote in 1930]. Here I would of course most easily obtain a suitable donor. And furthermore, they are more prone to spending their blood than complete outsiders. Thus, I have entirely left this task to the family of the sick person ... [I]t is in the patient's, his family's, or his friends' interest to see to it that there is a blood donor available (1930: 45–46).

Relying on relatives or friends was not without its problems. The patient might not have had any close relatives or friends nearby. They might have had a communicable disease. Sometimes friends or relatives even refused: 'Twice I have seen a downright refusal to find a donor to a severely ill relative [von Stapelmohr reported]. Once, a transfusion from the patient's healthy children would have saved the soon thereafter dead mother' (1930: 46).

Also, as was increasingly realized during the interwar years, even close relatives did not always have the same blood type as the patient. Landsteiner's discovery of what he thought were three different blood types dates back to 1901; others soon found a fourth type, and in the mid-1930s all four types received the designations used today (A, B, AB and O). It would take some years, however, before Landsteiner's discovery became part of routine clinical practice. Rietz and others conducting transfusions during and immediately after the First World War did not, and could not, test for blood type compatibility; as it turned out they were simply lucky in their choice of donors. Even later, blood typing was sometimes not done because of a lack of time. In these instances, doctors relied on the 'biological test', which involved starting with a transfusion of small amounts of blood to check for any unwanted reactions (Odelberg 1920: 397, Vidfelt 1928: 1430, cf. Diamond 1980: 675, Schneider 1997: 113).

Blood typing was established as a more or less standard practice during the 1920s. Swedish hospitals most often used commercial kits of test sera; the first such kits came from places like Vienna, although Swedish brands became available later. When in a hurry, doctors used already-identified 'universal donors' (i.e., those with blood type O). But there were still complications, as there seemed to exist incompatible sub-groups (partially explained with the discovery of the Rh system in 1940). Moreover, everyday practices were sometimes quite disorganized: mistakes were made in blood typing, blood samples were mixed up, outdated and inefficient tests were used, sterilization procedures were incomplete, and there was contamination from donors. Blood transfusion remained a dangerous practice, particularly for the recipient, although the donors also risked feeling weak, feeling pain, or even fainting (Forssman and Fogelgren 1927, Johansson 1929, Nilsson 1936: 219).

As blood transfusion became more commonplace, donors other than close relatives had to be found. Hospitals began to turn to persons who were part of some kind of hierarchical social structure, who could be expected to be rather healthy, and who were easily accessible. One such category was other patients staying in the hospital for bone fractures or other accidents. A second frequently-used group was hospital staff, such as doctors, medical students and nurses. Large hospitals kept a list of donors with blood type O available among its staff for use in urgent situations, a practice that lasted well into the 1940s. 'During the early 1940s [one doctor later recalled], medical students often constituted the blood reserve. It happened during many lectures, that an operating nurse would put her head in through the door and cry: 'We need someone with blood group O to operation immediately'. Therefore, all students had to be blood typed at the latest before the start of the surgical course' (Thorén 1993: 126).

The use of hospital staff was not uniformly accepted. Von Stapelmohr, for one, was strongly against it. He argued that doctors and nurses were needed for hospital care and should not be seen as 'blood letting cisterns' (von Stapelmohr 1930: 45). He preferred a third category of donors, which was relatively accessible and whose medical status was fairly well known: public servants such as the police, firemen or members of the military. In fact, their involvement as blood donors was quite common in the 1930s in several Swedish cities – a practice that helped characterize blood donation as a civic duty, a notion that would be prominent during the Second World War (albeit more in combatant countries than in neutral Sweden).

Creating a Donor Corps

The next attempt at increasing the number of donors was to extend the search among the general public. Major influences for this approach came from the United States and Great Britain. 'Professional donors' were employed by some large American hospitals as far back as the 1920s. Such donors had to come immediately when needed, were bled once a month or even more often, and were paid about 35 dollars for each donation. American donors, however, were a mixed group and included workers and medical students, but also alcoholics. This posed particular problems during the Great Depression, as far too much blood-letting took place from weak individuals or those with an increased risk of various contagious diseases. In addition, a number of disreputable blood procurement agents were operating in larger American cities, despite efforts by the medical authorities to put the practice on a sounder basis (Nemo 1934, Lederer 2008, Schneider 2003, Starr 1998).

The British had used blood transfusion during the First World War, bleeding slightly wounded soldiers (of which there were many) who were willing to give blood out of curiosity, solidarity or because of the extra leave blood donors were provided. In peacetime, however, it was more difficult to recruit donors. A prominent figure within the early British blood service, Geoffrey Keynes (a medical doctor and brother of the economist John Maynard Keynes), argued in 1922:

> [It is perhaps natural] that occasionally a man should feel some repugnance to taking part in a strange performance which he but dimly understands. To the young, on the other hand, the procedure may appeal by its faint flavour of adventure (Keynes 1922: 98).

British hospitals sometimes had to advertise for donors, but there was a strong call for an American-style corps of professional donors: healthy, blood-typed individuals able to be called on short notice, and comfortable with 'the strange performance'. In 1921, the first British blood centre was created by an idealistic and enterprising lower civil servant, Percy Lane Oliver. It later evolved into a major blood donation centre, with donors recruited through various existing organizations such as the Boy Scouts, the YMCA and fire halls. Oliver and his wife worked for free, and financed the centre via donations and through the sale of used aluminium foil. Oliver was very much against the for-profit professional blood centres which existed in other British cities, and where donors were paid up to three guineas for their donations. Instead, Oliver wanted to encourage the 'unselfishness' of the donor, create a blood donor community, raise the status of blood donors in society, and improve the way they were treated by surgeons and in hospitals (Sköld 1939a, Schneider 2003, Gunson and Dodsworth 1996).

Oliver's centre came to influence work at the first Swedish blood donation centre, or blood donor service, which was established in 1934, at St. Göran's hospital in Stockholm. Like the London centre and several others abroad, it was established by an enterprising individual, a young doctor named Erik Sköld. Sköld managed to persuade the hospital's managers to invest in a centre for 'uniformly examined blood donors' and overcame the resistance of other hospitals in the city who wanted to handle recruitment themselves (but who, according to Sköld, had varying and questionable criteria for which individuals could be accepted as donors). Sköld initially did all the practical work himself – from producing test sera, to blood-typing donors, to organizing and producing donor registry cards. Donors, who in 1935 numbered 150 individuals, were recruited from fire fighters, members of the Red Cross, medical students and unemployed persons, thus 'belonging to the most diverse occupations' (Sköld 1935: 395). They were medically examined and required to sign a declaration of health, stating that they did not suffer from syphilis, malaria, asthma, tuberculosis or hay fever. Sköld's vision was something that resembled a professional donor corps: 'It is to be hoped, that after a while there will be a crystallization of an elite group among the donors with the best physical and psychic conditions and the right sense of responsibility for their task' (Sköld 1935: 400).

For some time after its establishment, the Stockholm blood donor service (which soon moved to St. Erik's hospital) was used only to procure donors. Hospitals in Stockholm would phone the centre to requisition a donor of the right blood type. The number of transfusions for which the service supplied donors grew from six in 1934 to about 1,800 in 1939 and more than 5,300 in 1943. In the 1940s, the number of blood donors increased significantly in Sweden, as a result of large organizational and propaganda efforts during the Second World War (more about this below).

A blood donor registered with the Stockholm centre was expected to be able to respond at short notice. He or she needed to be reachable by telephone, either directly or through a neighbour, and always had to carry a donation card that included a photo and various medical and other information. Donors were expected to lead healthy and orderly lives and avoid catching venereal diseases (which tests could not identify immediately). Indeed, a 1946 brochure from the Stockholm blood administration admonished prospective candidates: 'Such [contamination] is normally contracted when under the influence of alcohol, wherefore the blood donor should exercise restraint in this matter' (Sköld 1946). Thus, the ideal donor was a disciplined and well-intentioned person who was willing to suffer some inconvenience in support of others in need. Despite these efforts, however, hospitals and blood centres could not rely solely on the donors' sense of solidarity and compassion for their fellow human beings; various incentives also had to be offered.

Keeping Donors

The donor Arne Tallberg, cited above, remembered blood donation during the 1920s and 1930s as a selfless and unpaid deed, maintaining that 'There was never a question of getting paid for the blood you gave to a fellow being' (Tallberg 1962: 10). This, however, was not altogether the case.

Relatives and friends of the patient were normally not paid for their blood. But convalescing patients who donated blood at the Sahlgrenska hospital in Gothenburg in the 1920s received 'a small encouragement in the form of a steak and a beer. Nowadays they also receive 15 crowns which is entered as pharmaceutical costs' (Johansson 1929: 214–215). Some doctors spoke of the danger of being too generous to donors. Some cited examples from the United States where, according to one Swedish doctor, a donor could be paid between 40 and 400 dollars – creating the risk that young people could abuse the system. This doctor also provided a moral example from his own experience:

> It happened once in Landskrona in 1925, that a patient did not have any relatives within easy reach. Through advertising at the local regiment, several [individuals] volunteered and after a suitable group had been found, one donor was selected. A rumour then spread that he would ask for 200 crowns for the procedure, but after us having made an agreement with the regimental head to offer him about a week's time off and 25 crowns, no further or higher demands were made (von Stapelmohr 1930: 46).

Erik Sköld, who tried to attract donors from voluntary organizations, also hinted at the difficulty of recruiting and, more importantly, maintaining suitable donors. In this case, payment was considered necessary, and as blood donation became more common in the late 1930s and in the 1940s, the sum of 25–30 Swedish crowns seems to have become the standard fee for a typical transfusion (*Betänkande* 1951: 9).

Was this 'blood for sale', as had been occurring in the United States? Sköld and others tended to downplay the role of money, and argued that many Swedish donors gave blood for idealistic reasons. While this was probably often the case, payment was not unimportant. In 1945, 25–30 Swedish crowns was the equivalent of about 500 Swedish crowns or €50 today. Donors could be bled as often as once a month, and it was reported that students used money from blood donations to help pay for their studies. Moreover, once it became the norm, it seemed difficult to stop paying donors, at least in peacetime (*Betänkande* 1951: 31).

Providing payment for blood donations underlined the fact that, by the end of the interwar period, donation had become a more anonymous and de-personalized procedure than was previously the case. Indirect transfusion kept the donor and recipient in different rooms, donors and patients would normally never see each other, and Sköld, for one, was adamant that the donor 'should under no circumstances be informed of the recipient's name and diagnosis' (Sköld 1939a: 304).The procedure could not be too anonymous and impersonal, however. 'Care work' was needed to ensure that the increasingly routine procedure remained a valuable one for the donors. (cf. Jonvallen 2005). Otherwise, it was feared that donors might tire of the practice and decide not to return. This was, at least, the message given by Sköld to the hospitals using the services of his blood centre.

Clearly drawing inspiration from Percy Lane Oliver's London centre (which he visited in 1938), Sköld argued that blood donors should be met by a friendly nurse accompanying them to the site of donation. They should be spared from witnessing unpleasant hospital scenes, such as operations and sick patients, and should be bled only by an experienced person using high-quality instruments. Moreover, aside from exceptional situations, they should never have their veins exposed. 'It has been shown that such an operation makes blood donation highly unpopular and, in addition, prevents the blood donor from being available many times. It also involves a risk of infection and work incapacity', he argued in a memorandum to hospitals in 1939 (Sköld 1939a: 304).

It is little wonder that Sköld became highly critical of experiments being undertaken by some Stockholm physicians in the late 1930s involving the injection of heparin into blood donors. Heparin is a blood-thinning substance extracted from sources such as ox liver, which Swedish scientists managed to produce in a pure and relatively cheap form in the 1930s. It was considered a promising substitute for sodium citrate for preventing collected blood from coagulating, even by Sköld himself (Sköld 1936, 1939a). But at two Swedish hospitals the substance was also injected into some 150 donors, thus inducing them into a 'haemophiliac condition' wherein their blood would not coagulate. This blood was then tapped and used, either directly or indirectly, with a flask and syringe. The experimenting physicians were enthusiastic, as the procedure gave them sufficient time to not have to expose the veins of the donor and patient, and reduced the chances of the blood coagulating. The procedure also allowed them to use 'slow-bleeding donors'. In addition, the simplicity of the method supposedly rendered it very practical in cases of accident or in the event of war: 'All a doctor need take along for a blood transfusion are a syringe and heparin ampoule ... and such blood transfusions could be done on the spot' (Hedenius 1936: 266–267, see also Hedenius 1937, Schuberth 1938). But Sköld who accepted the use of heparin in blood already collected, was highly sceptical to its being injected into donors, and voiced his objections at a meeting of the Swedish Medical Association: What would be the consequences if the donor was wounded while in his haemophiliac condition, or if he had an ulcer or burst haemorrhoids – might he not then bleed to death? Sköld also reported that a few donors had had negative experiences with this procedure:

> One was naturally quite angry, since he had to refrain from a previously accepted invitation, because it took him three whole hours to stop a bleeding after a shaving nick that occurred four hours after he was heparinized. Another blamed a nausea and diarrhoea on the injection (Sköld 1938: 36).

Once again, Sköld objected to practices that could give blood donation a bad reputation and threaten his creation of a steady corps of donors. In this case, the organizer of an efficient blood centre opposed physicians applying experimental procedures, and won. The heparinization of donors was soon abandoned. Since the medical use of human blood was increasing at the time, most physicians realized that anything that would frighten prospective blood donors and make blood donation unpopular had to be avoided. The seriousness of the situation was underlined by the advent of the Second World War. The imperative to find as many donors as possible was clear; as a result, procedures had to be simple, efficient and unobtrusive.

Organizing Mass Recruitment

During the First World War, citrated blood had been collected in one place and then transported to field hospitals. It could keep for up to 14 days (albeit with diminished efficacy). For various reasons, the practice was not revived until the late 1930s, as doctors preferred warm, fresh blood that could be transfused directly or indirectly. Then again, it was wartime conditions that gave rise to the collection of blood from large numbers of donors and then storing it before use.

During the Spanish Civil War (which started in 1936), the Republican army created an advanced organization for blood donation and transfusion. Blood was collected from a large number of voluntary donors and sent in large ampoules and refrigerated cars to the fighters on the various fronts. Efficient propaganda was used to recruit donors and in Barcelona alone there were about 14,000 female donors. The technology used involved mixing blood from five or six donors (only type O-type donors were used), filtering it, adding sodium citrate and transferring the blood to ampoules in which the air pressure was raised to two atmospheres immediately before sealing. An ingenious tube and syringe system then enabled quick use of the ampoules in field conditions (Jorda 1939, Starr 1998).

The process was widely reported, and inspired blood donation organizations outside Spain as well (e.g. Sköld 1939b). The organizer of the process, F. Duran Jorda, fled to England and later helped organize the British blood service during the Second World War. By 1939, Sweden, too, had to make provisions for possible future needs (Sköld 1939b, Nordlander 1944, Palmer 1940, Widström 1942), and the Medical Board of the Army Administration stepped in to organize the mass blood-typing of conscripts, standardize methods, and expand its recruitment of donors. By end of 1939, eleven blood donation centres had been established at various hospitals across the country. In 1942 an additional eight were created under the military administration. All conscripts and military personnel were blood-typed, as were a number of voluntary citizens. Completely new methods to recruit blood donors were utilized: folders and posters, radio programmes, and the mobilization of the Red Cross, other voluntary organizations, public authorities and even factory managers. The war atmosphere helped mobilize donors, but other incentives proved necessary, too. Donors received an extra portion of rationed food (meat and wheat meal) for each blood donation (Molin 1943: 46).

In 1944, there were about 30,000 voluntary donors registered and blood typed in Sweden (Nordlander 1944: 189), a significant increase on the few thousand donors in the interwar years. Recruitment, however, was uneven. In some cities with blood donation centres, seven per cent of the population was registered as blood donors, whereas in others the rate was barely one per cent. As one author exclaimed in the journal *Vårt Försvar* (Our Defence) in 1943, 'much remains to be accomplished' (Molin 1943: 46). Not surprisingly, the city of Boden, which was home to a large military contingent and was in close proximity to the Finnish border, was the top donor city (Nordlander 1944: 189). In 1939, the war between Finland and the Soviet Union involved many Swedes, as Swedish blood and plasma was sent to Finland and Swedish doctors treated wounded Finnish soldiers, both in Finland and across the border in Sweden (Unonius, Schröder and Elving 1941, Odén 1945, Molin 1943).

From Bodies to Bottles to Banks

Mass recruitment went hand-in-hand with technical and organizational changes. Before the 1930s blood was 'stored' in the donors' bodies, or intermittently in ampoules and syringes, but not in 'banks'. What was then to be called 'stored blood' had been used since the early 1930s in the Soviet Union where physicians organized blood banks with refrigerated blood from recently deceased individuals, so called 'cadaver blood'. About 2,500 such transfusions were completed (Starr 1998: 70). The practice did not really catch on anywhere else; Swedish doctors, among others, found it unworkable for both psychological and organizational reasons (e.g., Schuberth 1940: 906).

The first blood centres using blood that had been stored for weeks, rather than blood from 'walk-in' donors, were established on a large scale in the USSR in the 1930s. This inspired doctors in the United States to set up the first American blood bank in Chicago in 1937 (Starr 1998: 71). This was soon followed by other cities in the US. These were banks in the proper sense of the term, since individuals were expected to make deposits of blood, or pay with money or their own blood after drawing upon the banks' resources (Lederer 2008). In Sweden, there was a gradual transition from fresh blood to what was called 'depot blood' during the 1940s. Some large hospitals increasingly relied upon donors who gave regularly, and not only in situations of emergency. Their blood was then stored in what was also here called a blood bank. In the Swedish context, this term was not entirely accurate as nobody made 'deposits' in the bank, and patients did not have to pay for drawing upon the bank's blood supply.

The large ampoules used to store blood in the Spanish Civil War were not considered suitable in the Swedish context. Instead, a simpler and ingenious solution was developed by using ordinary soda water bottles and corks fitted with stoppers, needles, a siphon tube and a balloon pump (see Figure 9.4). Blood was collected straight into the bottle, which included a citrate solution or heparin (which stored the blood for a few days without deterioration), or from 1943 onwards, an ACD (Acid citrate-dextrose) solution. This was an efficient solution that impeded coagulation and preserved the red blood cells for up to two weeks. The bottles of stored or preserved blood were then kept in refrigerators. If the need arose, the

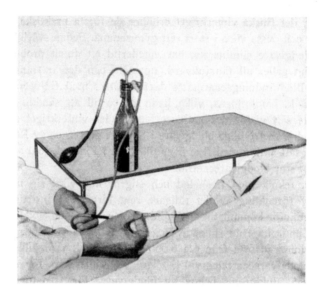

Figure 9.4   Blood transfusion with soda water bottle
Source: Molin 1943: 39.

bottles could be transported to the field hospitals in 'ordinary ice-cream vans' and
then used directly for transfusion purposes (Sköld 1939b: 1730, 1944: 186–188).
A committee set up by the Army Administration recommended the soda water
bottle principle as standard practice in 1939. It was exported to Finland during
the Finnish Winter War in 1939 and succeeded in that context (Unonius, Schröder
and Elving 1941: 1048). By 1948, however, the soda water bottles were felt to
have a number of technical and practical shortcomings, provoking the creation
of a new state committee. In 1950, the committee had designed a new kind of
bottle, in three sizes, to be manufactured by Swedish firms, and used for all kinds
of medical transfusion and infusion purposes. This bottle soon became a standard
among Nordic countries (Grönwall et al. 1950), and was the established method in
the major hospitals across Sweden (*Betänkande* 1951). In 1947, one surgeon at the
Karolinska Institute in Stockholm highlighted the changes as follows:

> While a transfusion only a decade ago was a rather complicated operation which
> demanded important preparations and was normally conducted in the operating
> theatre by a surgeon with considerable assistance, etc., the physician now only
> needs to fetch a blood bottle from the depot and administer it, most often in the
> sick ward. The procedure is little more complicated than a common intravenous
> injection (Palmlöv 1947: 883).

Conclusion: Re-ordering Bodies and Techniques

From just a few hundred transfusions in the 1920s and 1930s, by the end of the Second World War the practice of blood transfusion became an established, major medical treatment. In 1949, at least 65,000 transfusions were made in Sweden, mostly with whole blood in bottles. Plasma donation (which commenced during the war) was still a minor practice, and took place mainly in the larger hospitals. In the late 1940s, there were only about 30,000 registered blood donors in the country – a figure that was considered far too low (barely more than during the war) and a cause for concern (*Betänkande* 1951).

By this point in time, the interwar debates over which methods or apparatuses to employ during blood transfusions (which we have outlined in this article) were over. The complicated and sometimes invasive procedures of the 1920s and 1930s were succeeded by a simpler practice that could be performed by assistants and nurses; the dramatic procedure had become a routine one. Instead of moving blood by stitching the donor's artery to the recipient's vein, using ampoules and syringes, or screwing two-way taps, the physicians now performed a simple injection, or administered a drip. The transfusion took place in the ward, and no longer in the operating theatre, and instead of searching for a suitable donor among relatives, nurses or local fire fighters, the doctor retrieved a bottle from the depot.

Thus, multiple and unstable orders were gradually replaced by something more uniform and standardized. As blood transfusion became more entrenched in everyday clinical practices, on a large scale and in various settings, it changed its character. In terms used by Moreira (2000: 440) it was no longer part of a 'fluid space of objects' but started to show characteristics of a more stabilized, extended 'network', where procedures, representations, institutions, instruments and techniques went together and depended upon one another.

These changes in transfusion practices had several interesting social and cultural corollaries. I will discuss how the meaning of donation, as a medico-technically constituted act and social phenomenon, was reconstituted during this period in three interconnected ways.

First, there was a *reordering of relationships*. Donors in the early interwar years were physically and socially close to the patient needing the blood transfusion. Their emotional empathy could be assumed; they were relatives or friends, or other patients in possibly similar but less life-threatening conditions, or members of some caring or helping profession. They also often had to be physically close to the sick person, sometimes practically tethered to them. Even when indirect methods were used, the donor's connection to the recipient was close, in both time and space. Doctors – and perhaps also donors and patients – saw this intimacy as problematic; this was coupled with a gradual reordering of blood transfusion techniques and organization which was both a precondition for, and a result of, mass recruitment of donors. All told, these trends pushed the practice of transfusion towards anonymity and distance. The act of donation was disconnected from the actual transfusion, and mediated through a special donor service and blood banks.

It was no longer a transfer made to an identifiable person in close and immediate need but rather to a bottle in a depot, whose final use would not be known and could take place up to a couple of weeks later.

Secondly, the new practices meant that *donor identities* changed as well. Donors, especially from the late 1930s onwards were not isolated individuals recruited in an *ad hoc* manner. Instead, donors became part of an organized system of recruitment, and were the tested and accepted providers of specific amounts of correctly classified blood. Technologies of blood donation thus contributed to form novel identities, and shape a particular subject: the *modern blood donor*. This move was uncontroversial in homogeneous Sweden, although less so in Germany (where only blood from pure 'Aryans' was collected) or the United States (where blood from whites and blacks was separated as late as the 1950s) (cf. Lederer 2008, Starr 1998).

The social role as a blood donor assumed the readiness to treat one's body as a producer of blood, and to be the willing provider of a bodily fluid to the medical system and, eventually, to the blood component industry. This was not an obvious identity to assume in the general population. Prospective donors had to be motivated and organized. Monetary compensation, cost-free health checks and a shift towards less invasive medical practices for donation were necessary preconditions in the Swedish context, coupled with intense propaganda and blood donation campaigns. The particular conditions of the Second World War helped make the disconnection of an individual body part vital and relevant, both for individual donors and for the body politic. Blood donation was heralded as a civic duty and a sign of citizenship and solidarity, in Sweden as elsewhere.

Thus the practice of transfusion had definitely changed. The act of donation was no longer the concern only of individual surgeons, hospitals or donors. It had – and this is my third point – become a matter of *national public policy*. The ever-expanding need for blood within the medical system could no longer be met locally, but needed increasing financial resources, new kinds of training and regional and national coordination. As a result, the war years and the early post-war period saw efforts towards nationwide standardization of the technologies to be used, such as blood bottles, infusion techniques and methods of blood type classification. The period also saw attempts to increase collaboration between hospitals and regions in the collection and use of blood, increase the efficiency of blood and plasma collection, and the introduction of campaigns to convince the Swedish population at large to be more generous with their blood, or as it was phrased, more 'blood-minded' (*Betänkande* 1951: 30). These were still only 'partial accomplishments' (Law 1994), and future re-orderings and changes were to come. Nevertheless, by now, the Swedish state – first the military, then various civil medical authorities – had entered the scene. From this point onwards, the blood of the many was considered a national resource, and the practices of blood donation and of moving blood became a wider public concern.

References

Berg, M. and Mol, A. (eds). 1998. *Differences in Medicine: Unraveling practices, techniques, and bodies.* Durham: Duke University Press.

Berner, B. forthcoming. *Ge blod! Ge liv? Berättelser om blodgivning, altruism och medicinsk praktik.* Lund: Arkiv.

Betänkande angående transfusionsverksamhetens organisation. 1951. Avgivet av delegerade, tillsatta av Medicinalstyrelsen och Försvarets sjukvårdsstyrelse, Stockholm.

Dahlgren, L. 1930. Blodtransfusion från tre olika givare, sammanlagt en liter, inom loppet av fem timmar. *Svenska Läkartidningen*, 27(51), 1646–1651.

Diamond, L.K. 1980. A history of blood transfusion, in *Blood, Pure and Eloquent. A Story of Discovery, of People, and of Ideas*, edited by M.M. Wintrobe. New York: McGraw-Hill Book Company, 659–688.

Forssman, J. and Fogelgren, G. 1927. Dödsfall efter blodtransfusion från person till person av 'samma' blodgrupp. En varning och förslag. *Svenska Läkartidningen*, 24(38), 1082–1088.

Gärdstam, R. and Lilliestierna, H. 1932. Erfarenheter vid transfusion av citratblod. *Nordisk Medicinsk Tidskrift*, 6–10.

Grönwall, A., Lundberg, Å., Wilander, O. and Ahlström, R. 1950. Flaska och aggregat för infusionsändamål. *Svenska Läkartidningen*, 47, 867–879.

Gunson, H.H. and Dodsworth, H. 1996. Towards a national blood transfusion service in England and Wales, 1900–1946. *Transfusion Medicine*, 6(suppl. 1), 4–16.

Healy, K. 2000. Embedded altruism: Blood collection regimes and the European Union's donor population. *American Journal of Sociology*, 105(6), 1633–1657.

Heath, C., Luff, P. and Sanchez Svensson, M. 2003. Technology and medical practice. *Sociology of Health & Illness*, 25 (Silver Anniversary Issue), 75–96.

Hedenius, P. 1936. A new method of blood transfusion. *Acta Medica Scandinavica*, LXXXIX (III-IV), 263–267.

Hedenius, P. 1937. Blodtransfusion med heparisering av givaren. *Nordisk Medicinsk Tidskrift*, 13, 1328–1330.

Johansson, S. 1929. I blodtransfusionsfrågan. Summarisk redogörelse för 221 blodtransfusionsfall. *Hygiea*, 91(6), 209–239.

Jonvallen, P. 2005. *Testing Pills, Enacting Obesity. The work of localizing tools in a clinical trial.* Linköping: Linköping University Press.

Jorda, F.D. 1939. The Barcelona blood-transfusion service. *The Lancet*, 773–775.

Keynes, G. 1922. *Blood Transfusion.* London: Henry Frowde and Hodder and Stoughton.

Kubanyi, E. 1928. *Die Bluttransfusion.* Berlin and Wien: Urban and Schwarzenberg.

Law, J. 1994. *Organizing Modernity.* Oxford: Blackwell.

Lederer, S.E. 2008. *Flesh and Blood. Organ transplantation and blood transfusion in twentieth-century America*. Oxford and New York: Oxford University Press.

Liedholm, K. 1936. Erfarenheter av blodtransfusion enligt Beck. *Nordisk Medicinsk Tidskrift*, 12-II(49), 2013–2014.

Loodts, P. 2009. *Médicins de la Grande Guerre* [Online]. Available at: http:// www.1914-1918.be/photo.php?image=photos2/soigner_transfusion_sang/ transfusion_007.jpg [accessed: 17 May 2009].

Maluf, N.S.R. 1954. History of blood transfusion. *Journal of the History of Medicine*, 9(1), 59–107.

Molin, B. 1943. Blodtransfusionen inom krigssjukvården. *Vårt försvar*, 3, 30–47.

Moreira, T. 2000. Translation, difference and ontological fluidity: Cerebral angiography and neurosurgical practice (1926–45). *Social Studies of Science*, 30(3), 421–446.

Nemo, C.V. 1934. I sell blood. *The American Mercury*, 31, 194–203.

Nilsson, F. 1936. Om komplikationer vid blodtransfusion. *Nordisk Medicinsk Tidskrift*, 212–221.

Nordlander, O. 1944. Sjukvårdsstyrelsens blodgivareverksamhet. *Nordisk Medicin*, 21(6), 189–190.

Odelberg, A. 1920. Blodtransfusionen, dess teknik och indikationer *Hygiea*, 82(12), 385–394.

Odén, G. 1945. Några erfarenheter av krigssjukvård från finska gränsen hösten 1944, in *Göteborgs Läkaresällskap 1845–1945*, edited by S. Eckerström. Göteborg: Wezäta, 92–99.

Palmer, I. 1940. Frontorganisationen av blodtransfusion. *Svenska Läkartidningen*, 37, 907–911.

Palmlöv, A. 1947. Erfarenheter av blodtransfusioner under 6 års tid vid en kirurgisk avdelning. *Hygiea,* 109(15), 883–889.

Pelis, K. 1997. Blood clots: The nineteenth-century debate over the substance and means of transfusion in Britain. *Annals of Science*, 54(44), 331–360.

Pelis, K. 2001. Taking credit: The Canadian Army medical corps and the British conversion to blood transfusion in WWI. *Journal of the History of Medicine*, 56(3), 238–277.

Rietz, T. 1916. Om direkt blodöverföring. *Allmänna Svenska Läkartidningen*, 13(50), 1456–1462.

Rietz, T. 1921. Erfarenheter med blodöverföring, föredrag 26 april 1921. *Svenska läkaresällskapets förhandlingar*, 151–167.

Schneider, W.H. 1997. Blood Transfusion in peace and war, 1900–1918. *Social History of Medicine*, 10(1), 105–126.

Schneider, W.H. 2003. Blood transfusion between the wars. *Journal of the History of Medicine*, 58(2), 187–224.

Schuberth, O. 1938. Kan heparinet medföra risk för blodgivaren? *Nordisk Medicinsk Tidskrift,* 156.

Schuberth, O. 1940. Chock och blodtransfusion. *Svenska Läkaretidningen*, 37, 900–907.

Schuberth. O. and Söderlund, G. 1935. 500 blodtransfusioner. Teknik, Komplikationer. Indikationer. Resultat. *Nordisk Medicinsk Tidskrift,* 9(16), 601–608.

Sköld, E. 1935. Organisation av en 'blodgivarecentral' i Stockholm. *Svenska Läkartidningen*, 32, 393–401.

Sköld, E. 1936. Blodtransfusioner med heparin. *Nordisk Medicinsk Tidskrift*, 1659–1661.

Sköld, E. 1938. Diskussion. *Nordisk Medicinsk Tidskrift*, 34–35.

Sköld, E. 1939a. Blodgivarecentraler och transfusionsteknik, Intryck från en studieresa. *Svenska Läkartidningen,* 36(6), 273–304.

Sköld, E. 1939b. Infusion och transfusion I krig. *Svenska Läkartidningen,* 36(39), 1725–1733.

Sköld, E. 1944. *On Haemophilia in Sweden and its Treatment by Blood Transfusion.* Stockholm: P.A. Norstedt and Söner.

Sköld, E. 1946. *Meddelande till blodgivare, Sjukhusdirektionens blodgivarcentral.* Stockholm.

Söderlund, G. 1930. Om blodtransfusion i kirurgisk praxis. *Hygiea*, 92(13), 513–535.

Starr, D. 1998. *Blood. An Epic History of Medicine and Commerce.* New York: Knopf.

Sundell, C.G. 1935. Kan praktikern utanför sjukhus, t.ex. i patientens hem, utföra blodtransfusion? *Nordisk medicinsk tidskrift*, 2031–2032.

Tallberg, A. 1962. Att ge sitt blod. *Byggnadsarbetaren*, 20, 10.

Thorén, L. 1993. Blodtransfusionens historia fram till 1940. *Nordisk medicinhistorisk årsbok*, 113–128.

Tillgren, J. 1936. Diskussion. *Nordisk Medicinsk Tidskrift*, 12-II(49), 2014.

Timmermans, S. and Berg, M. 2003. The practice of medical technology. *Sociology of Health and Illness,* 25(Silver Anniversary Issue), 97–114.

Unonius, E., Schröder, I. and Elving H. 1941. Erfarenheter rörande blodgivare och blodtransfusion i krig. *Nordisk Medicin,* 1046–1055.

Vidfelt, G. 1928. Bidrag till frågan om tekniken vid blodtransfusion. *Svenska Läkartidningen*, 25(48), 1430–1431.

von Stapelmohr, S. 1930. Blodtransfusion. *Medicinska föreningens tidskrift*, 8(1), 1–11 and 8(2), 39–50.

Waldby, C., Rosengarten, M., Treloar, C. and Fraser, S. 2004. Blood and bioidentity: Ideas about self, boundaries and risk among blood donors and people living with Hepatitis C. *Social Science and Medicine,* 59(7), 1461–1471.

Widström, G. 1942. Synpunkter på infusion och transfusion, särskilt med hänsyn till fältförhållanden. *Nordisk Medicin*, 64–68.

Epilogue
Moving Nature/Culture

Lucy Suchman

Nature/culture is moving at the interface of bodies and machines. Investments in contemporary technoscience concentrate their sights on the fields of medicine, pressing for further elaboration and more intimate entanglements of bio and techno. In laboratories, surgeries and clinics the recombination of synthetic and organic in the name of remediated bodies proceeds apace, simultaneously opening up and closing down possibilities for what a healthy body could be. And incorporated into these sites of reconfigured potentiality and control, whether as patients or as witnesses, we are (as Petra Jonvallen, in this volume, makes poignantly clear) deeply moved. In the movement toward more intensive entanglements of the biological and the technological the possibilities for life, for who lives and how, are affected.

This is, at least in part, why even those of us not directly engaged in research on medical practices may find ourselves moved by work in this area. It is hardly a mystery that the field of medicine affords such fertile ground for science and technology studies (STS). Feminist STS in particular has a deep and ongoing commitment to the project of tracing how bodies are figured in technoscience, and medicine is among the most consequential arenas in which those figurations come to matter. Meeting as professionals, patients and their kin, persons very differently situated variously restage and/or transform together the historically and culturally constituted practices that comprise medical regimes. Bodies are central to these encounters, from the embodied practices of medicine and care giving to the lived bodies of those who desire to sustain, or to recover, a state of health. And in the case of modern biomedicine, the legibility and accessibility of the body are mediated through the machine.

Medical practice comprises a site, then, in which the boundary between bodies and machines comes into relief, only to be rendered more contingent. So, for example, the relation between the body of the pregnant woman and the ultrasound image of the foetus can only be understood by incorporating the embodied skills of the nurse midwife who moves the transducer and is in turn moved by what she sees (Sandell this volume). The bodies of surgeon and operative patient, similarly, are mutually articulated (joined together and made intelligible) at the interface of hands and instruments (Prentice this volume). Acts, persons and substances once registered as life giving can be recoded as risky through technologies of institutional distribution (Berner this volume), and the difference between human and machine itself is made and unmade in laboratory practices (Kruse this volume.) The body/

machine boundary is reconfigured from a static place to something performed in time, as the interface through which subjects and objects are both differentiated and aligned.

These contingencies become particularly salient in the context of learning, in the processes through which the body of the medical practitioner is sculpted in repeated encounters with the objects of her professional practice (Prentice this volume). Here machines, in the form of simulators, appear as potential proxies for the body of the patient, stand-ins whose value turns on their capacity to simulate the latter's materiality on one hand, while remaining machinically insensate to suffering or moral implications of success and failure on the other. The criteria of adequacy for medical simulation are not representational but phenomenological, as the simulated object must be responsive to the actions of the medical 'user' (via hands, or instrument) in a way that is, at the same time, responsible to the body of the prospective patient. Medical simulators are quintessential examples of technologies understood as 'rematerialized figurations' (a slight transformation on Haraway's 'materialized refigurations' (1997: 23), see Suchman 2007: 1)), understandings of bodies built out of the specific materialities and capacities of computational hardware and software. And as the process of their construction makes clear, the object of simulation is a patient body within the temporally unfolding practice of a medical procedure (Johnson this volume). Medical simulators, in Johnson's phrasing, recreate not human anatomies, but practice-specific knowledges and methods of intervention. The simulator must operate as part of an apparatus in the Baradian sense (2007), an arrangement through which medical practitioners, instruments and patient bodies are articulated and made agentially real. When practice-specific knowledge is materialized as the simulated patient body, it is a medically specific phenomenon, not an ontologically independent anatomy that is realized.

Performing the Body/Machine Interface

Ethnographically based studies of medical simulation further elaborate how, as biomedicine renders the 'internal' parts of the body available to view or discussion, they become available as well for treatment, for connection to new and different objects and courses of action than was the case before (Prentice, Sandell, Johnson this volume, see also Cussins [Thompson] 1998). Within professional institutions, action's accountability is elaborated from the reflexive enactment of a mutually intelligible interaction order, to a bureaucratic framework for regulatory control (see Goodwin and Mort this volume); one through which threats to reason – insofar as that is seen as separate from and sovereign over corporeality – are contained. The latter include moments of transition from self to other, inside to outside (Jonvallen this volume). Things that don't fit, in turn, assume critical importance both as problems and as resources for their resolution, enacting the bounds of the normal whether in the immediacy of an urgent intervention, or in the wider constitution of professional practice, health and disease. In these encounters possibilities for knowing and acting are inseparable from the technologies through which bodies are read (as in pain, or on the threshold of dying), and actions made medically accountable. The coherence of patient bodies is at once the condition of possibility and the ongoing achievement of medical intervention. Bodies and machines share this dependence on the material-semiotics of storytelling (see Orr 1996).

Reiterating the normal is essential here, from the developing foetus (Sandell this volume), to the pubescent sexual body (Roberts this volume) to the mature human anatomy (Prentice, Johnson this volume). Integral to the construction of appropriate objects for medical intervention, the normal body and its others are at once phenomenologically, historically, culturally and materially enacted through conjoinings of persons and instruments, measured and calibrated. Within these regimes, the normal body is not innocent but infused with politics, and the warrant for intervention is often far from self-evident. Our collective investments in the practical construction of boundaries delineating the healthy from the pathological makes this particularly tricky terrain, requiring a critical project that reworks the normal/pathological dichotomy into a careful differentiation among conditions of suffering, and conditions of possibility for greater well being. Central to the latter is the articulation of cases in which intervention's object must be not the remediation of bodies identified as out of bounds, but rather the remaking of boundaries through which their pathology is delineated.

Medical interventions make evident the contingencies of the otherwise taken for granted as singular, and unambiguously bounded, body. In surrendering themselves to a form of strategic objectification in exchange for the promise of effective interventions from the medical profession (Cussins [Thompson] 1998, Thompson [Cussins] 2005), patients simultaneously work to hold onto their status as agential subjects. Medical professionals, in their turn, assume responsibility for bodies in their care within the subject positions afforded them by prevailing institutional arrangements. Variously represented and multiply materialized, the performance of the body as a coherent entity one and the same with the person is an ongoing achievement of organizational and affective labour. It is not the fixity of boundaries or even the unity of the patient body that sustains bodily integrity, but rather the persistence of necessary relations and connections. The body/machine interface is reconfigured from a static place to something performed in time, in the ontological choreographies through which bodies and technologies are both differentiated and aligned.

In her investigation of these choreographies, Charis Thompson has taught us to be wary of any simple assumption that medical interventions necessarily objectify patients and thereby strip them of their agency, or even of any unquestioned associations of agency with the good. Objectification does not, she argues, inherently or necessarily lead to alienation, nor does it stand always in opposition to subjectivity or personhood. Similarly identity, or 'self', is enacted on specific occasions and has irreducibly collective, moral and temporal dimensions:

> ... the subject is dependent on the constant ontological dance between ourselves and our environments that changes how many descriptions we fall under, of how many parts we are built, and how integrated we are or need to be ... It is the genius of the [clinical] setting – its techniques – that allows these ontological variations to be realized and to multiply. By passing through them a patient embodied new options for her long term self (Cussins [Thompson] 1998: 169–170).

Taking temporality and intercorporeality seriously implies a radical shift both theoretically and methodologically (Sundén this volume). Thompson follows out the implications of this shift for the field of medical ethics in particular. Ethical action on her analysis requires recognition of the always present possibility of alienating and/or generative recombinations of bodies and machines, turning attention from a figure of the patient as unitary and rational actor to the 'conditions for the maintenance of synecdoche'; that is, of the relations of parts and wholes (Cussins [Thompson] 1998: 200). How to get the choreography right is inseparable, moreover, from the question of who adjudicates which configurations count as desirable or not. We need always to hold open the possibility that there may be good grounds, in specific cases, for resistance to ontological innovation (Thompson [Cussins] 2005: 9).

Technology and Medical Practice: Some Questions

Like bodies (and machines), the singularity and coherence of 'medicine' is articulated not as a prior condition but as an effect of professional and bureaucratic discourses that are enabling of institutional arrangements, but also obscure the messy contingencies, internal contradictions, affective complexities and practical achievements of medicine-in-practice. To do justice to these realities requires multiple forms of engagement, from specific locations in the midst of temporally unfolding encounters and events, to close readings of historical and organizational records, to theoretically informed reflections on conceptual, practical and political implications. As new conceptualizations and empirical specificities are generated from these studies, so are research questions clarified:

- How do discourses and technological devices make bodies, both multiplying and also fixing them?
- When is 'the patient' a salient identification and for whom, and how are the many ways in which lived bodies exceed that identification relevant for medical practice?
- What if medical simulations acknowledged their specific provenance, rather than presuming universality?
- What if we understand simulations not as self-standing representations, but as materializations of the experiences/practices of their makers; at the moment, predominantly medical researchers, computer scientists and engineers?

- How might we further elucidate the co-constitution of knowledge about the body, the objects of knowledge and the professional identities – and skilled bodies– of the knowers?
- How might an appreciation for all knowledges as situated work to expand the range of 'authoritative knowledges' (Jordan 1993) be recognized within the medical encounter?
- What would forms of accountability look like based not on practitioners' mediation of the gaps and contradictions between idealized prescriptions and realities of practice, but as an articulation of the latter based in legitimation of situated knowledges?
- What about an approach that took 'best practice' not as decontextualized and normalized prescriptions, but as experience recounted in regular occasions of mutual learning among practitioners?

If we understand that each proposal for remaking subjects and objects comes from somewhere, out of specific imaginaries and interests, the questions to ask are not is this new technology or technique desirable, or an improvement, but by whom is it imagined, for whom, and under what assumptions about current and future practice does it hold its promise? To answer that question requires commitment to a knowledge politics that respects what Helen Verran (2001) names 'disconcertment', that prioritizes means of working knowledges together (Verran 1998), and that acknowledges and respects the leakiness of boundaries in practice (e.g. between 'the medical' and the rest) (Jonvallen this volume). As Johnson (this volume) points out, understanding medical knowledge as an effect of practice-specific experience opens up a space for asking just how, and by whom, medical procedures are experienced, and whose experience is articulated in new technological formations. Read broadly, this argument has implications for how we might think about many forms of reconfiguration at the interface of bodies and machines.

References

Barad, K. 2007. *Meeting the Universe Half-Way*. Durham: Duke University Press.

Cussins [Thompson], C. 1998. Ontological Choreography: Agency for women patients in an infertility clinic, in *Differences in Medicine*, edited by M. Berg and A. Mol. Durham: Duke University Press, 166–201.

Haraway, D. 1997. *Modest_Witness@Second_Millenium.FemaleMan_Meets_Onco Mouse: Feminism and Technoscience*. New York: Routledge.

Jordan, B. 1993. *Birth in Four Cultures*. Prospect Heights: Waveland Press.

Orr, J. 1996. *Talking About Machines: An ethnography of a modern job*. Ithaca, New York: ILR Press.

Suchman, L. 2007. *Human-Machine Reconfigurations*. New York: Cambridge University Press.

Thompson [Cussins], C. 2005. *Making Parents: The ontological choreography of reproductive technologies*. Cambridge: MIT Press.

Verran, H. 1998. Re-imagining land ownership in Australia. *Postcolonial Studies*, 1, 237–254.

Verran, H. 2001. *Science and An African Logic*. Chicago: University of Chicago.

Index